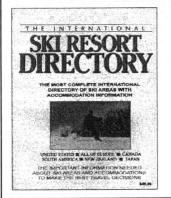

Fly For Less
1997

The Ultimate Guide to Bargain Airfares - and the Consolidators & Wholesalers who sell them!

Gary E. Schmidt

Travel Publishing, Inc. **St. Paul, Minnesota**

The information presented is not meant to endorse or recommend any firm listed in the publication. The author has provided the intellectual effort required to gather, organize, and compile the information deemed to be most relevant for travelers and travel agencies in considering a business transaction with a consolidator or wholesaler firm. The information presented was provided by the companies listed, and the ratings contributed by the travel agent subscribers of the *Index to Air Travel Consolidators & Wholesalers*, an edition designed for the travel professional. All information is subject to change. Users of the publication are urged to verify all details with all firms listed before completing a business transaction.

ISBN: 0-9649733-2-4

1. Airlines - Fares 2. Travel Directories 3. Schmidt, Gary E.
4. Title

Executive Editor/Design: Pamela Erwin
Editor: Kimberly A. Dineen

Printed in the United States of America

Fly For Less Presents:

*The Travel Agent
Referral Service

We always recommend using a travel agent to access the consolidator airfares - you'll still get a great fare and will benefit from their professional service. So, if you're having trouble  finding a good travel agent who is willing to help you check the consolidators you're interesting in -

Call 1(800)241-9299

. . .and we will be happy to locate a travel agent in your area from our professional database of agents who actively use consolidators to get the lowest fares for their clients. This is a _free_ service, courtesy of Travel Publishing, Inc.

* Travel Publishing referral service is based on consolidator use only and is not meant to suggest a certain quality of work or an overall endorsement of the agency.

Online Systems Group, Inc.

The Internet Travel Guide
http://www.osweb.com/

*Featuring: Airlines/Car Rentals/Cruise Lines/Hotels
Tour Operators/Tourist Offices/Travel Agencies . . .
Interactive Area: Photo Contest/Send Postcards via the Web.*

Table of Contents

Preface

Our primary goal in creating *Fly For Less* is to give the traveler more control over airfare. We want to expose the bargain airfare industry *in full* and raise consumer awareness of *all* the ticket prices available - not just those *published* by the airlines. Plus, we want to provide the instruction and the assurance the traveler needs to use consolidators and wholesalers well, and with confidence.

To do this, we have provided an *Introduction* explaining airline industry pricing and the role of the consolidator & wholesaler industry. Plus, we have gathered the corporate and sales information for each firm, so that you know all the options and can draw your own conclusions about who to do business with. All company profile information was contributed by the consolidator firms. Consolidator and wholesaler firms who were contacted but chose not to provide their information are so noted with an asterisk in the *Consolidators & Wholesalers by Location Index.*

For added assurance, we've included the results of the *Travel Agent Ratings*, drawn from the opinions of our travel agent subscriber base for the *Index to Air Travel Consolidators & Wholesalers,* our original guide designed for travel professionals. In future editions of *Fly For Less,* we plan to represent the opinions of our consumer customer base as well. So, if you have a problem with a firm - even if it is only poor service or poor attitude, please tell us about it. And, likewise, if you find a company you want to recommend, send us a note or call. Suppliers fear the power of the press and we have already made great strides through the Travel Agent Ratings in holding the suppliers accountable for service and performance.

One final note: The inclusion of companies within this publication is in no way meant to imply endorsement or recommendation. It's still a relatively new industry, and despite the growing number of good reliable consolidators, we advise *extreme caution and a thorough examination of the information provided in all cases*. We also urge you to work through your travel agent, so that any risk involved is shared. Read the *Introduction* and all instructional sections carefully, to ensure a complete understanding of the industry and the information provided, before proceeding.

Gary E. Schmidt

Part I

Introduction

You live in Dallas. You want a flight to Paris. What should you expect to pay?

Amazingly, *what you pay* will depend more on what you are *willing to pay, how determined you are to get a lower fare, and how good a shopper you are*, than what it *actually costs* the airline to provide the seat.

Everybody wants to find the *lowest ticket fare* available, but the problem is most travellers have no idea what the lowest possible fare is, and they stop looking too soon. The airline assigns up to 10 different *published* prices for each flight, sometimes ranging over 300% in difference. So, how can you know if you're paying too much? Basically, you're paying too much if you buy your tickets through the airline without checking further, because this book contains nearly 200 consolidator and wholesaler firms who sell tickets for the airlines at up to 50% less than the airline's lowest published fares. Here's how it works.

The Pricing Game - *How published airfares are established*

One of the biggest misconceptions about the airline industry is that there is a set pricing system for their tickets. The airlines view their product as a "perishable commodity". That is, once the plane starts rolling away from the gate, the unsold seat is gone; it's lost and cannot be sold again. So, if there is any chance that an empty seat can be sold before a flight takes off, even if it means lowering the price far below the previously published fares, the airlines will do it. As long as it puts extra money in their pocket, they are happy.

The first step the airlines make in selling a flight is to establish literally *dozens of different ticket prices* for what would be considered an *identical service*. This is what they call "yield management". Based on past sales trends, airline computers estimate the number of people willing to pay the various levels of fares for the available seats on a particular flight. Then they determine their pricing according to *the likelihood of selling* that particular seat at the designated fare, rather than on the actual cost of the service. So, every time a traveler agrees to pay $1,500 dollars for seat 13A, when the person in 13B has paid $500, it is confirming their assumption that at least one person would be willing to pay a premium price for the ticket.

Here's a sample analysis: to sell the most possible seats from 150 seats available on a plane flying from Dallas to Chicago, the computers predict that eight people will pay top dollar for first class; 15 will pay full coach or full priced general seating - because they decided to make the trip at the last minute and think they don't have a choice; 30 will pay about 75% of the full coach - because they think that's the best price available; another 50 will pay 60% of coach for the same reasons; another 30 just won't fly unless they can get a "good deal" - about 45% of coach; and then finally the airlines will price fifteen seats at 38% of the full coach fare so they can be competitive in their advertising.

To further confuse the matter, the airlines constantly move unsold seats in their inventory from one category to another - up until the day of departure. If a week before the flight leaves, they find nobody is paying the 75% of coach fare, but that there is a demand for the 40% of coach fare, they move some of the seats. They are constantly changing the ticket prices - as many as 25,000 fare changes daily. But don't be fooled, the airlines rarely advertise their best price. They don't want you to know just how low they are willing to go to sell the ticket. In case you're wondering why the last 10 tickets for the Dallas/Chicago flight were unaccounted for - read on. The airlines have one more sales trick up their sleeve.

How the really low, *unpublished* airfares are created

Remarkably, all of the above airline pricing strategies occur only to the general *published* air fares. There is a whole other realm of prices in existence that the airlines offer secretly through consolidator and wholesaler companies: these are the *unpublished fares*. They are almost always lower than the ones the airlines advertise in the papers as their best deals and are never included with the information the airlines transmit through CRS (Computer Reservations Systems) to travel agents or on the online services.

These deals take two forms: the airlines will give the reseller a *higher commission (percentage on each ticket sold)* or they will offer a *lower fare*. It's more common for the deals to involve higher commissions. In either case, *the fare that you pay* is a number subsequently created by the consolidator or wholesaler, and it may be a unique offer.

Some limitations may apply regarding frequent flyer mile terms, cancellation, or the ability to upgrade, depending on the individual policies of the consolidator or wholesaler you buy from. And it may require some flexibility in your scheduled travel time. But, once you've purchased the ticket, whether it's through

2

the airline for a premium, or through a consolidator/wholesaler, you share the same status with the airline as anyone else boarding the plane. There is no disadvantage for smart shopping.

Generally, consolidators offer the greatest savings on international flights, particularly to Europe or Asia, while wholesalers tend to have the best bargains for domestic flights. During some fare wars, however, the airlines have offered even greater bargains.

Welcome to the world of unpublished airfares. Now, all you need to know is *where* to get them....and *who* NOT to get them from.

Who are the Players?

It's important to understand who does what in the travel industry, in order to decide who is offering you the best deal. Here is the breakdown:

We know who the **airlines** are: they are the ones trying to get you to pay the highest fare for their tickets. With the exception of certain rare instances, they will never offer you the lowest price available on a ticket.

We also know who **travel agencies** are: traditionally, they are the retail sales outlet for the airlines. The airlines pay travel agencies commissions for selling and processing tickets. Since most don't charge fees for running tickets, their work is free to you. The airlines provide agents with computer systems that conveniently list all the thousands of *published* airfares and schedules. But, don't be mistaken, travel agents are not employed by the airlines. A good travel agent knows that they are working for you, and should be willing to go the extra mile with consolidators/wholesalers to save you money. *The fares won't be on their CRS system, so it will involve some extra phone calls.* The agent will still earn a commission from the sale. In fact, consolidator commissions are often higher than the airlines. Many agents, however, are reluctant to suggest using consolidators, and prefer to earn credit with the airlines on the sale, so it's up to you to ask.

Don't let an agent's reluctance dissuade you from working through a travel agency. If they discourage using consolidators, find a new travel agent. It is worth more than you may think. Anytime you purchase a ticket, especially from a firm that may be thousands of miles away, there is some risk. Even with the most reliable company a misunderstanding can occur. A travel agent would be more adept at making the arrangements, and their agency would share that risk with you.

The second reason to use a travel agent is simply for the good service. Normally, you won't find the best fare with one phone call. Moreover, you may need accommodations and local transportation. Let the agent do the work and research. It's free, and they may be able to offer inside knowledge and advice about consolidator/wholesaler firms and their fares to help find the best deals.

Working in-between the airlines and the travel agents are the **consolidators, wholesalers, tour operators, and brokers.** Once you enter this area of the industry, definitions tend to get blurred. For our purposes, all of these companies sell airline tickets, but only consolidators, wholesalers, and tour operators do so through a special deal with the airline. These companies working between the airlines and the travel agencies often operate as more than one of the above business categories. A great many tour operators are also consolidators and most are also wholesalers. Some travel agencies will do all of the above.

What exactly is a Consolidator?

Consolidators are a completely legitimate and much accepted part of the travel industry. Every airline has at least one consolidator working for them, whether they will admit it or not, and most travel agencies purchase tickets from them. They have been officially acknowledged by the Department of Transportation as a beneficial part of the travel industry for the airlines, the travel agencies, and the traveler.

The term "consolidator" was originally created to describe a firm that has entered into an agreement with an airline to sell a large volume of the airline's tickets, primarily for routes or in markets where the airline was experiencing a low volume of sales. In other words, they sell tickets the airlines can't sell, for prices the airlines don't want the general public to know are available. The original consolidator agreements were made with foreign airlines. Consolidators acted as their sales arms. So, domestic airlines picked up the practice as a defensive measure. Because of this, some airline people still refer to them as the "ethnic market".

To many longtimers in the travel industry, the term "consolidators" carries a stigma. They are sometimes referred to as "bucket shops", based on earlier days when stock brokers threw penny stocks into a bucket and peddlers were allowed to resell them for whatever they could get. Consolidators were created out of essentially the same process in the airline industry and, until recently, were considered just as risky to buy from. Travel agents had no way to distinguish the good companies from the fly by night operators who advertised low fares and then didn't deliver. These unscrupulous companies have made it particularly difficult for the good ones to gain acceptance. And the airlines offer no help to legitimize their trade, because they want their more expensive fares to sell first. Most airlines refuse to even acknowledge that they sell through consolidators and they commonly require the consolidators to agree to contracts prohibiting any mention of their name when advertising their fares.

Unfortunately, the industry is still plagued by *marginal and unstable businesses* and no business sector can fully shed the past, so don't be surprised if your travel agent acts reluctant to check a consolidator for you. If they do seem hesitant, chances are they haven't used the *Index to Air Travel Consolidators*, our original guide designed for the travel professional. The policing powers created in the *Index* have made tremendous strides in helping agents recognize the quality players in the business and have helped to raise the overall industry image. Travel Agents are using consolidators more than ever with the *Index* and their clients are getting great prices.

Today consolidators form a huge and powerful (but still largely unknown) air travel marketing force. They offer a tremendous savings to the traveler willing to take a few extra steps in making their flight arrangements. This book is geared to helping you do so with as much confidence and as little effort as possible.

And a Broker?

We need to mention a broker because anyone shopping for cheap air fares will run across one. You should know what distinguishes them from a consolidator. A consolidator *should* have a contract with an airline to sell below published fare. They do not actually "buy" any tickets, but rather just book them for the airline as a travel agency would. Many, however will buy tickets from other consolidators and resell them to travel agencies or to the public, which is actually acting as a *broker*.

Brokers are often low capitalized, low overhead players in the industry that earn money by finding their clients sources of cheap unpublished fares (usually the companies listed in this book). They are individuals who are knowledgeable about these sources and they will run ads in the travel sections of newspapers.

When you contact them they will purchase the ticket you want and charge you a little more than they paid (their profit for the work). They usually only get the ticket after you've sent them the money. Anytime you do business with someone you aren't familiar with, there is risk involved. So, if you have *Fly For Less,* there is little reason to work through a broker. A travel agent can offer you the same assistance, at less of a risk, and usually for no extra charge.

Who are the Wholesalers and Tour Operators?

Most wholesalers are also tour operators. There are virtually no true or pure wholesalers. A tour operator sells "packages." That is, they sell air, hotel, car and other elements of a trip to a traveler at one package price.

To be able to offer "tour packages" for less than the price of purchasing the items individually, tour operators obtain volume discounts, including a significant discount on the air portion of their package. They approach the airline and agree to purchase a minimum number of seats to specific destinations - many also use charters airlines. The volume purchase earns the tour operator a very low fare; well below most published fares and, to maximize the volume of sales, the tour operator will also sell "air only" or an airline ticket without the car, hotel or other parts of the travel package, qualifying them as a wholesaler.

Although many use the term "consolidator" and "wholesaler" interchangeably, wholesalers do differ from consolidators primarily through the terms of the agreement they have with the airline, and because consolidators do not sell tour packages.

How to *Fly For Less* with this Manual

Using this book is the easiest part of the whole process. Read *Understanding the Profiles* carefully for a complete overview of factors to consider relating to a firm's reliability. Then, when you're ready to find a company who can offer you a good fare, look up the region, country or city destination you're seeking in the *Destination Index*. Don't worry about your departure city; the consolidator will factor in the price of getting you to their main departure point. Make a list of the companies serving your destination and then turn to their profile pages. Check out all the details, including their *average rating*, then be sure to go to the actual rating section for a better understanding of the ratings received.

Once you have developed a list of companies you would be interested in, contact a travel agency you trust (even if the firm listed will sell direct to the public). Start by getting the airline's best published fare for the flight, then tell the agent you also want to know the best fares available from the company you've identified. Make sure your travel agent has explained all terms of the transaction to you before booking with a consolidator. If you go directly to the consolidator, make sure you communicate all details clearly and verify everything.

Then, enjoy your trip.

Part II

The Profiles

UNDERSTANDING THE PROFILES

The following pages provide a detailed explanation of the profile information. Each section contains a description of the data we've included and suggestions for interpretation. Read the pages carefully to ensure proper understanding and usage of the information provided.

1. THE CONTACT INFORMATION

All contact information provided by the firm has been presented. Firms that sell only through travel agents may have intentionally chosen not to include their (800)number. Also, only the three main branches of any firm are listed under branch offices. If three are listed, but none are local, you should verify that there is not an additional branch in your area.

FIRM: Jetset Tours Inc.

1(800) 638-3273

ADDRESS: 122 S. Michigan Ave., Ste. 1290
Chicago, IL 60603
PHONE: 312-362-9960
FAX: 312-362-9119
Branch Offices:
5120 W. Goldleaf Circle, #310
Los Angeles, CA 90056
800-453-8738

2. TRAVEL AGENT RATING

This is the overall average of the total ratings received from the travel agent subscribers of our professional manual, the Index to Air Travel Consolidators. The ratings are compiled twice a year and are only included within a two year time period of receipt. Some firms have not been rated. They are primarily firms who sell to the general public and are not commonly used by travel agencies. Consult the Ratings Section for a better understanding of the average rating; an explanation of the ratings system and a complete analysis are provided. Always consider the number of ratings received in the Ratings Section to comprise the average. These ratings are based on the opinions of travel agents only and should be regarded within the context of all information provided.

TRAVEL AGENT RATING
Overall Average
8.15
DETAILED ANALYSIS
OF RESULTS IN RATINGS
SECTION

3. CORPORATE INFORMATION

This information helps you verify the stability of the company. Bond coverage, escrow, and security reflect the company's financial security. This effects reimbersment, should the company fail in the midst of your transaction. Accreditation with ARC (Airline Reporting Corp.) indicates that the firm is licensed by the airlines to run tickets. If they list no ARC accreditation, chances are they are buying their tickets through another consolidator that can print and sell tickets, qualifying them as a broker. An IATAN endorsement (International Air Travel Association Network) indicates that the firm has met the organizations criteria based on the sale of international air, qualified fulltime management personal, proper handling of ticket supplies, a minimum sales requirement of $25,000 in working capital, and a minimum tangable net worth of $30,000. Pay attention to correlation regarding size, years in business, annual sales, and the number of ratings received. If a firm reports a large sales volume, check to see if the size of the staff would support it, and look at how many ratings were received on the company.

> ### CORPORATE INFORMATION
> Owner: Jetset Travel Holdings
> Gen Mgr: Ross Webster
> Number of staff: 112
> Date Originated: 1978
> Annual Sales: Over $25 million
> Bond Coverage: USTOA
> Accredited: ARC & IATAN
> Escrow: (NP)
> Security: (NP)

4. DESTINATIONS

Only general regions served by the firm are given here, and are categorized as follows: Europe, Mid East, Orient, Africa, Latin America, South Pacific, North America, and the Caribbean. In cases where a consolidator serves only a limited area, the country may be listed. For countries and specific cities served by each firm, see the Destination Index. For a definition of each region see the Destination Table of Contents at the front of the Index. It's important to note that not all destinations are served by each airline listed, but will be served by at least one.

DESTINATIONS
EUROPE, MID EAST,
ORIENT, AFRICA,
LATIN AMERICA,
SOUTH PACIFIC

(For a complete list of the exact cities served within each region, see Destination Index)

5. AIRLINES

The firms have agreements to sell tickets for the airlines listed (for explanation of agreements, see the Introduction). The airline codes are defined in the Index Section.

> **AIRLINES**
> QF, NZ, CO, UA, BA , LH, CP, MH, CX, VASP, Asiana, Air Pacific, AN, SA, GA
> *(Airline codes defined in Index)*

The ability to book business or first class tickets may vary among airlines listed - always ask. Charter airlines are not required to follow the scheduling requirements of the primary airlines, but, where available, can be a good alternative.The airlines are an excellent reference for reliability of a firm. If the firm consents, request the name of their sales contact at the airline. If the firm does not want you to contact the airlines for references, it may be because of an antidisclosure agreement with the airline. You may want to request another type of reference, such as a travel agency who uses them.

> Firm books Business Class: *(NP)*   First Class: *(NP)*
> Airlines may be contacted for references: **Yes**
> Percent of sales through Scheduled Air: *100%*

6. SALES POLICIES

Consolidator firms are not governed by the same policies as the airlines, so this information is to alert you of any special transaction charges or procedures which may effect your purchase. Always verify the details of your order (ticket delivery methods and charges, minimal or maximum advance confirmation time, cancellation policy, frequent flyer policy, etc.), and ask about any special charges. Fees for credit card orders are common, but we recommend always purchasing with a credit card to have the added assurance of protection, should something go wrong. Airline perks, such as frequent flyer miles, depend on the terms of the consolidators agreement with the airline and availability may vary among the airlines listed.

> **SALES POLICIES**
> Tickets delivered: *immediately after payment rcd.*
>   By: *Overnight $15.00*
> Fee charged for credit card payment: *(NP)*
> Flight confirmed: *At booking*
> Is a fare receipt provided? *(NP)*
> Cancellation Policy: *(NP)*
> Frequent Flyer Miles offered? *(NP)*

7. ORDERS ACCEPTED

The firm accepts orders by these methods only. These terms refer strictly to the travel agency for those consolidators or wholesalers who sell to travel agents only.

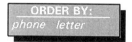

8. PAYMENT ACCEPTED

The firm accepts these forms of payment only. Always check to see if there are any special charges for certain types of payments. We recommend using a credit card wherever possible, regardless of any additional charges. Net 10 days is standard invoicing procedure where listed.

9. COMMENT

This section is provided to allow the consolidator to present any additional information or special policies to the listing that they feel is important for you to know about them.

> Comment: Offices: Los Angeles, San Francisco, Seattle, Chicago, New York, Houston, Orlando, San Diego, Washington D.C., Portland, Vancouver & Toronto - call 1-800-NETFARE.

10. (NP)

Where this symbol appears, the firm chose not to provide the requested information. In some cases, the questions do not apply to the specific firm, or other legitimate reasons may exist. If you feel significant information has been omitted, you should inquire with the firm. The company should be willing to cooperate.

(NP): Requested information not provided by firm.

Profiles of
Firms That Sell to the
General Public

FIRM: AESU

RES PHONE: 1-800-638-7640

ADDRESS: 2 Hamill Road, Ste. 248
　　　　　 Baltimore, MD 21210
　PHONE: 410-323-4416
　　FAX: 410-323-4498

Branch Offices:

Travel Agent Rating
Overall Average

7.09

*(Detailed analysis of
results in Ratings
Section)*

CORPORATE INFORMATION

Owner: Fritz Satran
Gen Mgr: (NP)
Number of staff: 30
Date originated: 1977
Annual sales: $10 - 25 million
Bond coverage: $75,000
Accredited: ARC & IATAN
Escrow: (NP)
Security: (NP)

DESTINATIONS
EUROPE

*(For a complete list of the exact
cities served within each region, see
the Destination Index)*

AIRLINES
KLM, BA, Icelandic, Delta, Air New Zealand, TWA, Lufthansa, AL, Northwest

(Airline codes defined in Index)

Firm books business class: (NP)　　　First class: (NP)
Airlines may be contacted for references: Yes
Percentage of sales through scheduled air: 100%

SALES POLICIES

Tickets delivered: 15 days before departure
　　Delivered by: *Overnight*　　　*$10.00*
　　　　　　　　 First class　　　*no charge*

Fee charged for credit card payment: 2.5%
Flight confirmed: 30 days before departure
Is a printed receipt provided? No
Cancellation policy: Varies by airline

Frequent flyer miles offered? Yes
　　　　　　　 Varies by airline

ORDER BY:

PAYMENT FORMS
ACCEPTED

Comment:

(NP) = Firm did not provide requested information.

FIRM: Adventure Int'l Travel Service

RES PHONE: 1-800-542-2487

ADDRESS: 14305 Madison Avenue,
Lakewood, OH 44107
PHONE: 216-228-7171
FAX: 216-228-7170

Branch Offices:

CORPORATE INFORMATION

Owner: Paul J. Hudak
Gen Mgr: Paul J. Hudak
Number of staff: 6
Date originated: 1971
Annual sales: $1 - 4 million
Bond coverage: $30,000
Accredited: ARC & IATAN
Escrow: (NP)
Security: (NP)

DESTINATIONS
EUROPE

(For a complete list of the exact cities served within each region, see the Destination Index)

AIRLINES
OK, KL, OS, LH, GU, SU, AY

(Airline codes defined in Index)

Firm books business class: (NP)   First class: (NP)
Airlines may be contacted for references: No
Percentage of sales through scheduled air: 50%

SALES POLICIES

Tickets delivered: 5 to 7 days before departure
Delivered by: *Overnight*   *$15.00*
First class   *no charge*
Other   *billed*

Fee charged for credit card payment:
Flight confirmed: 7 - 90 days before departure
Is a printed receipt provided? (NP)
Cancellation policy: (NP)

Frequent flyer miles offered? (NP)

ORDER BY:

PAYMENT FORMS ACCEPTED

Comment:

(NP) = Firm did not provide requested information.

FIRM: Air Brokers Int'l, Inc.

RES PHONE: 1-800-883-3273

ADDRESS: 323 Geary St., Ste.411
San Francisco, CA 94102
PHONE: 415-397-1383
FAX: 415-397-4767

Branch Offices:

Travel Agent Rating
Overall Average

7.17

(Detailed analysis of results in Ratings Section)

CORPORATE INFORMATION

Owner: Evertsen & Kontis
Gen Mgr: E. Evertsen
Number of staff: 10
Date originated: 1987
Annual sales: $5 - 10 million
Bond coverage: $75,000
Accredited: ARC & IATAN
Escrow: (NP)
Security: $75,000 ARC bond

DESTINATIONS

ROUND THE WORLD, ORIENT, SOUTH PACIFIC

(For a complete list of the exact cities served within each region, see the Destination Index)

AIRLINES
Most scheduled airlines

(Airline codes defined in Index)

Firm books business class: Yes First class: Yes
Airlines may be contacted for references: Yes
Percentage of sales through scheduled air: 100%

SALES POLICIES

Tickets delivered: ASAP
Delivered by: *Overnight* *$7.00*

FED EX

Fee charged for credit card payment:
Flight confirmed: 21 days before departure
Is a printed receipt provided? Yes
Cancellation policy: 30%

Frequent flyer miles offered? Yes
Varies by airline

ORDER BY:
phone letter fax

PAYMENT FORMS ACCEPTED
*Credit card
Personal check*

Comment:

(NP) = Firm did not provide requested information.

FIRM: Air Travel Discounts, Inc.

RES PHONE: 1-800-888-2621

ADDRESS: 141 E. 44th St., #702
New York, NY 10017
PHONE: 212-922-1326
FAX: 212-922-1547
Branch Offices:

Travel Agent Rating
Overall Average
6.25
(Detailed analysis of results in Ratings Section)

CORPORATE INFORMATION

Owner: A. Khandekar
Gen Mgr: Chris D'Souza
Number of staff: 10
Date originated: 1990
Annual sales: $10 - 25 million
Bond coverage: $25,000
Accredited: ARC & IATAN
Escrow: (NP)
Security: Air travel has average bank
balance of $250,000

DESTINATIONS
EUROPE, MID EAST, ORIENT, AFRICA

(For a complete list of the exact cities served within each region, see the Destination Index)

AIRLINES
AF, LH, BA, SN, EK, UA, AA, US, SQ, KE, OZ, CX, RJ, SA, AR, RG, DC, TW, OS, OK, GU, AI
(Airline codes defined in Index)

Firm books business class: No   First class: No
Airlines may be contacted for references: Yes
Percentage of sales through scheduled air: 100%

SALES POLICIES

Tickets delivered: Two days after payment
Delivered by: *Overnight*   *$10.00*

Fee charged for credit card payment: (NP)
Flight confirmed: At booking
Is a printed receipt provided? Yes
Cancellation policy: Varies by airline

Frequent flyer miles offered? Yes
Varies by airline

ORDER BY:
phone letter fax

PAYMENT FORMS ACCEPTED
*Credit card
Cash
Personal check*

Comment: *Also last minute specials available on domestic long-haul flights.*

(NP) = Firm did not provide requested information.

18

FIRM: **Alek's Travel**

RES PHONE: 1-800-929-7768

ADDRESS: 519 A South Andrews Avenue
              Fort Lauderdale, FL 33301
    PHONE: 305-462-6767
      FAX: 305-462-8691
Branch Offices:

CORPORATE INFORMATION

Owner: Jean Purre Orfanides
Gen Mgr: Blandon Tissier
Number of staff: 3
Date originated: 1989
Annual sales: $1 - 4 million
Bond coverage: $20,000
Accredited: ARC & IATAN
Escrow: (NP)
Security: (NP)

DESTINATIONS
EUROPE

(For a complete list of the exact cities served within each region, see the Destination Index)

AIRLINES
(NP)

(Airline codes defined in Index)

Firm books business class: (NP)   First class: (NP)
Airlines may be contacted for references: No
Percentage of sales through scheduled air: (NP)

SALES POLICIES

Tickets delivered: (NP)
      Delivered by: *Overnight*   *$15.00*
                  First class

Fee charged for credit card payment: (NP)
Flight confirmed: 2 days before departure
Is a printed receipt provided? (NP)
Cancellation policy: (NP)

Frequent flyer miles offered? (NP)

ORDER BY:

PAYMENT FORMS ACCEPTED

Comment:

(NP) = Firm did not provide requested information.

19

FIRM: All Destinations

RES PHONE: 1-800-228-1510

ADDRESS: 19 Scodon Dr.
Ridgefield, CT 06877
PHONE: 203-744-3100
FAX: 203-744-1320
Branch Offices:

Travel Agent Rating
Overall Average
8.5
(Detailed analysis of results in Ratings Section)

CORPORATE INFORMATION
Owner: Susan Resch /Allyson Catarzao
Gen Mgr: Allyson Catarzao
Number of staff: 4
Date originated: 1989
Annual sales: $1 - 4 million
Bond coverage: $20,000
Accredited: ARC
Escrow: (NP)
Security: (NP)

DESTINATIONS
CARIBBEAN

(For a complete list of the exact cities served within each region, see the Destination Index)

AIRLINES
American, US Air

(Airline codes defined in Index)

Firm books business class: (NP)   First class: (NP)
Airlines may be contacted for references: (NP)
Percentage of sales through scheduled air: (NP)

SALES POLICIES

Tickets delivered: 7 - 10 days before departure
Delivered by: *Overnight*
First class $15.00

Fee charged for credit card payment: (NP)
Flight confirmed: 24 hours
Is a printed receipt provided? (NP)
Cancellation policy: (NP)

Frequent flyer miles offered? (NP)

ORDER BY:

PAYMENT FORMS ACCEPTED

Comment:

(NP) = Firm did not provide requested information.

FIRM: Alpha Travel

RES PHONE: 1-800-793-8424

ADDRESS: 3000 Windy Hill Rd, Ste. T-7
Marietta, GA 30067
PHONE: 404-988-9982
FAX: 404-988-9986

Branch Offices:

CORPORATE INFORMATION

Owner: Kevin Rustom
Gen Mgr: Kevin Rustom
Number of staff: 6
Date originated: 1989
Annual sales: $1 - 4 million
Bond coverage: $20,000
Accredited: ARC & IATAN
Escrow: (NP)
Security: (NP)

DESTINATIONS
EUROPE, MID EAST, ORIENT, AFRICA

(For a complete list of the exact cities served within each region, see the Destination Index)

AIRLINES
Alitalia, Royal Jordanian, Saudi Airlines, Air Afrique, KLM Royal Dutch Airlines

(Airline codes defined in Index)

Firm books business class: (NP)   First class: (NP)
Airlines may be contacted for references: Yes
Percentage of sales through scheduled air: 100%

SALES POLICIES

Tickets delivered: One day after booking
Delivered by: *Overnight $9.00*

Certified mail no charge
Fee charged for credit card payment: (NP)
Flight confirmed: At booking
Is a printed receipt provided? Yes
Cancellation policy: Airlines fare rules apply, plus
service fee

Frequent flyer miles offered? Yes
Varies by airline

ORDER BY:

PAYMENT FORMS ACCEPTED

Comment:

(NP) = Firm did not provide requested information.

FIRM: Alta Tours

RES PHONE: 1-800-338-4191

ADDRESS: 870 Market St., Ste. 784
San Francisco, CA 94102
PHONE: 415-777-1307
FAX: 415-434-2684

Branch Offices:

CORPORATE INFORMATION

Owner: Eugenio Ovalle
Gen Mgr: Joan Ovalle
Number of staff: (NP)
Date originated: 1975
Annual sales: $1 - 4 million
Bond coverage: $65,000
Accredited: ARC & IATAN
Escrow: (NP)
Security: (NP)

DESTINATIONS
EUROPE, LATIN AMERICA

(For a complete list of the exact cities served within each region, see the Destination Index)

AIRLINES
United Lan Chile, Ladeco Airlines, TWA

(Airline codes defined in Index)

Firm books business class: (NP)   First class: (NP)
Airlines may be contacted for references: Yes
Percentage of sales through scheduled air: (NP)

SALES POLICIES

Tickets delivered: (NP)
Delivered by: *Overnight*   *$12.00*

Fee charged for credit card payment:
Flight confirmed: (NP)
Is a printed receipt provided? (NP)
Cancellation policy: (NP)

Frequent flyer miles offered? (NP)

ORDER BY:

PAYMENT FORMS ACCEPTED

Comment:

(NP) = Firm did not provide requested information.

FIRM: AmeriCorp Travel Professionals

RES PHONE: 1-800-299-LATI

ADDRESS: 2351 W. Northwest Highway, MD-54
Dallas, TX 75220
PHONE: 214-956-9112
FAX: 214-357-2580

Branch Offices:

Travel Agent Rating
Overall Average
9
(Detailed analysis of results in Ratings Section)

CORPORATE INFORMATION

Owner: Lee Brown
Gen Mgr: Yolanda
Number of staff: 6
Date originated: 1990
Annual sales: $5 - 10 million
Bond coverage: $25,000
Accredited: ARC & IATAN
Escrow: $10,000
Security: Tickets issued immediately

DESTINATIONS

C.I.S., ORIENT, AFRICA, LATIN AMERICA, MEXICO

(For a complete list of the exact cities served within each region, see the Destination Index)

AIRLINES

CO, TA, GU, LA, ML, AA, UA, TR, VP, RG, CF, PL, AM, TK, AY, AV, VA

(Airline codes defined in Index)

Firm books business class: Yes   First class: Yes
Airlines may be contacted for references: Yes
Percentage of sales through scheduled air: 100%

SALES POLICIES

Tickets delivered: Two weeks before departure
Delivered by: *Overnight* $5.00
First class $3.00

Fee charged for credit card payment:
Flight confirmed: At booking
Is a printed receipt provided? Yes
Cancellation policy: $25 - minimum fee

Frequent flyer miles offered? Yes
Varies by airline

ORDER BY:
phone letter fax

PAYMENT FORMS ACCEPTED
*Credit card
Personal check*

Comment:

(NP) = Firm did not provide requested information.

FIRM: Asensio Tours & Travel Corp

RES PHONE: 1-800-221-7679

ADDRESS: 445 Fifth Ave #14A
New York, NY 10016
PHONE: 212-213-4310
FAX: 212-689-3021

Branch Offices:

Travel Agent Rating
Overall Average
9
(Detailed analysis of results in Ratings Section)

CORPORATE INFORMATION

Owner: J. C. Rivero/Hector Hermida
Gen Mgr: (NP)
Number of staff: 7
Date originated: 1962
Annual sales: $5 - 10 million
Bond coverage: ARC bond
Accredited: ARC & IATAN
Escrow: (NP)
Security: (NP)

DESTINATIONS
LATIN AMERICA

(For a complete list of the exact cities served within each region, see the Destination Index)

AIRLINES
AR, AA, RG, UA, LA, VP, UC

(Airline codes defined in Index)

Firm books business class: Yes   First class: Yes
Airlines may be contacted for references: Yes
Percentage of sales through scheduled air: 100%

SALES POLICIES

Tickets delivered: Yes
Delivered by: *Overnight*   *$12.00*

Fee charged for credit card payment:
Flight confirmed: Yes
Is a printed receipt provided? Yes
Cancellation policy: Varies by airline

Frequent flyer miles offered? Yes
Varies by airline

ORDER BY:
phone   fax

PAYMENT FORMS ACCEPTED
*Credit card
Personal check*

Comment:

(NP) = Firm did not provide requested information.

FIRM: Borgsmiller Travels

RES PHONE: 1-800-228-0585

ADDRESS: 702 S Illinois Ave.
Carbondale, IL 62901
PHONE: 618-529-5511
FAX: 618-549-1438
Branch Offices:

CORPORATE INFORMATION

Owner: Dirk Borgsmiller
Gen Mgr: Dirk Borgsmiller
Number of staff: 5
Date originated: 1986
Annual sales: $1 - 4 million
Bond coverage: $40,000
Accredited: ARC & IATAN
Escrow: (NP)
Security: (NP)

DESTINATIONS
MALAYSIA

(For a complete list of the exact cities served within each region, see the Destination Index)

AIRLINES
Malaysian Airlines

(Airline codes defined in Index)

Firm books business class: (NP)   First class: (NP)
Airlines may be contacted for references: Yes
Percentage of sales through scheduled air: 100%

SALES POLICIES

Tickets delivered: (NP)
Delivered by: *Overnight*   *$13.00*

2 day   *$8.00*

Fee charged for credit card payment:
Flight confirmed: (NP)
Is a printed receipt provided? (NP)
Cancellation policy: (NP)

Frequent flyer miles offered? (NP)

ORDER BY:

PAYMENT FORMS ACCEPTED

Comment:

(NP) = Firm did not provide requested information.

FIRM: British Network, LTD

RES PHONE: 1-800-274-8583

ADDRESS: The Mews, 594 Valley Rd
Upper Montclair, NJ 07043
PHONE: 201-744-8814
FAX: 201-744-0531
Branch Offices:

Travel Agent Rating
Overall Average
8.5
(Detailed analysis of results in Ratings Section)

CORPORATE INFORMATION

Owner: Joseph D. Kloza
Gen Mgr: (NP)
Number of staff: 9
Date originated: 1990
Annual sales: $1 - 4 million
Bond coverage: Yes
Accredited: ARC
Escrow: (NP)
Security: (NP)

DESTINATIONS
EUROPE

(For a complete list of the exact cities served within each region, see the Destination Index)

AIRLINES
AA, and others

(Airline codes defined in Index)

Firm books business class: No   First class: (NP)
Airlines may be contacted for references: Yes
Percentage of sales through scheduled air: 100%

SALES POLICIES

Tickets delivered: ASAP
Delivered by: *Overnight*   *$10.00*

Certified   *no charge*

Fee charged for credit card payment:
Flight confirmed: ASAP
Is a printed receipt provided? Yes
Cancellation policy: (NP)

Frequent flyer miles offered? Yes
Varies by airline

ORDER BY:

PAYMENT FORMS ACCEPTED

Comment:

(NP) = Firm did not provide requested information.

26

FIRM: CWT/Maharaja

RES PHONE: 1-800-223-6862

ADDRESS: 34 W 33rd St., Ste. 1014
New York, NY 10001
PHONE: 212-695-8435
FAX: 212-695-8627

Branch Offices:

Travel Agent Rating
Overall Average
6
(Detailed analysis of results in Ratings Section)

CORPORATE INFORMATION

Owner: (NP)
Gen Mgr: Ray Sanghvi
Number of staff: (NP)
Date originated: 1975
Annual sales: $5 - 10 million
Bond coverage: (NP)
Accredited: (NP)
Escrow: (NP)
Security: (NP)

DESTINATIONS

EUROPE, MID EAST, ORIENT, AFRICA, LATIN AMERICA, SOUTH PACIFIC, NORTH AMERICA

(For a complete list of the exact cities served within each region, see the Destination Index)

AIRLINES
All major airlines

(Airline codes defined in Index)

Firm books business class: (NP)   First class: (NP)
Airlines may be contacted for references: Yes
Percentage of sales through scheduled air: 98%

SALES POLICIES

Tickets delivered: Immediately
Delivered by: *Overnight*   *$10.00*

Fee charged for credit card payment:
Flight confirmed: Immediately
Is a printed receipt provided? (NP)
Cancellation policy: (NP)

Frequent flyer miles offered? (NP)

ORDER BY:

PAYMENT FORMS ACCEPTED

Comment:

(NP) = Firm did not provide requested information.

FIRM: Campus Travel Center/Euroflgts

RES PHONE: 1-800-328-3359

ADDRESS: 2506 Riverside Ave So.
Minneapolis, MN 55454
PHONE: 612-338-5616
FAX: 612-338-6798
Branch Offices:

Travel Agent Rating
Overall Average
8
(Detailed analysis of results in Ratings Section)

CORPORATE INFORMATION

Owner: Gloria J. Hiner
Gen Mgr: John M. Hiner
Number of staff: 10
Date originated: 1972
Annual sales: $5 - 10 million
Bond coverage: $70,000
Accredited: ARC & IATAN
Escrow: (NP)
Security: (NP)

DESTINATIONS
EUROPE, SOUTH PACIFIC

(For a complete list of the exact cities served within each region, see the Destination Index)

AIRLINES
AA, NW, Air Paraguay

(Airline codes defined in Index)

Firm books business class: No   First class: (NP)
Airlines may be contacted for references: Yes
Percentage of sales through scheduled air: 100%

SALES POLICIES

Tickets delivered: Two weeks before departure
Delivered by: *Overnight*   *$10.00*

Fee charged for credit card payment:
Flight confirmed: Immediately
Is a printed receipt provided? (NP)
Cancellation policy: (NP)

Frequent flyer miles offered? Yes
Varies by airline

ORDER BY:

PAYMENT FORMS ACCEPTED

Comment:

(NP) = Firm did not provide requested information.

FIRM: Cathay Travel

RES PHONE: 1-800-

ADDRESS: 108 N. Ynez Ave #201
Monterey Park, CA 91754
PHONE: 818-571-6727
FAX: 818-571-1831

Branch Offices:

CORPORATE INFORMATION

Owner: (NP)
Gen Mgr: Virginia Chan
Number of staff: 6
Date originated: 1982
Annual sales: $1 - 4 million
Bond coverage: (NP)
Accredited: ARC & IATAN
Escrow: (NP)
Security: (NP)

DESTINATIONS

ORIENT, LATIN AMERICA, NORTH AMERICA

(For a complete list of the exact cities served within each region, see the Destination Index)

AIRLINES
TZ, FF

(Airline codes defined in Index)

Firm books business class: Yes   First class: (NP)
Airlines may be contacted for references: Yes
Percentage of sales through scheduled air: 99%

SALES POLICIES

Tickets delivered: Upon payment
Delivered by: *Overnight*   *$10.00*

Two days within $6.00

Fee charged for credit card payment:
Flight confirmed: At booking
Is a printed receipt provided? (NP)
Cancellation policy: (NP)

Frequent flyer miles offered? No

ORDER BY:

fax

PAYMENT FORMS ACCEPTED

Credit card
COD

Comment:

(NP) = Firm did not provide requested information.

FIRM: Cedok Central European Tours

RES PHONE: 1-800-800-8891

ADDRESS: 10 E. 40th St., 36th Floor
NY, NY 10016
PHONE: 212-689-9720
FAX: 212-491-0597

Branch Offices:

CORPORATE INFORMATION

Owner: Cedok Travel Corp.
Gen Mgr: Vladimir Hulpach, Pres.
Number of staff: 8
Date originated: 1990
Annual sales: $1 - 4 million
Bond coverage: $20,000
Accredited: ARC & IATAN
Escrow: (NP)
Security: (NP)

DESTINATIONS
EUROPE, MID EAST

(For a complete list of the exact cities served within each region, see the Destination Index)

AIRLINES
OK, LH, AY

(Airline codes defined in Index)

Firm books business class: (NP)   First class: (NP)
Airlines may be contacted for references: No
Percentage of sales through scheduled air: 100%

SALES POLICIES

Tickets delivered: Two weeks before departure
        Delivered by:

Fee charged for credit card payment: (NP)
Flight confirmed: Two weeks before departure
Is a printed receipt provided? No
Cancellation policy: (NP)

Frequent flyer miles offered? (NP)

ORDER BY:

PAYMENT FORMS ACCEPTED

Comment:

(NP) = Firm did not provide requested information.

FIRM: Central Tours

RES PHONE: 1-800-783-9882

ADDRESS: 73-75 Ferry St.
Newark, NJ 07105
PHONE: 201-344-2489
FAX: 201-344-7115

Branch Offices:

Travel Agent Rating
Overall Average
8
*(Detailed analysis of
results in Ratings
Section)*

CORPORATE INFORMATION

Owner: Lino Vazquez
Gen Mgr: A.J. Vazquez
Number of staff: 5
Date originated: 1958
Annual sales: $1 - 4 million
Bond coverage: $75,000
Accredited: ARC & IATAN
Escrow: Yes
Security: (NP)

DESTINATIONS
EUROPE, LATIN AMERICA

*(For a complete list of the exact
cities served within each region, see
the Destination Index)*

AIRLINES
IB, TW, CO, TP

(Airline codes defined in Index)

Firm books business class: No   First class: No
Airlines may be contacted for references: No
Percentage of sales through scheduled air: 80%

SALES POLICIES

Tickets delivered: Upon payment
Delivered by: *Overnight*

Fee charged for credit card payment: 3%
Flight confirmed: One week before departure
Is a printed receipt provided? No
Cancellation policy: Varies

Frequent flyer miles offered? Yes
Varies by airline

ORDER BY:
phone letter fax

**PAYMENT FORMS
ACCEPTED**
*Credit card
Cash
COD*

Comment:

(NP) = Firm did not provide requested information.

FIRM: **Chartours**

RES PHONE: 1-800-323-4444

ADDRESS: 562 Mission St.
San Francisco, CA 94105
PHONE: 415-495-8881
FAX: 415-543-8010
Branch Offices:

Travel Agent Rating
Overall Average
8.4
(Detailed analysis of results in Ratings Section)

CORPORATE INFORMATION

Owner: Gisele Freedman
Gen Mgr: Cathy Anderson
Number of staff: 10
Date originated: 1965
Annual sales: $5 - 10 million
Bond coverage: (NP)
Accredited: ARC & IATAN
Escrow: (NP)
Security: (NP)

DESTINATIONS

EUROPE, MID EAST, ORIENT, AFRICA, LATIN AMERICA, SOUTH PACIFIC, NORTH AMERICA

(For a complete list of the exact cities served within each region, see the Destination Index)

AIRLINES
United Airlines, LH, KL

(Airline codes defined in Index)

Firm books business class: No   First class: No
Airlines may be contacted for references: No
Percentage of sales through scheduled air: 80%

SALES POLICIES

Tickets delivered: (NP)
Delivered by: *Overnight*
First class

Fee charged for credit card payment:
Flight confirmed: (NP)
Is a printed receipt provided? (NP)
Cancellation policy: (NP)

Frequent flyer miles offered? (NP)

ORDER BY:

PAYMENT FORMS ACCEPTED

Comment:

(NP) = Firm did not provide requested information.

FIRM: Chisholm Travel, Inc.

RES PHONE: 1-800-631-2824

ADDRESS: 230 N. Michigan Ave., Ste. 2012
Chicago, IL 60601
PHONE: 312-263-7900
FAX: 312-759-9234
Branch Offices:

CORPORATE INFORMATION

Owner: Beverly Lynch
Gen Mgr: Andrew Greskovich
Number of staff: 8
Date originated: 1992
Annual sales: $5 - 10 million
Bond coverage: $60,000
Accredited: ARC & IATAN
Escrow: No
Security: (NP)

DESTINATIONS
ORIENT, SOUTH PACIFIC

(For a complete list of the exact cities served within each region, see the Destination Index)

AIRLINES
UA, KE, JL, CX, MH, GA, NZ

(Airline codes defined in Index)

Firm books business class: Yes   First class: Yes
Airlines may be contacted for references: Yes
Percentage of sales through scheduled air: 100%

SALES POLICIES

Tickets delivered: (NP)
Delivered by: *(NP)*

Fee charged for credit card payment: (NP)
Flight confirmed: (NP)
Is a printed receipt provided? (NP)
Cancellation policy: (NP)

Frequent flyer miles offered? Yes

ORDER BY:
phone letter fax

PAYMENT FORMS ACCEPTED
*Credit card
Personal check*

Comment:

(NP) = Firm did not provide requested information.

FIRM: Compare Travel

RES PHONE: 1-800-

ADDRESS: 5 N. Wabash Ave., Ste 818
Chicago, IL 60602
PHONE: 312-853-1144
FAX: 312-853-2446
Branch Offices:

Travel Agent Rating
Overall Average
7.5
(Detailed analysis of results in Ratings Section)

CORPORATE INFORMATION

Owner: Ted Habib
Gen Mgr: Manuel
Number of staff: 8
Date originated: 1984
Annual sales: $10 - 25 million
Bond coverage: $100,000
Accredited: ARC & IATAN
Escrow: (NP)
Security: (NP)

DESTINATIONS AROUND THE WORLD

(For a complete list of the exact cities served within each region, see the Destination Index)

AIRLINES
AZ, NW, TG, IB, CX, AF, OA, NZ, RJ, BG, TR, GA, KU, KF
(Airline codes defined in Index)

Firm books business class: Yes   First class: Yes
Airlines may be contacted for references: Yes
Percentage of sales through scheduled air: 100%

SALES POLICIES

Tickets delivered: Upon payment
Delivered by: *Overnight*

Second day   *$5.00*

Fee charged for credit card payment: 4%
Flight confirmed: At booking
Is a printed receipt provided? Yes
Cancellation policy: Varies by ticket

Frequent flyer miles offered? Yes
Varies by airline

ORDER BY:
phone   *fax*

PAYMENT FORMS ACCEPTED
Credit card
Personal check

Comment: *We have 42 offices in 42 countries.*

(NP) = Firm did not provide requested information.

FIRM: Costa Azul Travel

RES PHONE: 1-800-332-7202

ADDRESS: 4221 Wilshire Blvd.
Los Angeles, CA 91001
PHONE: 213-525-3331
FAX: 213-525-1584
Branch Offices:

Travel Agent Rating
Overall Average
4.67
*(Detailed analysis of
results in Ratings
Section)*

CORPORATE INFORMATION

Owner: (NP)
Gen Mgr: Lili Altman
Number of staff: (NP)
Date originated: 1982
Annual sales: Over $25 million
Bond coverage: (NP)
Accredited: ARC & IATAN
Escrow: (NP)
Security: (NP)

DESTINATIONS
EUROPE, MID EAST, AFRICA, LATIN AMERICA

*(For a complete list of the exact
cities served within each region, see
the Destination Index)*

AIRLINES
Mexicana, American, Continental, etc.

(Airline codes defined in Index)

Firm books business class: (NP)   First class: (NP)
Airlines may be contacted for references: Yes
Percentage of sales through scheduled air: 100%

SALES POLICIES

Tickets delivered: (NP)
Delivered by: *Overnight*   *$10.00*

Fee charged for credit card payment:
Flight confirmed: (NP)
Is a printed receipt provided? (NP)
Cancellation policy: (NP)

Frequent flyer miles offered? (NP)

ORDER BY:

PAYMENT FORMS
ACCEPTED

Comment:

(NP) = Firm did not provide requested information.

FIRM: Cut Rate Travel

RES PHONE: 1-800-388-0575

ADDRESS: 1220 Montgomery Dr.
Deerfield, IL 60015
PHONE: 708-405-0587
FAX: 708-405-0587
Branch Offices:

CORPORATE INFORMATION

Owner: Marshall Schaffer
Gen Mgr: Marshall Schaffer
Number of staff: 2
Date originated: 1984
Annual sales: $1 - 4 million
Bond coverage: No
Accredited:
Escrow: No
Security: Written confirmations offered

DESTINATIONS

EUROPE, MID EAST, ORIENT, LATIN AMERICA, SOUTH PACIFIC

(For a complete list of the exact cities served within each region, see the Destination Index)

AIRLINES

TG, DL, GF, MH, NW, LH, TW, SR, AF, TE, AC, AR, SA, AZ, OS, BA, CP, CX, CI, LY, AY, JL, KL, LA, LO, SQ

(Airline codes defined in Index)

Firm books business class: Yes   First class: Yes
Airlines may be contacted for references: Yes
Percentage of sales through scheduled air: 90%

SALES POLICIES

Tickets delivered: As soon as possible
Delivered by: *Overnight*   *$10.00*
First class   *no charge*

Fee charged for credit card payment: 3%
Flight confirmed: Up to six months before leaving
Is a printed receipt provided? Yes
Cancellation policy: Varies

Frequent flyer miles offered? No

ORDER BY:

phone letter fax

PAYMENT FORMS ACCEPTED

Credit card
Personal check

Comment:

(NP) = Firm did not provide requested information.

FIRM: DERAIR

RES PHONE: 1-800-717-4247

ADDRESS: 11933 Wilshire Blvd.
Los Angeles, CA 90025
PHONE: 310-479-4411
FAX: 310-479-2239

Branch Offices:
9501 W. Devon Ave.
Rosemont, IL 60018
800-717-4247

Travel Agent Rating
Overall Average
8.13
(Detailed analysis of results in Ratings Section)

CORPORATE INFORMATION

Owner: Corporation
Gen Mgr: Heinz Niederhoff, Pres.
Number of staff: 124
Date originated: 1982
Annual sales: $10 - 25 million
Bond coverage: N/A
Accredited: ARC & IATAN
Escrow: N/A
Security: USTOA $1,000,000

DESTINATIONS
EUROPE, MID EAST, AFRICA

(For a complete list of the exact cities served within each region, see the Destination Index)

AIRLINES
DL, LH, NW, UA, US, TW, AC, IB, LT, BA, NZ, OS, RJ

(Airline codes defined in Index)

Firm books business class: No   First class: No
Airlines may be contacted for references: Yes
Percentage of sales through scheduled air: 100%

SALES POLICIES

Tickets delivered: Upon payment
Delivered by: *Overnight*   *$10.00*
First class   *no charge*

Fee charged for credit card payment: $20
Flight confirmed: At booking
Is a printed receipt provided? Yes
Cancellation policy: $150-200 if ticket is issued; some non-refundable

Frequent flyer miles offered? Yes
Except TW, BA, IB, LT, RJ

ORDER BY:
phone letter fax

PAYMENT FORMS ACCEPTED
Credit card

Comment:

(NP) = Firm did not provide requested information.

FIRM: Democracy Travel

RES PHONE: 1-800-

ADDRESS: 4818 Macarthur Blvd.
Washington, DC 20007
PHONE: 202-965-7200
FAX: 202-342-0471

Branch Offices:

CORPORATE INFORMATION

Owner: Roy Goldman
Gen Mgr: Roy Goldman
Number of staff: 6
Date originated: 1981
Annual sales: $1 - 4 million
Bond coverage: Yes
Accredited: ARC & IATAN
Escrow: No
Security: Member ARC, IATAN, ASTA, UNIGLOBE, CLIA.

DESTINATIONS

EUROPE, MID EAST, AFRICA, LATIN AMERICA, SOUTH PACIFIC

(For a complete list of the exact cities served within each region, see the Destination Index)

AIRLINES

BA, EK, GF, MH, MK, MD, CI, TG, BR, TK, FI

(Airline codes defined in Index)

Firm books business class: (NP)   First class: (NP)
Airlines may be contacted for references: Yes
Percentage of sales through scheduled air: 99%

SALES POLICIES

Tickets delivered: (NP)
Delivered by: *Overnight*   *$8.00*
First class   *no charge*

Fee charged for credit card payment: Yes
Flight confirmed: (NP)
Is a printed receipt provided? Yes
Cancellation policy: 25% minimum

Frequent flyer miles offered? Yes
Varies by ticket/fare

ORDER BY:

PAYMENT FORMS ACCEPTED

Comment: *'Round the world/Circle Pacific specialists.*

(NP) = Firm did not provide requested information.

FIRM: Destinations Unlimited

RES PHONE: 1-800-338-7987

ADDRESS: 3603 4th Ave.
San Diego, CA 92103-4196
PHONE: 619-299-5161
FAX: 619-299-5195

Branch Offices:
4688 Convoy St., Ste. 105
San Diego, CA 92111
619-260-4930

Travel Agent Rating
Overall Average
8.33
(Detailed analysis of results in Ratings Section)

CORPORATE INFORMATION

Owner: Sung Ho Chun
Gen Mgr: Kee Y. Song
Number of staff: 9
Date originated: 1978
Annual sales: $5 - 10 million
Bond coverage: $100,000
Accredited: ARC & IATAN
Escrow: (NP)
Security: (NP)

DESTINATIONS
ORIENT

(For a complete list of the exact cities served within each region, see the Destination Index)

AIRLINES
KE, OZ, SQ, CI

(Airline codes defined in Index)

Firm books business class: Yes   First class: Yes
Airlines may be contacted for references: Yes
Percentage of sales through scheduled air: 95%

SALES POLICIES

Tickets delivered: Upon payment
Delivered by: *Overnight*   *$12.00*
First class   *no charge*

Fee charged for credit card payment: no charge
Flight confirmed: At booking
Is a printed receipt provided? Yes
Cancellation policy: Same as airline's policy

Frequent flyer miles offered? Yes
No specific terms

ORDER BY:
phone letter fax

PAYMENT FORMS ACCEPTED
Credit card
Personal check

Comment:

(NP) = Firm did not provide requested information.

FIRM: Dial Europe Inc.

RES PHONE: 1-800-

ADDRESS: 515 Madison Ave., Ste. 917
New York, NY 10022
PHONE: 212-758-5310
FAX: 212-935-7468

Branch Offices:

Travel Agent Rating
Overall Average

7.83

(Detailed analysis of results in Ratings Section)

CORPORATE INFORMATION

Owner: Ibolya Brunzvik
Gen Mgr: Ed Mehler
Number of staff: 10
Date originated: 1978
Annual sales: $5 - 10 million
Bond coverage: $20,000
Accredited: IATAN
Escrow: (NP)
Security: (NP)

DESTINATIONS
EUROPE, MID EAST, ORIENT

(For a complete list of the exact cities served within each region, see the Destination Index)

AIRLINES
TW, OA, AY, IB, DL, UA, BA, MS, Ariana

(Airline codes defined in Index)

Firm books business class: Yes   First class: Yes
Airlines may be contacted for references: Yes
Percentage of sales through scheduled air: 100%

SALES POLICIES

Tickets delivered: (NP)
        Delivered by: *Overnight*
                First class

Fee charged for credit card payment: (NP)
Flight confirmed: (NP)
Is a printed receipt provided? (NP)
Cancellation policy: $100 fee

Frequent flyer miles offered? Yes
                Varies by airline

ORDER BY:

PAYMENT FORMS ACCEPTED
Personal check
COD

Comment:

(NP) = Firm did not provide requested information.

FIRM: Egypt Tours & Travel

RES PHONE: 1-800-523-4978

ADDRESS: 4353 N Harding Ave.
Chicago, IL 60618
PHONE: 312-463-4999
FAX: 312-463-4001
Branch Offices:

Travel Agent Rating
Overall Average
8
(Detailed analysis of results in Ratings Section)

CORPORATE INFORMATION

Owner: (NP)
Gen Mgr: Jim Onan
Number of staff: 3
Date originated: 1991
Annual sales: Under $1 Million
Bond coverage: (NP)
Accredited: IATAN
Escrow: (NP)
Security: (NP)

DESTINATIONS
MID EAST

(For a complete list of the exact cities served within each region, see the Destination Index)

AIRLINES
MS, KLM, BA, Austrian Airlines

(Airline codes defined in Index)

Firm books business class: Yes   First class: (NP)
Airlines may be contacted for references: Yes
Percentage of sales through scheduled air: 80%

SALES POLICIES

Tickets delivered: 10 days before departure
Delivered by: *Overnight* $7.00
First class

Fee charged for credit card payment:
Flight confirmed: 15 days before departure
Is a printed receipt provided? No
Cancellation policy: (NP)

Frequent flyer miles offered? No

ORDER BY:

PAYMENT FORMS ACCEPTED

Comment:

(NP) = Firm did not provide requested information.

FIRM: Euram Tours Inc

RES PHONE: 1-800-848-6789

ADDRESS: 1522 K. St. N.W. Ste. 430
Washington, DC 20005
PHONE: 202-789-2255
FAX: 202-842-0608

Branch Offices:
2nd Reservations Office
Los Angeles, CA
800-555-3872

Travel Agent Rating
Overall Average

8.05

(Detailed analysis of results in Ratings Section)

CORPORATE INFORMATION

Owner: R. David Scott
Gen Mgr: Wendy Beacher Tuthill
Number of staff: 94
Date originated: 1981
Annual sales: Over $25 million
Bond coverage: Maximum
Accredited: ARC & IATAN
Escrow: Yes
Security: Summer Charter program - all
monies held in escrow.

DESTINATIONS

EUROPE, MID EAST, AFRICA, LATIN AMERICA, SOUTH PACIFIC

(For a complete list of the exact cities served within each region, see the Destination Index)

AIRLINES
SU, AR, AT, IT, NH, AA, BA, CO, DL, FI, KL, LH, NW, SN, SQ, SR, TR, TW, UA, US, QF, VP

(Airline codes defined in Index)

Firm books business class: Yes   First class: (NP)
Airlines may be contacted for references: Yes
Percentage of sales through scheduled air: 80%

SALES POLICIES

Tickets delivered: 7 to 10 days before departure
Delivered by: *Overnight*   *no charge*

Fee charged for credit card payment:
Flight confirmed: Immediately
Is a printed receipt provided? Yes
Cancellation policy: Varies by airline

Frequent flyer miles offered? Yes
Varies by airline

ORDER BY:

PAYMENT FORMS ACCEPTED

Comment:

(NP) = Firm did not provide requested information.

FIRM: Everest Travel Inc.

RES PHONE: 1-800-

ADDRESS: 3350 Peachtree Rd NE, Ste. 120
Atlanta, GA 30326
PHONE: 404-231-5222
FAX: 404-231-9745

Branch Offices:

Travel Agent Rating
Overall Average
6.86
(Detailed analysis of results in Ratings Section)

CORPORATE INFORMATION

Owner: Asmish Dharamrup
Gen Mgr: Franklin
Number of staff: 12
Date originated: 1982
Annual sales: $5 - 10 million
Bond coverage: No
Accredited: ARC & IATAN
Escrow: (NP)
Security: (NP)

DESTINATIONS

EUROPE, MID EAST, ORIENT, AFRICA, LATIN AMERICA, SOUTH PACIFIC, NORTH AMERICA

(For a complete list of the exact cities served within each region, see the Destination Index)

AIRLINES
Lufthansia, British Airways, KLM

(Airline codes defined in Index)

Firm books business class: (NP)   First class: (NP)
Airlines may be contacted for references: Yes
Percentage of sales through scheduled air: 100%

SALES POLICIES

Tickets delivered: Same day
Delivered by: *Overnight First class*

Fee charged for credit card payment:
Flight confirmed: Same day
Is a printed receipt provided? (NP)
Cancellation policy: (NP)

Frequent flyer miles offered? (NP)

ORDER BY:

PAYMENT FORMS ACCEPTED

Comment:

(NP) = Firm did not provide requested information.

FIRM: Fantasy Holidays

RES PHONE: 1-800-645-2555

ADDRESS: 400 Jericho Turnpike Ste 301
Jericho, NY 11753
PHONE: 516-935-8500
FAX: 516-932-4622

Branch Offices:

Travel Agent Rating
Overall Average
8.33
(Detailed analysis of results in Ratings Section)

CORPORATE INFORMATION

Owner: John DeLeo
Gen Mgr: N/A
Number of staff: 20
Date originated: 1981
Annual sales: Over $25 million
Bond coverage: $70,000
Accredited: ARC & IATAN
Escrow: Only charters
Security: ASTA top member

DESTINATIONS
WESTERN EUROPE

(For a complete list of the exact cities served within each region, see the Destination Index)

AIRLINES
AA, CO, TW, UA

(Airline codes defined in Index)

Firm books business class: No   First class: No
Airlines may be contacted for references: Yes
Percentage of sales through scheduled air: 60%

SALES POLICIES

Tickets delivered: Upon payment
Delivered by: *Overnight*   *no charge*

Fee charged for credit card payment: no charge
Flight confirmed: At booking
Is a printed receipt provided? Yes
Cancellation policy: Varies by airline

Frequent flyer miles offered? Yes
Varies by airline

ORDER BY:
phone

PAYMENT FORMS ACCEPTED
Credit card
Personal check

Comment:

(NP) = Firm did not provide requested information.

FIRM: Fare Deals Ltd.

RES PHONE: 1-800-347-7006

ADDRESS: 10806 Reisterstown Rd.
Owing Mills, MD 21117
PHONE: 410-581-8787
FAX: 410-581-1093

Branch Offices:

CORPORATE INFORMATION

Owner: Darlene Fisher, Martin Sitnick
Gen Mgr: Darlene Fisher
Number of staff: 12
Date originated: 1990
Annual sales: $5 - 10 million
Bond coverage: (NP)
Accredited: ARC & IATAN
Escrow: Yes
Security: Escrow account for passenger
funds

DESTINATIONS
EUROPE, ORIENT, AFRICA, LATIN AMERICA, NORTH AMERICA, CARIBBEAN

(For a complete list of the exact cities served within each region, see the Destination Index)

AIRLINES
All major international carriers and charter airlines

(Airline codes defined in Index)

Firm books business class: Yes   First class: Yes
Airlines may be contacted for references: Yes
Percentage of sales through scheduled air: 85%

SALES POLICIES

Tickets delivered: Upon payment
Delivered by: *Overnight*   *$10.00*
First class   *no charge*

Fee charged for credit card payment:
Flight confirmed: Up to six months
Is a printed receipt provided? Yes
Cancellation policy: Set by airline; fees vary

Frequent flyer miles offered? Yes
Varies by airline

ORDER BY:
phone letter fax

PAYMENT FORMS ACCEPTED
Credit card
Personal check

Comment:

(NP) = Firm did not provide requested information.

FIRM: Favored Holidays Inc.

RES PHONE: 1-800-

ADDRESS: 2403 E 22nd St.
Brooklyn, NY 11235
PHONE: 718-934-8881
FAX: 718-934-4115

Branch Offices:

Travel Agent Rating
Overall Average
9.5
(Detailed analysis of results in Ratings Section)

CORPORATE INFORMATION

Owner: Favored Holidays
Gen Mgr: Marina Shkolnik
Number of staff: 4
Date originated: 1991
Annual sales: $1 - 4 million
Bond coverage: $70,000
Accredited: ARC & IATAN
Escrow: (NP)
Security: (NP)

DESTINATIONS

EUROPE, MID EAST, ORIENT, AFRICA, LATIN AMERICA, SOUTH PACIFIC, NORTH AMERICA

(For a complete list of the exact cities served within each region, see the Destination Index)

AIRLINES
AF, LH, AY, TK, IB, AZ, GU, SK, SU

(Airline codes defined in Index)

Firm books business class: Yes   First class: (NP)
Airlines may be contacted for references: Yes
Percentage of sales through scheduled air: 100%

SALES POLICIES

Tickets delivered: No limit
Delivered by: *Overnight*   *$10.00*

Fee charged for credit card payment:
Flight confirmed: No limit
Is a printed receipt provided? No
Cancellation policy: Varies by airline

Frequent flyer miles offered? Yes
Varies by airline

ORDER BY:

PAYMENT FORMS ACCEPTED

Comment:

(NP) = Firm did not provide requested information.

FIRM: Four Seasons Travel

RES PHONE: 1-800-

ADDRESS: 2300 W Meadowview Rd
Greensboro, NC 27407
PHONE: 910-292-1887
FAX: 910-852-6089

Branch Offices:

Travel Agent Rating
Overall Average

2

(Detailed analysis of results in Ratings Section)

CORPORATE INFORMATION

Owner: M.Hilton/B. Beck/R. Crawford
Gen Mgr: Mary Hilton
Number of staff: 5
Date originated: 1991
Annual sales: $5 - 10 million
Bond coverage: $1,000,000
Accredited: ARC & IATAN
Escrow: (NP)
Security: (NP)

DESTINATIONS

EUROPE, ORIENT, LATIN AMERICA

(For a complete list of the exact cities served within each region, see the Destination Index)

AIRLINES

Air India, Korean Air, United, Singapore, Varig, Brazilian, Gulf Air

(Airline codes defined in Index)

Firm books business class: (NP)   First class: (NP)
Airlines may be contacted for references: No
Percentage of sales through scheduled air: 100%

SALES POLICIES

Tickets delivered: (NP)
Delivered by: *Overnight*   *no charge*

Fee charged for credit card payment:
Flight confirmed: (NP)
Is a printed receipt provided? (NP)
Cancellation policy: (NP)

Frequent flyer miles offered? (NP)

ORDER BY:

PAYMENT FORMS ACCEPTED

Comment:

(NP) = Firm did not provide requested information.

FIRM: The French Experience

RES PHONE: 1-800-

ADDRESS: 370 Lexington Ave.
New York, NY 10017
PHONE: 212-986-3800
FAX: 212-986-3808

Branch Offices:

CORPORATE INFORMATION

Owner: Brigitte Sayagh & Francois Petitot
Gen Mgr: (NP)
Number of staff: 10
Date originated: 1982
Annual sales: $1 - 4 million
Bond coverage: No
Accredited: No
Escrow: No
Security: Reservations made on scheduled air flights.

DESTINATIONS
EUROPE

(For a complete list of the exact cities served within each region, see the Destination Index)

AIRLINES
AF, KL, DL, FF, BA, CO, LH, AA, etc.

(Airline codes defined in Index)

Firm books business class: No   First class: No
Airlines may be contacted for references: Yes
Percentage of sales through scheduled air: 100%

SALES POLICIES

Tickets delivered: (NP)
      Delivered by: *Overnight*   *$9.00*

Fee charged for credit card payment: (NP)
Flight confirmed: (NP)
Is a printed receipt provided? (NP)
Cancellation policy: Depends on the airline

Frequent flyer miles offered? Yes
            Varies by airline

ORDER BY:
phone   fax

PAYMENT FORMS ACCEPTED
*Credit card
Personal check*

Comment:

(NP) = Firm did not provide requested information.

FIRM: GIT Travel

RES PHONE: 1-800-228-1777

Travel Agent Rating
Overall Average
8.25
(Detailed analysis of results in Ratings Section)

ADDRESS: 7000 Peachtree Dunwoody Rd. Bldg II
Atlanta, GA 30328
PHONE: 404-399-6404
FAX: 404-399-6957

Branch Offices:
2880 Mollomb Br. Road, Ste.
Alpharetta, GA 30202

CORPORATE INFORMATION

Owner: Micmar J. Walsh
Gen Mgr: Betty Adams
Number of staff: 5
Date originated: 1985
Annual sales: $5 - 10 million
Bond coverage: $70,000
Accredited: ARC & IATAN
Escrow: Yes
Security: (NP)

DESTINATIONS

EUROPE, MID EAST, AFRICA, LATIN AMERICA

(For a complete list of the exact cities served within each region, see the Destination Index)

AIRLINES
BA, LH, KLM

(Airline codes defined in Index)

Firm books business class: (NP)   First class: (NP)
Airlines may be contacted for references: Yes
Percentage of sales through scheduled air: 95%

SALES POLICIES

Tickets delivered: One week after order
Delivered by: *Overnight*   *$9.00*

Fee charged for credit card payment: (NP)
Flight confirmed: One week before departure
Is a printed receipt provided? Yes
Cancellation policy: Only if voided in one week

Frequent flyer miles offered? No

ORDER BY:

PAYMENT FORMS ACCEPTED

Comment: *Group discounts*

(NP) = Firm did not provide requested information.

FIRM: GTI Travel Consolidators

RES PHONE: 1-800-829-8234

ADDRESS: 515 E. 8th St.
Holland, MI 49423
PHONE: 616-396-1234
FAX: 616-396-7720

Branch Offices:

Travel Agent Rating
Overall Average
10
(Detailed analysis of results in Ratings Section)

CORPORATE INFORMATION

Owner: Corporation
Gen Mgr: Tom Harrington
Number of staff: 11
Date originated: 1979
Annual sales: $5 - 10 million
Bond coverage: $70,000
Accredited: ARC & IATAN
Escrow: (NP)
Security: Tickets are issued and sent out
upon receipt of payment.

DESTINATIONS

EASTERN EUROPE, ORIENT

(For a complete list of the exact cities served within each region, see the Destination Index)

AIRLINES
KL, DL, OK, SU, PR, OS, TK, GA, NW

(Airline codes defined in Index)

Firm books business class: Yes   First class: Yes
Airlines may be contacted for references: Yes
Percentage of sales through scheduled air: 100%

SALES POLICIES

Tickets delivered: Upon payment
Delivered by: *Overnight*   *no charge*

Fee charged for credit card payment: $15.00
Flight confirmed: At booking
Is a printed receipt provided? Yes
Cancellation policy: Varies by airline

Frequent flyer miles offered? Yes
Varies by airline

ORDER BY:
phone letter fax

PAYMENT FORMS ACCEPTED
Cash
Personal check

Comment:

(NP) = Firm did not provide requested information.

FIRM: **Garden State Travel**

RES PHONE: 1-800-537-2420

ADDRESS: 581 West Side Ave
Jersey City, NJ 07304
PHONE: 201-333-1232
FAX: 201-333-0122
Branch Offices:

Travel Agent Rating
Overall Average
10
(Detailed analysis of results in Ratings Section)

CORPORATE INFORMATION

Owner: Vid M. Figueras
Gen Mgr: Lisa Valencia
Number of staff: 8
Date originated: 1985
Annual sales: $5 - 10 million
Bond coverage: $25,000
Accredited: ARC & IATAN
Escrow: (NP)
Security: (NP)

DESTINATIONS

ORIENT

(For a complete list of the exact cities served within each region, see the Destination Index)

AIRLINES

Philippine Airlines, Korean Air, Northwest, MA, China, United Airlines

(Airline codes defined in Index)

Firm books business class: (NP)   First class: (NP)
Airlines may be contacted for references: Yes
Percentage of sales through scheduled air: (NP)

SALES POLICIES

Tickets delivered: ASAP
Delivered by: *Overnight*   *$15.00*
First class   *no charge*

Fee charged for credit card payment: (NP)
Flight confirmed: One week before departure
Is a printed receipt provided? (NP)
Cancellation policy: (NP)

Frequent flyer miles offered? (NP)

ORDER BY:

PAYMENT FORMS ACCEPTED

Comment:

(NP) = Firm did not provide requested information.

FIRM: General Tours

RES PHONE: 1-800-221-2216

ADDRESS: 53 Summer St.
              Keene, NH 03431
   PHONE: 603-357-5033
      FAX: 603-357-4548

Branch Offices:

Travel Agent Rating
Overall Average
7.22
(Detailed analysis of results in Ratings Section)

CORPORATE INFORMATION

Owner: Robert Drumm & Partners
Gen Mgr: Robert Drumm, President
Number of staff: 30
Date originated: 1947
Annual sales: $10 - 25 million
Bond coverage: (NP)
Accredited: ARC
Escrow: Yes
Security: First of America escrow
              account

DESTINATIONS

EUROPE, MID EAST, AFRICA, INDIA

(For a complete list of the exact cities served within each region, see the Destination Index)

AIRLINES

Delta, Swissair, Finnair, LOT, SK, Royal Air Maroc, Air India

(Airline codes defined in Index)

Firm books business class: (NP)   First class: (NP)
Airlines may be contacted for references: Yes
Percentage of sales through scheduled air: (NP)

SALES POLICIES

Tickets delivered: 72 hours after booking
      Delivered by:

              Fed Ex 2-day
Fee charged for credit card payment: (NP)
Flight confirmed: At booking
Is a printed receipt provided? Yes
Cancellation policy: Varies; dependent on how
                          much notice we're given.

Frequent flyer miles offered? Yes

ORDER BY:

PAYMENT FORMS ACCEPTED

Comment:

(NP) = Firm did not provide requested information.

FIRM: **Getaway Travel Intl. Inc.**

RES PHONE: 1-800-683-6336

ADDRESS: 250 Catalonia Ave Ste. 805
Coral Gables, FL 33134
PHONE: 305-446-7855
FAX: 305-444-6647

Branch Offices:

Travel Agent Rating
Overall Average
7
(Detailed analysis of results in Ratings Section)

CORPORATE INFORMATION

Owner: Serge D'Adesky
Gen Mgr: Serge D'Adesky
Number of staff: 6
Date originated: 1983
Annual sales: $1 - 4 million
Bond coverage: $40,000
Accredited: ARC & IATAN
Escrow: (NP)
Security: (NP)

DESTINATIONS

MID EAST, ORIENT, AFRICA, LATIN AMERICA

(For a complete list of the exact cities served within each region, see the Destination Index)

AIRLINES

AF, AA, BA, LH, LT, IB, TK, KE, CI, DL, UA, CM, TA, GY, LR, AV, VX, OD, RG, UC, LA

(Airline codes defined in Index)

Firm books business class: (NP)   First class: (NP)
Airlines may be contacted for references: Yes
Percentage of sales through scheduled air: 95%

SALES POLICIES

Tickets delivered: Immediately upon payment
Delivered by: *Overnight $10.00*
First class
UPS/land   no charge
Fee charged for credit card payment: (NP)
Flight confirmed: No limit
Is a printed receipt provided? No
Cancellation policy: $30 to $50 - plus airline fees

Frequent flyer miles offered? Yes
Varies by airline

ORDER BY:

PAYMENT FORMS ACCEPTED

Comment: *We offer Sabre agents free software giving them live access to database of over 15,000 net fares.*

(NP) = Firm did not provide requested information.

FIRM: **Group & Leisure**

RES PHONE: 1-800-874-6608

ADDRESS: P.O. Box 1384
Blue Springs, MO 64013
PHONE: 816-224-3717
FAX: 816-228-2650
Branch Offices:

CORPORATE INFORMATION

Owner: Donna Jerome
Gen Mgr: (NP)
Number of staff: (NP)
Date originated: 1989
Annual sales: Under $1 million
Bond coverage:
Accredited: ARC & IATAN
Escrow: Yes
Security: Escrow accounts or credit card
payments

DESTINATIONS
EUROPE, ORIENT, LATIN AMERICA, NORTH AMERICA, CARIBBEAN

(For a complete list of the exact cities served within each region, see the Destination Index)

AIRLINES
All major air carriers, such as TW, NW, AA, DL, US, BA

(Airline codes defined in Index)

Firm books business class: Yes   First class: Yes
Airlines may be contacted for references: Yes
Percentage of sales through scheduled air: 95%

SALES POLICIES

Tickets delivered: Two weeks before departure
Delivered by: *Overnight*
First class

Fee charged for credit card payment: (NP)
Flight confirmed: At booking
Is a printed receipt provided? Yes
Cancellation policy: Depends on fare

Frequent flyer miles offered? Yes
Varies by airline

ORDER BY:
phone letter fax

PAYMENT FORMS ACCEPTED
*Credit card
Personal check*

Comment:

(NP) = Firm did not provide requested information.

FIRM: Guardian Travel Service Inc.

RES PHONE: 1-800-741-3050

ADDRESS: 7360 Gulf Blvd.
Petersburg Beach, FL 33706
PHONE: 813-367-5622
FAX: 813-367-4597

Branch Offices:

Travel Agent Rating
Overall Average
5
(Detailed analysis of results in Ratings Section)

CORPORATE INFORMATION

Owner: Fran Stutz
Gen Mgr: Fran Stutz
Number of staff: 4
Date originated: 1981
Annual sales: $1 - 4 million
Bond coverage: (NP)
Accredited: ARC & IATAN
Escrow: Yes
Security: (NP)

DESTINATIONS
EUROPE

(For a complete list of the exact cities served within each region, see the Destination Index)

AIRLINES
AC, AY, AZ, BA, FI, LT, BD

(Airline codes defined in Index)

Firm books business class: No   First class: (NP)
Airlines may be contacted for references: Yes
Percentage of sales through scheduled air: 80%

SALES POLICIES

Tickets delivered: Three weeks before departure
Delivered by: *Overnight $10.00*
First class   no charge

Fee charged for credit card payment: no charge
Flight confirmed: At booking
Is a printed receipt provided? (NP)
Cancellation policy: Varies by airline

Frequent flyer miles offered? Yes

ORDER BY:
phone letter fax

PAYMENT FORMS ACCEPTED
*Credit card
Personal check*

Comment:

(NP) = Firm did not provide requested information.

FIRM: Hana Travel Inc.

RES PHONE: 1-800-962-8044

ADDRESS: 1207 Old McHenry Rd Ste.214
Buffalo Grove, IL 60089
PHONE: 708-913-1177
FAX: 708-913-5492

Branch Offices:

CORPORATE INFORMATION

Owner: Sonnia Bach
Gen Mgr: Debra Mykleby
Number of staff: (NP)
Date originated: (NP)
Annual sales: $5 - 10 million
Bond coverage: (NP)
Accredited: ARC
Escrow: (NP)
Security: (NP)

DESTINATIONS
ORIENT

(For a complete list of the exact cities served within each region, see the Destination Index)

AIRLINES
Most major airlines

(Airline codes defined in Index)

Firm books business class: (NP)   First class: (NP)
Airlines may be contacted for references: No
Percentage of sales through scheduled air: (NP)

SALES POLICIES

Tickets delivered: (NP)
Delivered by: *Overnight*   *$10.00*
First class   *no charge*

Fee charged for credit card payment:
Flight confirmed: (NP)
Is a printed receipt provided? (NP)
Cancellation policy: (NP)

Frequent flyer miles offered? Yes
Varies by airline

ORDER BY:

PAYMENT FORMS ACCEPTED

Comment:

(NP) = Firm did not provide requested information.

FIRM: Hari World Travels, Inc.

RES PHONE: 1-800-

ADDRESS: 30 Rockefeller Plaza, Shop 21N
New York, NY 10112
PHONE: 212-957-3000
FAX: 212-957-7921

Branch Offices:

Travel Agent Rating
Overall Average

7

(Detailed analysis of results in Ratings Section)

CORPORATE INFORMATION

Owner: Mr. Prem Cohly
Gen Mgr: Mrs. Teresita Flores
Number of staff: 20
Date originated: 1982
Annual sales: Over $25 million
Bond coverage: $80,000
Accredited: ARC & IATAN
Escrow: (NP)
Security: (NP)

DESTINATIONS

EUROPE, MID EAST, ORIENT, AFRICA, LATIN AMERICA, SOUTH PACIFIC, NORTH AMERICA

(For a complete list of the exact cities served within each region, see the Destination Index)

AIRLINES

Lufthansa, American, United, Swiss Air, Alitalia, Emirates, Delta, Kenyan Air, Korean Air

(Airline codes defined in Index)

Firm books business class: (NP)   First class: (NP)
Airlines may be contacted for references: Yes
Percentage of sales through scheduled air: (NP)

SALES POLICIES

Tickets delivered: At booking
Delivered by: *Overnight*   *$9.00*

Fee charged for credit card payment: (NP)
Flight confirmed: At booking
Is a printed receipt provided? (NP)
Cancellation policy: (NP)

Frequent flyer miles offered? (NP)

ORDER BY:

PAYMENT FORMS ACCEPTED

Comment:

(NP) = Firm did not provide requested information.

FIRM: Holbrook Travel Inc.

RES PHONE: 1-800-451-7111

ADDRESS: 3540 NW 13th St.
Gainesville, FL 32609
PHONE: 904-377-7111
FAX: 904-371-3710

Branch Offices:

Travel Agent Rating
Overall Average
9
(Detailed analysis of results in Ratings Section)

CORPORATE INFORMATION

Owner: Juan & Giovanna Holbrook
Gen Mgr: David Holbrook
Number of staff: 25
Date originated: 1974
Annual sales: $5 - 10 million
Bond coverage: Yes
Accredited: ARC
Escrow: (NP)
Security: (NP)

DESTINATIONS

AFRICA, LATIN AMERICA

(For a complete list of the exact cities served within each region, see the Destination Index)

AIRLINES
American, Delta,United (all major US carriers)

(Airline codes defined in Index)

Firm books business class: (NP)   First class: (NP)
Airlines may be contacted for references: Yes
Percentage of sales through scheduled air: (NP)

SALES POLICIES

Tickets delivered: Within two days
Delivered by:

Fee charged for credit card payment:
Flight confirmed: Within one day
Is a printed receipt provided? (NP)
Cancellation policy: (NP)

Frequent flyer miles offered? (NP)

ORDER BY:

PAYMENT FORMS ACCEPTED

Comment:

(NP) = Firm did not provide requested information.

FIRM: Holiday Travel International

RES PHONE: 1-800-775-7111

ADDRESS: 12239 US Route 30
North Huntingdon, PA 15642-1836
PHONE: 412-863-7500
FAX: 412-863-7590

Branch Offices:

Travel Agent Rating
Overall Average
8
(Detailed analysis of results in Ratings Section)

CORPORATE INFORMATION

Owner: Philip Petrulli
Gen Mgr: Jan Eddy
Number of staff: 14
Date originated: 1971
Annual sales: $10 - 25 million
Bond coverage: $100,000
Accredited: ARC & IATAN
Escrow: (NP)
Security: (NP)

DESTINATIONS
NORTH AMERICA

(For a complete list of the exact cities served within each region, see the Destination Index)

AIRLINES
TWA

(Airline codes defined in Index)

Firm books business class: Yes   First class: (NP)
Airlines may be contacted for references: Yes
Percentage of sales through scheduled air: 100%

SALES POLICIES

Tickets delivered: 21 to 30 days before departure
Delivered by: *Overnight $15.00*
First class   no charge

Fee charged for credit card payment: (NP)
Flight confirmed: Immediately
Is a printed receipt provided? Yes
Cancellation policy: (NP)

Frequent flyer miles offered? No

ORDER BY:

PAYMENT FORMS ACCEPTED

Comment: *Serves all TWA domestic cities.*

(NP) = Firm did not provide requested information.

FIRM: Homeric Tours, Inc.

RES PHONE: 1-800-223-5570

ADDRESS: 55 East 59th St.
New York, NY 10022
PHONE: 212-753-1100
FAX: 212-753-0319

Branch Offices:

CORPORATE INFORMATION

Owner: Nikos Tsakanikas
Gen Mgr: Tassoula Christofidis
Number of staff: (NP)
Date originated: 1969
Annual sales: Over $25 million
Bond coverage: (NP)
Accredited: ARC & IATAN
Escrow: Yes
Security: All payments deposited in DOT
approved charter escrow

DESTINATIONS
GREECE, PORTUGAL, MOROCCO, EGYPT

(For a complete list of the exact cities served within each region, see the Destination Index)

AIRLINES
OA, DL, TW, TP, AT, FF, WO

(Airline codes defined in Index)

Firm books business class: Yes   First class: Yes
Airlines may be contacted for references: Yes
Percentage of sales through scheduled air: 50%

SALES POLICIES

Tickets delivered: Two weeks before departure
Delivered by: *Overnight*   *$15.00*
First class   *no charge*

Fee charged for credit card payment: Yes
Flight confirmed: At booking
Is a printed receipt provided? No
Cancellation policy: (NP)

Frequent flyer miles offered? No

ORDER BY:
phone letter fax

PAYMENT FORMS ACCEPTED
Credit card
Personal check

Comment:

(NP) = Firm did not provide requested information.

FIRM: Hostway Tours

RES PHONE: 1-800-327-3207

ADDRESS: 2907 Stirling Rd.
Fort Lauderdale, FL 33312
PHONE: 305-966-8500
FAX: 305-966-7815

Branch Offices:

CORPORATE INFORMATION

Owner: Bruce Balter
Gen Mgr: Bruce Balter
Number of staff: 15
Date originated: 1979
Annual sales: $5 - 10 million
Bond coverage: (NP)
Accredited: ARC
Escrow: (NP)
Security: (NP)

DESTINATIONS

LATIN AMERICA, NORTH AMERICA

(For a complete list of the exact cities served within each region, see the Destination Index)

AIRLINES
Aeroflot, Continental, AA

(Airline codes defined in Index)

Firm books business class: (NP)   First class: (NP)
Airlines may be contacted for references: Yes
Percentage of sales through scheduled air: (NP)

SALES POLICIES

Tickets delivered: Upon payment
Delivered by:

UPS

Fee charged for credit card payment: (NP)
Flight confirmed: Upon payment
Is a printed receipt provided? (NP)
Cancellation policy: (NP)

Frequent flyer miles offered? Yes
Varies by airline

ORDER BY:

PAYMENT FORMS ACCEPTED

Comment:

(NP) = Firm did not provide requested information.

FIRM: Hudson Holidays

RES PHONE: 1-800-323-6855

ADDRESS: 7512 W Grand Ave.
　　　　 Elmwood Pk, IL 60635
　PHONE: 708-452-0600
　　FAX: 708-452-9264

Branch Offices:

Travel Agent Rating
Overall Average
7.38
*(Detailed analysis of
results in Ratings
Section)*

CORPORATE INFORMATION

Owner: George and Steve Hudson
Gen Mgr: Steve Hudson
Number of staff: 18
Date originated: 1987
Annual sales: $10 - 25 million
Bond coverage: $100,000
Accredited: ARC & IATAN
Escrow: (NP)
Security: (NP)

DESTINATIONS
EUROPE

*(For a complete list of the exact
cities served within each region, see
the Destination Index)*

AIRLINES
TZ, Most major international carriers

(Airline codes defined in Index)

Firm books business class: No　　　 First class: No
Airlines may be contacted for references: Yes
Percentage of sales through scheduled air: 80%

SALES POLICIES

Tickets delivered: Three weeks before departure
　　 Delivered by: *Overnight*　　　　 *$15.00*

Fee charged for credit card payment: yes
Flight confirmed: Up to 120 days before
Is a printed receipt provided? (NP)
Cancellation policy: Varies by airline

Frequent flyer miles offered? Yes
　　　　　　　 Varies by airline

ORDER BY:

**PAYMENT FORMS
ACCEPTED**

Comment:

(NP) = Firm did not provide requested information.

FIRM: ITS Tours & Travel

RES PHONE: 1-800-533-8688

ADDRESS: 1055 Texas Ave. Ste 104
College Station, TX 77840
PHONE: 409-964-9400
FAX: 409-693-9673

Branch Offices:

Travel Agent Rating
Overall Average
8.6
(Detailed analysis of results in Ratings Section)

CORPORATE INFORMATION

Owner: Michal Barszap
Gen Mgr: Andrew Loehrer
Number of staff: 22
Date originated: 1983
Annual sales: $5 - 10 million
Bond coverage: Yes
Accredited: ARC & IATAN
Escrow: (NP)
Security: Fully bonded as paid per
ARC/IATA requirements

DESTINATIONS
EUROPE

(For a complete list of the exact cities served within each region, see the Destination Index)

AIRLINES
AY, SU, DL, OK, KL

(Airline codes defined in Index)

Firm books business class: (NP)   First class: (NP)
Airlines may be contacted for references: Yes
Percentage of sales through scheduled air: 100%

SALES POLICIES

Tickets delivered: Upon payment
Delivered by: *Overnight*   *$15.00*
First class   *yes*

Fee charged for credit card payment:
Flight confirmed: One day, subject to availability
Is a printed receipt provided? (NP)
Cancellation policy: Fees for cancellation

Frequent flyer miles offered? Yes

ORDER BY:

PAYMENT FORMS ACCEPTED

Comment:

(NP) = Firm did not provide requested information.

FIRM: Inter Island Tours

RES PHONE: 1-800-245-3434

ADDRESS: 419 Park Ave. South
New York, NY 10016
PHONE: 212-686-4868
FAX: 212-532-4906
Branch Offices:

Travel Agent Rating
Overall Average
7
(Detailed analysis of results in Ratings Section)

CORPORATE INFORMATION

Owner: Bob Thorne
Gen Mgr: Greg Thorne
Number of staff: 9
Date originated: 1984
Annual sales: $1 - 4 million
Bond coverage: $75,000
Accredited: ARC & IATAN
Escrow: (NP)
Security: (NP)

DESTINATIONS
LATIN AMERICA, CARIBBEAN

(For a complete list of the exact cities served within each region, see the Destination Index)

AIRLINES
AA, TWA, UE

(Airline codes defined in Index)

Firm books business class: Yes First class: Yes
Airlines may be contacted for references: Yes
Percentage of sales through scheduled air: 20%

SALES POLICIES

Tickets delivered: Three weeks before departure
Delivered by: *Overnight* *$10.00*

Fee charged for credit card payment:
Flight confirmed: At booking
Is a printed receipt provided? No
Cancellation policy: Per our conditions of

Frequent flyer miles offered? Yes
Varies by airline

ORDER BY:
phone letter fax

PAYMENT FORMS ACCEPTED

Comment: *We are a preferred wholesaler for American Airlines to the Caribbean.*

(NP) = Firm did not provide requested information.

FIRM: Interworld Travel

RES PHONE: 1-800-468-3796

ADDRESS: 800 Douglas Rd., #140
Coral Gables, FL 33134
PHONE: 305-443-4929
FAX: 305-443-0351
Branch Offices:

CORPORATE INFORMATION
Owner: Robert Hubbard
Gen Mgr: (NP)
Number of staff: 6
Date originated: August 1985
Annual sales: $5 - 10 million
Bond coverage: Yes
Accredited: ARC & IATAN
Escrow: No
Security: (NP)

DESTINATIONS
EAST & WEST EUROPE, MID EAST, AFRICA, LATIN AMERICA

(For a complete list of the exact cities served within each region, see the Destination Index)

AIRLINES
BA, VS, NW, SA, IB, AA, UC

(Airline codes defined in Index)

Firm books business class: No   First class: No
Airlines may be contacted for references: Yes
Percentage of sales through scheduled air: 100%

SALES POLICIES
Tickets delivered: ASAP
Delivered by: *Overnight*   *$10.00*
First class   *no charge*

Fee charged for credit card payment: 4%
Flight confirmed: Varies from carrier to carrier
Is a printed receipt provided? Yes
Cancellation policy: Varies; usually $150 once ticketed

Frequent flyer miles offered? Yes
Varies by airline

ORDER BY:
phone letter fax

PAYMENT FORMS ACCEPTED
Credit card
Personal check

Comment:

(NP) = Firm did not provide requested information.

FIRM: **KTS Services**

RES PHONE: 1-800-531-6677

ADDRESS: 187-10 Hillside Ave.
Jamaica, NY 11432
PHONE: 718-454-2300
FAX: 718-454-9491
Branch Offices:

CORPORATE INFORMATION

Owner: Fred Kunzmann
Gen Mgr: (NP)
Number of staff: 4
Date originated: 1950
Annual sales: $1 - 4 million
Bond coverage: (NP)
Accredited: ARC & IATAN
Escrow: (NP)
Security: (NP)

DESTINATIONS
EUROPE

(For a complete list of the exact cities served within each region, see the Destination Index)

AIRLINES
LH

(Airline codes defined in Index)

Firm books business class: Yes   First class: (NP)
Airlines may be contacted for references: Yes
Percentage of sales through scheduled air: 100%

SALES POLICIES

Tickets delivered: Upon payment
Delivered by: *Overnight*   *no charge*

Fee charged for credit card payment: 3%
Flight confirmed: 360 days before departure
Is a printed receipt provided? No
Cancellation policy: Non-refundable

Frequent flyer miles offered? Yes
Varies by airline

ORDER BY:

PAYMENT FORMS ACCEPTED

Comment:

(NP) = Firm did not provide requested information.

FIRM: Kambi Travel Intl.

RES PHONE: 1-800-220-2192

ADDRESS: 1400 Mercantile Ln.Ste.234
        Landover, MD 20785
  PHONE: 301-925-9012
    FAX: 301-925-9211

Branch Offices:

CORPORATE INFORMATION

Owner: Patricia Brown
Gen Mgr: Robin Bhandari
Number of staff: 4
Date originated: 1991
Annual sales: $1 - 4 million
Bond coverage: $48,000
Accredited: ARC & IATAN
Escrow: (NP)
Security: (NP)

DESTINATIONS
EUROPE, ORIENT, AFRICA

(For a complete list of the exact cities served within each region, see the Destination Index)

AIRLINES
KL, CX, SN, RK, TG, BA

(Airline codes defined in Index)

Firm books business class: Yes   First class: Yes
Airlines may be contacted for references: Yes
Percentage of sales through scheduled air: 85%

SALES POLICIES

Tickets delivered: (NP)
    Delivered by: *Overnight*   *varies*

               Two day   *varies*
Fee charged for credit card payment: (NP)
Flight confirmed: 10 days before departure
Is a printed receipt provided? (NP)
Cancellation policy: Varies by airline

Frequent flyer miles offered? Yes
           Varies by airline

ORDER BY:
phone   *fax*

PAYMENT FORMS ACCEPTED
Credit card
Cash
Money order
Net 10 days
COD

Comment:

(NP) = Firm did not provide requested information.

FIRM: Katy Van Tours

RES PHONE: 1-800-808-8747

ADDRESS: 16360 Park TEW Place, Ste. 101
Houston, TX 77084
PHONE: 713-492-7032
FAX: 713-492-0586

Branch Offices:

CORPORATE INFORMATION

Owner: Fred Pelsinger
Gen Mgr: Elena S. Pelsinger
Number of staff: 6
Date originated: 1985
Annual sales: $1 - 4 million
Bond coverage: $25,000
Accredited: ARC & IATAN
Escrow: No
Security: (NP)

DESTINATIONS

EUROPE, MID EAST, ORIENT, LATIN AMERICA

(For a complete list of the exact cities served within each region, see the Destination Index)

AIRLINES
AR, LA, GU, LR, TA, UA, BA, CO

(Airline codes defined in Index)

Firm books business class: Yes   First class: Yes
Airlines may be contacted for references: Yes
Percentage of sales through scheduled air: 100%

SALES POLICIES

Tickets delivered: 21 days before departure
Delivered by: *Overnight*   *$5.00*
First class   *no charge*

Fee charged for credit card payment: 2%
Flight confirmed: 14 days or immediately
Is a printed receipt provided? Yes
Cancellation policy: 14 days

Frequent flyer miles offered? Yes
Varies by airline

ORDER BY:
phone letter fax

PAYMENT FORMS ACCEPTED
Credit card
Cash

Comment:

(NP) = Firm did not provide requested information.

FIRM: King Tut Travel & Tours

RES PHONE: 1-800-398-1888

ADDRESS: 38848 Bell St.
Fremont, CA 94538
PHONE: 510-791-2907
FAX: 510-791-2908

Branch Offices:

CORPORATE INFORMATION

Owner: Mohammed Elshesbini
Gen Mgr: Mohammed Elshesbini
Number of staff: 4
Date originated: 1987
Annual sales: $1 - 4 million
Bond coverage: (NP)
Accredited: ARC & IATAN
Escrow: (NP)
Security: Confirmed seats

DESTINATIONS
WORLDWIDE

(For a complete list of the exact cities served within each region, see the Destination Index)

AIRLINES
All

(Airline codes defined in Index)

Firm books business class: Yes   First class: Yes
Airlines may be contacted for references: Yes
Percentage of sales through scheduled air: 100%

SALES POLICIES

Tickets delivered: ASAP
    Delivered by: *Overnight*   *$15.00*

Fee charged for credit card payment: 4%
Flight confirmed: At booking
Is a printed receipt provided? Yes
Cancellation policy: Airline policy, plus $25

Frequent flyer miles offered? No

ORDER BY:
phone letter fax

PAYMENT FORMS ACCEPTED
Credit card

Comment:

(NP) = Firm did not provide requested information.

FIRM: Kompas Travel

RES PHONE: 1-800-233-6422

ADDRESS: 2826 E. Commercial Blvd.
Ft. Lauderdale, FL 33308
PHONE: 305-771-9200
FAX: 305-771-9841

Branch Offices:

CORPORATE INFORMATION

Owner: Predrag Krivokapic
Gen Mgr: Lilly Markovic
Number of staff: 4
Date originated: 1993
Annual sales: Under $1 million
Bond coverage: $20,000
Accredited: ARC & IATAN
Escrow: (NP)
Security: (NP)

DESTINATIONS
EUROPE

(For a complete list of the exact cities served within each region, see the Destination Index)

AIRLINES
BA, IB, LT, OA

(Airline codes defined in Index)

Firm books business class: No   First class: No
Airlines may be contacted for references: Yes
Percentage of sales through scheduled air: 100%

SALES POLICIES

Tickets delivered: Upon payment
Delivered by: *Overnight*   *charge*
First class   *no charge*

Fee charged for credit card payment: Yes
Flight confirmed: At booking
Is a printed receipt provided? No
Cancellation policy: Varies- $150 charge

Frequent flyer miles offered? No

ORDER BY:
phone letter fax

PAYMENT FORMS ACCEPTED
Credit card
Personal check

Comment:

(NP) = Firm did not provide requested information.

FIRM: Lotus

RES PHONE: 1-800-998-6116

ADDRESS: 18 E. 41st St., Ste. 401
New York, NY 10017
PHONE: 212-213-1625
FAX: 212-213-1660
Branch Offices:

CORPORATE INFORMATION
Owner: Danilo Stojanovic, CTC
Gen Mgr: Sonia Stojanovi
Number of staff: 6
Date originated: 1992
Annual sales: $1 - 4 million
Bond coverage: (NP)
Accredited: (NP)
Escrow: (NP)
Security: (NP)

DESTINATIONS
EUROPE, ORIENT, SOUTH PACIFIC

(For a complete list of the exact cities served within each region, see the Destination Index)

AIRLINES
AY, VS, OK, MA, OA, TK, LO, RO, OS, KL, IB, TP, LH, CY, GA, SQ, CY, KM, RJ

(Airline codes defined in Index)

Firm books business class: (NP)   First class: (NP)
Airlines may be contacted for references: Yes
Percentage of sales through scheduled air: 100%

SALES POLICIES

Tickets delivered: Within 7 days upon payment
Delivered by: *Overnight $9.00 - 13.00*

Fee charged for credit card payment: (NP)
Flight confirmed: Immediately if space available
Is a printed receipt provided? Yes
Cancellation policy: $25.00 - plus airline terms

Frequent flyer miles offered? Yes
Varies by airline

ORDER BY:

PAYMENT FORMS ACCEPTED

Comment:

(NP) = Firm did not provide requested information.

71

FIRM: Lucky Tours

RES PHONE: 1-800-932-6654

ADDRESS: 420 Box Butte Ave.
Alliance, NE 69301
PHONE: 308-762-3957
FAX: 308-762-5243

Branch Offices:

Travel Agent Rating
Overall Average
4
(Detailed analysis of results in Ratings Section)

CORPORATE INFORMATION

Owner: Mohamed El-khatib
Gen Mgr: Mohamed El-khatib
Number of staff: 7
Date originated: 1990
Annual sales: $1 - 4 million
Bond coverage: $10,000
Accredited: ARC & IATAN
Escrow: Yes
Security: Escrow account

DESTINATIONS
MID EAST

(For a complete list of the exact cities served within each region, see the Destination Index)

AIRLINES
MS, OA, WO, TW, AT, MH, RJ

(Airline codes defined in Index)

Firm books business class: Yes   First class: Yes
Airlines may be contacted for references: Yes
Percentage of sales through scheduled air: 100%

SALES POLICIES

Tickets delivered: Upon payment
    Delivered by: *Overnight*

Fee charged for credit card payment: (NP)
Flight confirmed: At booking
Is a printed receipt provided? Yes
Cancellation policy: According to airline policy

Frequent flyer miles offered? No

ORDER BY:
phone letter fax

PAYMENT FORMS ACCEPTED
Credit card
Cash
Personal check
Net 10 days

Comment: *We do not offer air only for other destinations (international) - only with tour packages.*

(NP) = Firm did not provide requested information.

FIRM: M & H Travel, Inc.

RES PHONE: 1-800-

ADDRESS: 275 Madison Ave. Rm. 605
New York, NY 10016
PHONE: 212-661-7171
FAX: 212-661-7437

Branch Offices:

Travel Agent Rating
Overall Average

7.71

*(Detailed analysis of
results in Ratings
Section)*

CORPORATE INFORMATION

Owner: Karl Kershaw
Gen Mgr: Irene Yu
Number of staff: 9
Date originated: 1988
Annual sales: $10 - 25 million
Bond coverage: (NP)
Accredited: ARC
Escrow: (NP)
Security: (NP)

DESTINATIONS

EUROPE, MID EAST, ORIENT, AFRICA

*(For a complete list of the exact
cities served within each region, see
the Destination Index)*

AIRLINES
AF

(Airline codes defined in Index)

Firm books business class: (NP)   First class: (NP)
Airlines may be contacted for references: Yes
Percentage of sales through scheduled air: 100%

SALES POLICIES

Tickets delivered: Varies
Delivered by: *Overnight*   *$13.00*

Fee charged for credit card payment:
Flight confirmed: Varies
Is a printed receipt provided? (NP)
Cancellation policy: (NP)

Frequent flyer miles offered? (NP)

ORDER BY:

PAYMENT FORMS
ACCEPTED

Comment:

(NP) = Firm did not provide requested information.

FIRM: Magical Holidays, Inc.

RES PHONE: 1-800-433-7773

ADDRESS: 501 Madison Ave.
New York, NY 10022
PHONE: 415-781-1345
FAX: 415-781-4544

Branch Offices:

Travel Agent Rating
Overall Average

9

(Detailed analysis of results in Ratings Section)

CORPORATE INFORMATION

Owner: Michael Hering
Gen Mgr: (NP)
Number of staff: 25
Date originated: 1980
Annual sales: Over $25 million
Bond coverage: $1 million +
Accredited: ARC & IATAN
Escrow: (NP)
Security: Fully bonded - over $1 million

DESTINATIONS

EUROPE, MID EAST, ORIENT, AFRICA, LATIN AMERICA

(For a complete list of the exact cities served within each region, see the Destination Index)

AIRLINES

BA, AF, KL, SA, KQ, UY, RK, SN, TP, SR, LZ, LH, UA, LR, AR, IB

(Airline codes defined in Index)

Firm books business class: No   First class: No
Airlines may be contacted for references: Yes
Percentage of sales through scheduled air: 100%

SALES POLICIES

Tickets delivered: Upon receipt of payment
Delivered by: *Overnight*   *$10*

Fee charged for credit card payment: 3%
Flight confirmed: At booking
Is a printed receipt provided? No
Cancellation policy: 25% - no med notes or
exceptions.

Frequent flyer miles offered? No

ORDER BY:

phone

PAYMENT FORMS ACCEPTED

*Credit car
Personal check*

Comment:

(NP) = Firm did not provide requested information.

FIRM: Marakesh Tourist Company

RES PHONE: 1-800-458-1772

ADDRESS: 3196 Kennedy Blvd.
Jersy City, NJ 07306
PHONE: 201-435-2800
FAX: 201-659-8246

Branch Offices:
Riham Travel 7B Damascus St.
Cairo, Egypt
011-202-259289

CORPORATE INFORMATION

Owner: Dr. Yehia Abdelal
Gen Mgr: Samir Mohamed
Number of staff: 5
Date originated: 1975
Annual sales: $5 - 10 million
Bond coverage: (NP)
Accredited: ARC & IATAN
Escrow: (NP)
Security: (NP)

DESTINATIONS

EUROPE, MID EAST, ORIENT, AFRICA, NORTH AMERICA, CARIBBEAN

(For a complete list of the exact cities served within each region, see the Destination Index)

AIRLINES

MS, AT, RJ, OA, TW, BA, SR, AF, KL, AZ, etc. All domestic.

(Airline codes defined in Index)

Firm books business class: Yes   First class: (NP)
Airlines may be contacted for references: Yes
Percentage of sales through scheduled air: 100%

SALES POLICIES

Tickets delivered: One week before departure
Delivered by: *Overnight*   *$10.00*
First class
Priority mail   *$3.00*
Fee charged for credit card payment: (NP)
Flight confirmed: Varies
Is a printed receipt provided? Yes
Cancellation policy: After ticketing, $150 for
change or cancellation.

Frequent flyer miles offered? No

ORDER BY:

PAYMENT FORMS ACCEPTED

Comment: *FAM trips to Egypt every Friday. Packages to Egypt and Morocco with add-on's.*

(NP) = Firm did not provide requested information.

FIRM: Mena Tours & Travel

RES PHONE: 1-800-937-6362

ADDRESS: 5209 N. Clark St.
Chicago, IL 60640
PHONE: 312-275-2125
FAX: 312-275-9927

Branch Offices:
2479 N. Clark
Chicago, IL 60640
800-536-6362

Travel Agent Rating
Overall Average
7.64
(Detailed analysis of results in Ratings Section)

CORPORATE INFORMATION

Owner: Jorge & Giselle Sanchez
Gen Mgr: Jorge Sanchez
Number of staff: 20
Date originated: 1965
Annual sales: $10 - 25 million
Bond coverage: Max per ARC
Accredited: ARC & IATAN
Escrow: (NP)
Security: (NP)

DESTINATIONS

EUROPE, LATIN AMERICA, NORTH AMERICA, CARIBBEAN

(For a complete list of the exact cities served within each region, see the Destination Index)

AIRLINES
UA, CO, RG, GU, AA, IB, UZ, TR, PL, AR, AV, CF, CM, LR

(Airline codes defined in Index)

Firm books business class: Yes   First class: Yes
Airlines may be contacted for references: Yes
Percentage of sales through scheduled air: 100%

SALES POLICIES

Tickets delivered: Yes, local
    Delivered by: *Overnight* $10.00
                  First class   no charge

Fee charged for credit card payment: (NP)
Flight confirmed: At booking
Is a printed receipt provided? Yes
Cancellation policy: Processing fee of $25, plus
                     tariff penalties.

Frequent flyer miles offered? Yes

ORDER BY:
phone letter fax

PAYMENT FORMS ACCEPTED
Credit card
Cash
Cashier's check
COD

Comment: *We specialize in Latin destinations. Our agents/consultants have lived, studied, as well as speak and understand the language and culture of destinations we sell.*

(NP) = Firm did not provide requested information.

FIRM: Midtown Travel Consultants

RES PHONE: 1-800-548-8904

ADDRESS: 1830 Piedmont Rd. NE, Ste. F
Atlanta, GA 30324
PHONE: 404-872-8308
FAX: 404-881-6322

Branch Offices:

Travel Agent Rating
Overall Average
7.25
(Detailed analysis of results in Ratings Section)

CORPORATE INFORMATION

Owner: Allen Barbee
Gen Mgr: Michael Malone
Number of staff: 7
Date originated: 1988
Annual sales: $5 - 10 million
Bond coverage: $70,000
Accredited: ARC & IATAN
Escrow: (NP)
Security: (NP)

DESTINATIONS

EUROPE, ORIENT, AFRICA, LATIN AMERICA

(For a complete list of the exact cities served within each region, see the Destination Index)

AIRLINES
LH, KE, JL, CX, SN, KL, SR, TW, AZ, AA, RG

(Airline codes defined in Index)

Firm books business class: Yes   First class: Yes
Airlines may be contacted for references: Yes
Percentage of sales through scheduled air: 100%

SALES POLICIES

Tickets delivered: ASAP
Delivered by: *Overnight*   *$20.00*
First class   *no charge*

Fee charged for credit card payment:
Flight confirmed: ASAP
Is a printed receipt provided? Yes
Cancellation policy: Non-refundable

Frequent flyer miles offered? Yes
Varies by airline

ORDER BY:
phone letter fax

PAYMENT FORMS ACCEPTED
Credit card
Cash
Money order
Cashier's check

Comment:

(NP) = Firm did not provide requested information.

FIRM: Millrun Tours

RES PHONE: 1-800-645-5786

ADDRESS: 333 N. Michigan Ave., Ste. 1825
Chicago, IL 60601
PHONE: 312-641-5914
FAX: 312-641-2840

Travel Agent Rating
Overall Average
6.43
(Detailed analysis of results in Ratings Section)

Branch Offices:

424 Madison Ave. Ste. 1200	545 Bolyston St. Ste. 904	9800 4th St. N., Ste.
New York, NY 10017	Boston, MA 02116	St. Petersburg, FL 33702
212-486-9840	617-262-4475	813-579-9300

CORPORATE INFORMATION

Owner: Issam Sawaya
Gen Mgr: Nagi Tabet
Number of staff: 10
Date originated: 1987
Annual sales: $10 - 25 million
Bond coverage: Yes
Accredited: ARC & IATAN
Escrow: Yes
Security: (NP)

DESTINATIONS
EUROPE, MID EAST, ORIENT, AFRICA

(For a complete list of the exact cities served within each region, see the Destination Index)

AIRLINES
AF, UY, AZ, OS, MS, EK, AY, GF, KL, LH, OA, RJ, SN, SR

(Airline codes defined in Index)

Firm books business class: Yes   First class: (NP)
Airlines may be contacted for references: Yes
Percentage of sales through scheduled air: 100%

SALES POLICIES

Tickets delivered: Upon payment
    Delivered by: *Overnight*   *$10.00*

        Second day   *$6.00*

Fee charged for credit card payment: Varies
Flight confirmed: When available
Is a printed receipt provided? Yes
Cancellation policy: $25.00 service charge

Frequent flyer miles offered? Yes
        Varies by airline

ORDER BY:

PAYMENT FORMS ACCEPTED

Comment:

(NP) = Firm did not provide requested information.

FIRM: **National Travel Centre**

RES PHONE: 1-800-228-6886

ADDRESS: 175 W. Jackson, #1266
Chicago, IL 60604
PHONE: 312-939-2190
FAX: 312-939-7789

Branch Offices:

CORPORATE INFORMATION

Owner: (NP)
Gen Mgr: Joyce Go
Number of staff: 3
Date originated: 1987
Annual sales: Under $1 million
Bond coverage: (NP)
Accredited: ARC
Escrow: (NP)
Security: Receipt

DESTINATIONS
ORIENT, SOUTH PACIFIC

(For a complete list of the exact cities served within each region, see the Destination Index)

AIRLINES
UA, NW, BR, OZ, KE

(Airline codes defined in Index)

Firm books business class: Yes   First class: Yes
Airlines may be contacted for references: Yes
Percentage of sales through scheduled air: 98%

SALES POLICIES

Tickets delivered: Upon payment
Delivered by:

Fee charged for credit card payment:
Flight confirmed: At booking
Is a printed receipt provided? Yes
Cancellation policy: $150 fee plus airline

Frequent flyer miles offered? Yes

ORDER BY:
phone letter fax

PAYMENT FORMS ACCEPTED
*Credit card
Personal check*

Comment:

(NP) = Firm did not provide requested information.

FIRM: New Frontiers

RES PHONE: 1-800-366-6387

ADDRESS: 12 E. 33rd St.
New York, NY 10016
PHONE: 212-779-0600
FAX: 212-779-1007

Branch Offices:

CORPORATE INFORMATION

Owner: Jacques Maillot
Gen Mgr: Claire Bouquet
Number of staff: 20
Date originated: 1967
Annual sales: $5 - 10 million
Bond coverage: $200,000
Accredited: (NP)
Escrow: BankAmerica
Security: All payments made payable to
BankAmerica Novelles Frontiers

DESTINATIONS
EUROPE

(For a complete list of the exact cities served within each region, see the Destination Index)

AIRLINES
AF, BA, CO, AA, BD

(Airline codes defined in Index)

Firm books business class: No   First class: No
Airlines may be contacted for references: Yes
Percentage of sales through scheduled air: 40%

SALES POLICIES

Tickets delivered: Upon payment
Delivered by: *Overnight $10 - 15.00*

Fee charged for credit card payment: no charge
Flight confirmed: Two days before departure
Is a printed receipt provided? No
Cancellation policy: Varies - some small fee,
others nonrefundable

Frequent flyer miles offered? Yes

ORDER BY:
phone letter fax

PAYMENT FORMS ACCEPTED
*Credit card
Cash*

Comment:

(NP) = Firm did not provide requested information.

FIRM: Overseas Express

RES PHONE: 1-800-343-4873

ADDRESS: 2705 W. Howard St.
Chicago, IL 60645
PHONE:
FAX: 312-262-4406
Branch Offices:

CORPORATE INFORMATION

Owner: Joseph T. Silliman
Gen Mgr: Joseph T. Silliman
Number of staff: 8
Date originated: 1987
Annual sales: $10 - 25 million
Bond coverage: $70,000 ARC
Accredited: ARC & IATAN
Escrow: No
Security: (NP)

DESTINATIONS
EUROPE, ORIENT, AFRICA, LATIN AMERICA

(For a complete list of the exact cities served within each region, see the Destination Index)

AIRLINES
AF, BA, SK, LH, MS, OS, SA, SN, MA, SR, KE, KL, UY, UM, AY, TP, TW, UA, MH, TG, TA
(Airline codes defined in Index)

Firm books business class: Yes   First class: Yes
Airlines may be contacted for references: Yes
Percentage of sales through scheduled air: 100%

SALES POLICIES

Tickets delivered: Upon payment
Delivered by: *Overnight*   *$6.00*

Fee charged for credit card payment: 3%
Flight confirmed: At booking
Is a printed receipt provided? Yes
Cancellation policy: Varies by airline

Frequent flyer miles offered? Yes
Varies by airline

ORDER BY:
letter fax

PAYMENT FORMS ACCEPTED
*Credit card
Cash*

Comment:

(NP) = Firm did not provide requested information.

FIRM: Overseas Travel

RES PHONE: 1-800-783-7196

ADDRESS: 16740 E. Iliff Ave.
         Aurora, CO 80013
   PHONE: 303-337-7196
     FAX: 303-696-1226

Branch Offices:

CORPORATE INFORMATION

Owner: Anwar Ahmed
Gen Mgr: Fauzia Ahmed
Number of staff: 8
Date originated: 1982
Annual sales: $5 - 10 million
Bond coverage: $40,000
Accredited: ARC & IATAN
Escrow: Yes
Security: (NP)

DESTINATIONS

**EUROPE, MID EAST,
ORIENT, AFRICA,
SOUTH PACIFIC**

*(For a complete list of the exact
cities served within each region, see
the Destination Index)*

AIRLINES
LH, TK, EK, PK, CX, TG, UC, PL, GF, UA, KU, KL, SV, PR

(Airline codes defined in Index)

Firm books business class: Yes   First class: Yes
Airlines may be contacted for references: Yes
Percentage of sales through scheduled air: 100%

SALES POLICIES

Tickets delivered: Upon payment
     Delivered by: *Overnight*   *$10.00*
                   First class   *no charge*

Fee charged for credit card payment: yes
Flight confirmed: At booking
Is a printed receipt provided? Yes
Cancellation policy: $150

Frequent flyer miles offered? Yes
                   Varies by airline

ORDER BY:
phone letter fax

PAYMENT FORMS ACCEPTED
*Credit card
Cash
COD*

Comment:

(NP) = Firm did not provide requested information.

FIRM: P & F International Inc.

RES PHONE: 1-800-822-3063

ADDRESS: 169 Norman Ave.
Brooklyn, NY 11222
PHONE: 718-383-5630
FAX: 718-389-2246

Branch Offices:

CORPORATE INFORMATION

Owner: Mazen Mohammed
Gen Mgr: Eduardo Sosa
Number of staff: 12
Date originated: 1988
Annual sales: $5 - 10 million
Bond coverage: $100,000
Accredited: ARC & IATAN
Escrow: (NP)
Security: (NP)

DESTINATIONS

EUROPE, MID EAST, ORIENT, LATIN AMERICA

(For a complete list of the exact cities served within each region, see the Destination Index)

AIRLINES

British Airways, Finnair, Royal Jordanian, Austrian Air, Iberia, Avianca, Delta,

(Airline codes defined in Index)

Firm books business class: (NP)   First class: (NP)
Airlines may be contacted for references: Yes
Percentage of sales through scheduled air: 100%

SALES POLICIES

Tickets delivered: (NP)
Delivered by: *Overnight*   *$8.50*

Fee charged for credit card payment: (NP)
Flight confirmed: (NP)
Is a printed receipt provided? (NP)
Cancellation policy: (NP)

Frequent flyer miles offered? (NP)

ORDER BY:

PAYMENT FORMS ACCEPTED

Comment:

(NP) = Firm did not provide requested information.

FIRM: PERS Travel, Inc.

RES PHONE: 1-800-583-0909

ADDRESS: 14114 Dallas Parkway, #100
Dallas, TX 75240
PHONE: 214-458-6877
FAX: 214-233-7075
Branch Offices:

CORPORATE INFORMATION

Owner: Catherine Danai
Gen Mgr: Catherine Danai
Number of staff: (NP)
Date originated: 1985
Annual sales: $1 - 4 million
Bond coverage: $20,000
Accredited: ARC & IATAN
Escrow: (NP)
Security: (NP)

DESTINATIONS

EUROPE, MID EAST, AFRICA, INDIA, COLOMBIA, VENEZUELA

(For a complete list of the exact cities served within each region, see the Destination Index)

AIRLINES
LH, AZ, TK, OS, DL, EK, KU

(Airline codes defined in Index)

Firm books business class: (NP)   First class: (NP)
Airlines may be contacted for references: Yes
Percentage of sales through scheduled air: 100%

SALES POLICIES

Tickets delivered: (NP)
Delivered by: *Overnight*   *$9.00*

Fee charged for credit card payment:
Flight confirmed: No advance
Is a printed receipt provided? (NP)
Cancellation policy: (NP)

Frequent flyer miles offered? No

ORDER BY:
phone letter fax

PAYMENT FORMS ACCEPTED
Credit card
Cash/money order
Cashier's check

Comment:

(NP) = Firm did not provide requested information.

FIRM: Palm Coast Tours & Travel

RES PHONE: 1-800-444-1560

ADDRESS: 4175 S. Congress Ave. #J-K
Lake Worth, FL 33461
PHONE: 407-433-1558
FAX: 407-433-0286

Branch Offices:

CORPORATE INFORMATION

Owner: Lee A. Smolinski
Gen Mgr: Lee A. Smolinski
Number of staff: 7
Date originated: 1988
Annual sales: $5 - 10 million
Bond coverage: Yes
Accredited: ARC & IATAN
Escrow: (NP)
Security: (NP)

DESTINATIONS
EUROPE, ORIENT, LATIN AMERICA

(For a complete list of the exact cities served within each region, see the Destination Index)

AIRLINES
Finnair, SK, Varig

(Airline codes defined in Index)

Firm books business class: (NP)   First class: (NP)
Airlines may be contacted for references: (NP)
Percentage of sales through scheduled air: (NP)

SALES POLICIES

Tickets delivered: Yes
        Delivered by: *Overnight*   *$10.00*
                          First class   *no charge*

Fee charged for credit card payment: (NP)
Flight confirmed: 2 days before departure
Is a printed receipt provided? (NP)
Cancellation policy: (NP)

Frequent flyer miles offered? (NP)

ORDER BY:

PAYMENT FORMS ACCEPTED

Comment:

(NP) = Firm did not provide requested information.

FIRM: Paul Laifer Tours Inc.

RES PHONE: 1-800-346-6314

ADDRESS: 106 Parsippany Rd.
Parsippany, NJ 07054
PHONE: 201-887-1188
FAX: 201-887-6118
Branch Offices:

Travel Agent Rating
Overall Average
7.33
(Detailed analysis of results in Ratings Section)

CORPORATE INFORMATION

Owner: Paul Laifer
Gen Mgr: Robert Laifer
Number of staff: 6
Date originated: 1992
Annual sales: $5 - 10 million
Bond coverage: No
Accredited: (NP)
Escrow: No
Security: (NP)

DESTINATIONS
EASTERN EUROPE

(For a complete list of the exact cities served within each region, see the Destination Index)

AIRLINES
MA, OK, SU, AY

(Airline codes defined in Index)

Firm books business class: Yes   First class: Yes
Airlines may be contacted for references: Yes
Percentage of sales through scheduled air: 100%

SALES POLICIES

Tickets delivered: Two weeks before departure
Delivered by: *Overnight*   *no charge*
First class   *no charge*

Fee charged for credit card payment: 2%
Flight confirmed: Immediately
Is a printed receipt provided? (NP)
Cancellation policy: Varies by airline

Frequent flyer miles offered? No

ORDER BY:
phone letter fax

PAYMENT FORMS ACCEPTED
Credit card

Comment:

(NP) = Firm did not provide requested information.

FIRM: Persvoyage Inc

RES PHONE: 1-800-455-7377

ADDRESS: 2 West 45th St, Ste 1703
New York, NY 10036
PHONE: 212-719-0900
FAX: 212-221-3548

Branch Offices:

555 Federal Hwy, Ste. 300 Boca Raton, FL 33432 407-347-0900	2 W. 45th St., Ste 1703 New York, NY 10036 212-719-0900	1000 16th St. NW, Ste Washington, D.C. 20036 202-822-6500

CORPORATE INFORMATION

Owner: Masoud Refghi
Gen Mgr: Masoud Refghi
Number of staff: 3
Date originated: 1974
Annual sales: $5 - 10 million
Bond coverage: (NP)
Accredited: ARC & IATAN
Escrow: (NP)
Security: N/A

DESTINATIONS
EUROPE, MID EAST

(For a complete list of the exact cities served within each region, see the Destination Index)

AIRLINES
Major carriers

(Airline codes defined in Index)

Firm books business class: (NP)   First class: (NP)
Airlines may be contacted for references: Yes
Percentage of sales through scheduled air: 90%

SALES POLICIES

Tickets delivered: (NP)
Delivered by: *Overnight* $9.00

Fee charged for credit card payment: (NP)
Flight confirmed: (NP)
Is a printed receipt provided? Yes
Cancellation policy: (NP)

Frequent flyer miles offered? No

ORDER BY:

PAYMENT FORMS ACCEPTED

Comment:

(NP) = Firm did not provide requested information.

FIRM: Picasso Travel

RES PHONE: 1-800-PICASSO

ADDRESS: 5250 W. Century Blvd. #626
Los Angeles, CA 90045
PHONE: 310-645-4400
FAX: 310-645-0412

Branch Offices:
330 Primrose Rd., #221
Burlingame, CA 94010
800-247-7283

136 E. 57th St., #1104
New York, NY
800-525-3632

Travel Agent Rating
Overall Average
7.19
(Detailed analysis of results in Ratings Section)

CORPORATE INFORMATION

Owner: Esin Ozyurtcu
Gen Mgr: Heather Fox
Number of staff: 45
Date originated: 1980
Annual sales: Over $25 million
Bond coverage: $80,000
Accredited: ARC & IATAN
Escrow: Yes
Security: (NP)

DESTINATIONS

EUROPE, MID EAST, ORIENT, AFRICA, LATIN AMERICA, SOUTH PACIFIC

(For a complete list of the exact cities served within each region, see the Destination Index)

AIRLINES

TW, UA, VP, RG, RK, AC, AZ, OZ, BA, DL, MS, LY, AY, GA, IB, KL, LH, LT, NZ, QF, SA, TK, SK

(Airline codes defined in Index)

Firm books business class: Yes   First class: Yes
Airlines may be contacted for references: Yes
Percentage of sales through scheduled air: 100%

SALES POLICIES

Tickets delivered: Upon payment
Delivered by: *Overnight*   *$10.00*
First class

Fee charged for credit card payment: Varies
Flight confirmed: At booking
Is a printed receipt provided? No
Cancellation policy: Varies by airline

Frequent flyer miles offered? Yes
Varies by airline

ORDER BY:
phone letter fax

PAYMENT FORMS ACCEPTED
Credit card
Personal check

Comment:

(NP) = Firm did not provide requested information.

FIRM: Pino Welcome Travel

RES PHONE: 1-800-247-6578

ADDRESS: 501 Fifth Avenue Ste. 803
New York, NY 10017
PHONE: 212-682-5400
FAX: 212-682-8880

Branch Offices:

Travel Agent Rating
Overall Average
5.2
*(Detailed analysis of
results in Ratings
Section)*

CORPORATE INFORMATION

Owner: Pino
Gen Mgr: Nathan
Number of staff: 20
Date originated: 1986
Annual sales: $5 - 10 million
Bond coverage: Yes
Accredited: ARC & IATAN
Escrow: (NP)
Security: (NP)

DESTINATIONS

**EUROPE, MID EAST,
ORIENT, AFRICA,
LATIN AMERICA,
SOUTH PACIFIC,
NORTH AMERICA**

*(For a complete list of the exact
cities served within each region, see
the Destination Index)*

AIRLINES
We use 33 airlines.

(Airline codes defined in Index)

Firm books business class: (NP)   First class: (NP)
Airlines may be contacted for references: (NP)
Percentage of sales through scheduled air: (NP)

SALES POLICIES

Tickets delivered: Immediately
Delivered by: *Overnight*   *$14.00*

Fee charged for credit card payment:
Flight confirmed: Immediately
Is a printed receipt provided? (NP)
Cancellation policy: (NP)

Frequent flyer miles offered? (NP)

ORDER BY:

PAYMENT FORMS
ACCEPTED

Comment:

(NP) = Firm did not provide requested information.

FIRM: Pinto Basto USA

RES PHONE: 1-800-526-8539

ADDRESS: 40 Prince St.
New York, NY 10012
PHONE: 212-226-9056
FAX: 212-966-1697

Branch Offices:

Travel Agent Rating
Overall Average
6
(Detailed analysis of results in Ratings Section)

CORPORATE INFORMATION

Owner: John Mcglade
Gen Mgr: Alan Davies
Number of staff: 7
Date originated: 1988
Annual sales: $5 - 10 million
Bond coverage: $100,000
Accredited: ARC & IATAN
Escrow: (NP)
Security: (NP)

DESTINATIONS

EUROPE, LATIN AMERICA

(For a complete list of the exact cities served within each region, see the Destination Index)

AIRLINES

United, Delta, Air Portugal, LACSA

(Airline codes defined in Index)

Firm books business class: (NP)   First class: (NP)
Airlines may be contacted for references: Yes
Percentage of sales through scheduled air: 100%

SALES POLICIES

Tickets delivered: Upon payment
Delivered by: *Overnight $9.00*
First class   no charge

Fee charged for credit card payment: (NP)
Flight confirmed: At booking
Is a printed receipt provided? (NP)
Cancellation policy: (NP)

Frequent flyer miles offered? (NP)

ORDER BY:

PAYMENT FORMS ACCEPTED

Comment:

(NP) = Firm did not provide requested information.

FIRM: **Pioneer Tours**

RES PHONE: 1-800-228-2107

ADDRESS: 2600 Gardeu Rd., Ste. 140
Monterey, CA 93940
PHONE: 408-648-8800
FAX: 408-648-8300

Branch Offices:

CORPORATE INFORMATION

Owner: Lynn Lozier
Gen Mgr: (NP)
Number of staff: 5
Date originated: (NP)
Annual sales: $1 - 4 million
Bond coverage: (NP)
Accredited: ARC & IATAN
Escrow: (NP)
Security: (NP)

DESTINATIONS
LATIN AMERICA

*(For a complete list of the exact
cities served within each region, see
the Destination Index)*

AIRLINES
AA, UA, LR, TA, ML

(Airline codes defined in Index)

Firm books business class: No   First class: No
Airlines may be contacted for references: Yes
Percentage of sales through scheduled air: 35%

SALES POLICIES

Tickets delivered: 3 to 30 days before departure
Delivered by: *Overnight $10.00*

UPS - 2nd day
Fee charged for credit card payment: 3%
Flight confirmed: At booking
Is a printed receipt provided? Yes
Cancellation policy: Varies

Frequent flyer miles offered? Yes
Varies by airline

ORDER BY:
phone letter fax

PAYMENT FORMS ACCEPTED
*Credit card
Personal check*

Comment:

(NP) = Firm did not provide requested information.

FIRM: Premier Travel Services Inc

RES PHONE: 1-800-545-1910

ADDRESS: 217 South 20th Street
Philadelphia, PA 19103
PHONE: 215-893-9966
FAX: 215-893-0357

Branch Offices:

Travel Agent Rating
Overall Average
10
(Detailed analysis of results in Ratings Section)

CORPORATE INFORMATION

Owner: Maureen Abrams
Gen Mgr: Maureen Abrams
Number of staff: 18
Date originated: (NP)
Annual sales: $10 - 25 million
Bond coverage: (NP)
Accredited: ARC & IATAN
Escrow: (NP)
Security: (NP)

DESTINATIONS

EUROPE, MID EAST, ORIENT, AFRICA, LATIN AMERICA, SOUTH PACIFIC

(For a complete list of the exact cities served within each region, see the Destination Index)

AIRLINES
AA, BA, SN, OA, CX, MH, VS, AZ, KE, SA

(Airline codes defined in Index)

Firm books business class: (NP)   First class: (NP)
Airlines may be contacted for references: Yes
Percentage of sales through scheduled air: 100%

SALES POLICIES

Tickets delivered: Immediately
Delivered by: *Overnight*   *$10.00*

Fee charged for credit card payment:
Flight confirmed: At booking
Is a printed receipt provided? (NP)
Cancellation policy: (NP)

Frequent flyer miles offered? (NP)

ORDER BY:

PAYMENT FORMS ACCEPTED

Comment:

(NP) = Firm did not provide requested information.

FIRM: Saga Tours

RES PHONE: 1-800-683-4200

ADDRESS: 292 Madison Avenue, 23rd Floor
New York, NY 10017
PHONE: 212-696-5200
FAX: 212-779-8383

Branch Offices:

Travel Agent Rating
Overall Average
4.5
(Detailed analysis of results in Ratings Section)

CORPORATE INFORMATION

Owner: A.K.Durrani/President
Gen Mgr: (NP)
Number of staff: 18
Date originated: 1987
Annual sales: $5 - 10 million
Bond coverage: $75,000
Accredited: ARC & IATAN
Escrow: (NP)
Security: (NP)

DESTINATIONS
EUROPE, MID EAST, ORIENT, AFRICA, LATIN AMERICA, SOUTH PACIFIC

(For a complete list of the exact cities served within each region, see the Destination Index)

AIRLINES
All major airlines, including PK

(Airline codes defined in Index)

Firm books business class: No   First class: (NP)
Airlines may be contacted for references: Yes
Percentage of sales through scheduled air: (NP)

SALES POLICIES

Tickets delivered: Upon payment
Delivered by: *Overnight*   *$9.00*
First class   *no charge*

Fee charged for credit card payment:
Flight confirmed: 30 days prior to departure
Is a printed receipt provided? (NP)
Cancellation policy: (NP)

Frequent flyer miles offered? Yes
Varies by airline

ORDER BY:

PAYMENT FORMS ACCEPTED

Comment:

(NP) = Firm did not provide requested information.

FIRM: Saltaire Travel

RES PHONE: 1-800-777-8926

ADDRESS: 1923 Mott Ave
Far Rockaway, NY 11691
PHONE: 718-327-4665
FAX: 718-327-6020
Branch Offices:

Travel Agent Rating
Overall Average
5
(Detailed analysis of results in Ratings Section)

CORPORATE INFORMATION

Owner: Igor Cotler
Gen Mgr: Lana Kreiman
Number of staff: 5
Date originated: 1990
Annual sales: $1 - 4 million
Bond coverage: (NP)
Accredited: ARC & IATAN
Escrow: (NP)
Security: (NP)

DESTINATIONS
RUSSIA

(For a complete list of the exact cities served within each region, see the Destination Index)

AIRLINES
Aeroflot, SK

(Airline codes defined in Index)

Firm books business class: (NP)   First class: (NP)
Airlines may be contacted for references: No
Percentage of sales through scheduled air: (NP)

SALES POLICIES

Tickets delivered: Fed Ex
Delivered by: *Overnight*   *$10.00 or more*

Fee charged for credit card payment: (NP)
Flight confirmed: (NP)
Is a printed receipt provided? (NP)
Cancellation policy: (NP)

Frequent flyer miles offered? (NP)

ORDER BY:

PAYMENT FORMS ACCEPTED

Comment:

(NP) = Firm did not provide requested information.

FIRM: Sharp Travel Washington

RES PHONE: 1-800-969-7427

ADDRESS: 7002 Little River Tnpk, Ste. 1
Annandale, VA 22003
PHONE: 703-941-2323
FAX: 703-941-2929

Branch Offices:

Travel Agent Rating
Overall Average
10
*(Detailed analysis of
results in Ratings
Section)*

CORPORATE INFORMATION

Owner: Jacob Hyo Lee
Gen Mgr: Zee Hee Lee
Number of staff: 9
Date originated: 1986
Annual sales: $5 - 10 million
Bond coverage: $70,000
Accredited: ARC & IATAN
Escrow: (NP)
Security: (NP)

DESTINATIONS
ORIENT

*(For a complete list of the exact
cities served within each region, see
the Destination Index)*

AIRLINES
Asiana Airline, Korean Air, NW, UA, JL

(Airline codes defined in Index)

Firm books business class: (NP)   First class: (NP)
Airlines may be contacted for references: No
Percentage of sales through scheduled air: (NP)

SALES POLICIES

Tickets delivered: Within two days
Delivered by: *Overnight*   *$10.00*

Fee charged for credit card payment: (NP)
Flight confirmed: Within two days
Is a printed receipt provided? (NP)
Cancellation policy: (NP)

Frequent flyer miles offered? (NP)

ORDER BY:

**PAYMENT FORMS
ACCEPTED**

Comment:

(NP) = Firm did not provide requested information.

95

FIRM: Skytours

RES PHONE: 1-800- 246-8687

ADDRESS: 26 Third St.
San Francisco, CA 94103
PHONE: 415-777-3544
FAX: 415-777-9290

Branch Offices:

CORPORATE INFORMATION
Owner: Henrick Hervall
Gen Mgr: Henrick Hervall
Number of staff: 6
Date originated: 1979
Annual sales: $1 - 4 million
Bond coverage: $75,000
Accredited: ARC & IATAN
Escrow: $30,000
Security: Escrow account

DESTINATIONS
EUROPE

(For a complete list of the exact cities served within each region, see the Destination Index)

AIRLINES
AF, KL, NW, BA, AY, UA, OZ, CP

(Airline codes defined in Index)

Firm books business class: No   First class: No
Airlines may be contacted for references: Yes
Percentage of sales through scheduled air: 80%

SALES POLICIES

Tickets delivered: Immediately
Delivered by:
First class

Fee charged for credit card payment: (NP)
Flight confirmed: Immediately
Is a printed receipt provided? Yes
Cancellation policy: Varies by airline

Frequent flyer miles offered? Yes
Varies by airline

ORDER BY:
phone letter fax

PAYMENT FORMS ACCEPTED
*Credit card
Personal check*

Comment:

(NP) = Firm did not provide requested information.

FIRM: South American Fiesta

RES PHONE: 1-800-334-3782

ADDRESS: 910 W Mercury Blvd.
Hampton, VA 23666
PHONE: 804-825-9000
FAX: 804-826-1747

Branch Offices:

Travel Agent Rating
Overall Average
8
(Detailed analysis of results in Ratings Section)

CORPORATE INFORMATION

Owner: Jesus Lopez
Gen Mgr: Silvia Lopez
Number of staff: 4
Date originated: (NP)
Annual sales: $1 - 4 million
Bond coverage: Yes
Accredited: ARC
Escrow: (NP)
Security: (NP)

DESTINATIONS
LATIN AMERICA

(For a complete list of the exact cities served within each region, see the Destination Index)

AIRLINES

Varig, LACSA, TACA, Faucett, Aerolineas Argentinas, Ladeco, Saeta, Aero Peru, Lan Chile, Aviateca, Nica, Copa, Aero Costa Rica, Lloyd, Aereo Bolivia

Firm books business class: (NP)   First class: (NP)
Airlines may be contacted for references: Yes
Percentage of sales through scheduled air: 100%

SALES POLICIES

Tickets delivered: (NP)
       Delivered by: *Overnight*   *$15.00*
                          First class   *no charge*

Fee charged for credit card payment: (NP)
Flight confirmed: Two days before departure
Is a printed receipt provided? (NP)
Cancellation policy: (NP)

Frequent flyer miles offered? (NP)

ORDER BY:

PAYMENT FORMS ACCEPTED

Comment:

(NP) = Firm did not provide requested information.

FIRM: South Pacific Express Travels

RES PHONE: 1-800-321-7739

ADDRESS: 150 Powell St., Ste. 406
San Francisco, CA 94102
PHONE: 415-982-6833
FAX: 415-989-7634

Branch Offices:

CORPORATE INFORMATION
Owner: Vanita Louie
Gen Mgr: David Louis
Number of staff: 17
Date originated: (NP)
Annual sales: $10 - 25 million
Bond coverage: $70,000
Accredited: ARC & IATAN
Escrow: (NP)
Security: Trust Account

DESTINATIONS
SOUTH PACIFIC, NORTH AMERICA

(For a complete list of the exact cities served within each region, see the Destination Index)

AIRLINES
(NP)

(Airline codes defined in Index)

Firm books business class: (NP)   First class: Yes
Airlines may be contacted for references: Yes
Percentage of sales through scheduled air: 100%

SALES POLICIES

Tickets delivered: Upon payment
Delivered by: *Overnight*   *$12.00 - 25.00*
First class

Fee charged for credit card payment: (NP)
Flight confirmed: At booking
Is a printed receipt provided? Yes
Cancellation policy: Varies per airline & destination

Frequent flyer miles offered? Yes

ORDER BY:
phone letter fax

PAYMENT FORMS ACCEPTED
Credit card
Personal check

Comment:

(NP) = Firm did not provide requested information.

FIRM: Specialty Tours Int'l USA Inc.

RES PHONE: 1-800-421-3913

ADDRESS: 8939 S. Sepulveda Blvd., #103
Los Angeles, CA 90045
PHONE: 310-568-8709
FAX: 310-568-9171

Branch Offices:

Australia	Canada	Japan
1-800-815-879	1-800-421-3913	0120-784-896

CORPORATE INFORMATION

Owner: Corporation
Gen Mgr: Peter Brunner
Number of staff: 2
Date originated: 1979
Annual sales: under $1 million
Bond coverage: Yes
Accredited: ARC
Escrow: (NP)
Security: (NP)

DESTINATIONS

EUROPE, ORIENT, SOUTH PACIFIC

(For a complete list of the exact cities served within each region, see the Destination Index)

AIRLINES
(NP)

(Airline codes defined in Index)

Firm books business class: Yes   First class: Yes
Airlines may be contacted for references: Yes
Percentage of sales through scheduled air: 40%

SALES POLICIES

Tickets delivered: Depends on routing
Delivered by: *Overnight*
First class

Fee charged for credit card payment: (NP)
Flight confirmed: Depends on routing
Is a printed receipt provided? Yes
Cancellation policy: No refunds

Frequent flyer miles offered? Yes
Varies by airline

ORDER BY:
phone letter fax

PAYMENT FORMS ACCEPTED
Cash
Personal check
Money order

Comment: *Ground and air custom itineraries*

(NP) = Firm did not provide requested information.

FIRM: Spector Travel of Boston

RES PHONE: 1-800-879-2374

ADDRESS: 31 St. James Ave.
Boston, MA 02116
PHONE: 617-338-0111
FAX: 617-338-0110
Branch Offices:

Travel Agent Rating
Overall Average
3.5
(Detailed analysis of results in Ratings Section)

CORPORATE INFORMATION

Owner: (NP)
Gen Mgr: (NP)
Number of staff: 10
Date originated: 1990
Annual sales: $1 - 4 million
Bond coverage: Yes
Accredited: ARC & IATAN
Escrow: (NP)
Security: (NP)

DESTINATIONS
AFRICA

(For a complete list of the exact cities served within each region, see the Destination Index)

AIRLINES
Major carriers

(Airline codes defined in Index)

Firm books business class: Yes   First class: (NP)
Airlines may be contacted for references: Yes
Percentage of sales through scheduled air: 100%

SALES POLICIES

Tickets delivered: Two weeks after payment
Delivered by: *Overnight*   *$10.00*

Fee charged for credit card payment:
Flight confirmed: Upon confirmation
Is a printed receipt provided? (NP)
Cancellation policy: Nonrefundable

Frequent flyer miles offered? Yes
Varies by airline

ORDER BY:

PAYMENT FORMS ACCEPTED

Comment: *One of the largest consolidators specializing in travel to and from Africa.*

(NP) = Firm did not provide requested information.

FIRM: Sunrise Tours

RES PHONE: 1-800-872-3801

ADDRESS: 390 5th Ave., Ste. 905
New York, NY 10018
PHONE: 212-947-3617
FAX: 212-947-3618

Branch Offices:
Affiliate office - St. Petersburg   Affiliate office - Moscow   Affiliate office - Brooklyn

Travel Agent Rating
Overall Average
6
(Detailed analysis of results in Ratings Section)

CORPORATE INFORMATION

Owner: Mila Granik
Gen Mgr: Jack Stepanian
Number of staff: 10
Date originated: 1987
Annual sales: $1 - 4 million
Bond coverage: (NP)
Accredited: ARC & IATAN
Escrow: (NP)
Security: (NP)

DESTINATIONS

EUROPE, MID EAST, ORIENT, AFRICA, LATIN AMERICA

(For a complete list of the exact cities served within each region, see the Destination Index)

AIRLINES

GU, GY, TP, AY, CM, GU, HY, IB, LR, OA, OK, RJ, SQ, SU, SV, TA, TK, UC, VA

(Airline codes defined in Index)

Firm books business class: Yes   First class: (NP)
Airlines may be contacted for references: Yes
Percentage of sales through scheduled air: 100%

SALES POLICIES

Tickets delivered: As per fare condition
Delivered by: *Overnight $7.00 - 15.00*

Priority mail $3.00
Fee charged for credit card payment: 4%
Flight confirmed: As per fare condition
Is a printed receipt provided? (NP)
Cancellation policy: Varies by airline and fare
condition

Frequent flyer miles offered? Yes
Varies by airline

ORDER BY:

PAYMENT FORMS ACCEPTED

Comment:

(NP) = Firm did not provide requested information.

FIRM: Supertravel

RES PHONE: 1-800-

ADDRESS: 13470 Washington Blvd., Ste. 101
Marina del Rey, CA 90292
PHONE: 310-301-4567
FAX: 310-301-4570

Branch Offices:
1811 N. Tahim Blvd., Ste. 3031
Phoenix, AZ 85028

CORPORATE INFORMATION

Owner: (NP)
Gen Mgr: (NP)
Number of staff: 4
Date originated: 1994
Annual sales: $1 - 4 million
Bond coverage: $20,000
Accredited: ARC & IATAN
Escrow: (NP)
Security: Trust account for passengers'
funds

DESTINATIONS
EUROPE, LATIN AMERICA

(For a complete list of the exact cities served within each region, see the Destination Index)

AIRLINES
CO, TW, AF, IW, SS, CO, TW, VP, VG, DL, UA, AA, IB, LH

(Airline codes defined in Index)

Firm books business class: Yes   First class: Yes
Airlines may be contacted for references: Yes
Percentage of sales through scheduled air: 90%

SALES POLICIES

Tickets delivered: Up to 60 days before
Delivered by: *Overnight*   *$7.00*

Fee charged for credit card payment:
Flight confirmed: At booking
Is a printed receipt provided? Yes
Cancellation policy: Non-refundable

Frequent flyer miles offered? Yes

ORDER BY:
phone letter fax

PAYMENT FORMS ACCEPTED
~~Cash~~
Personal check

Comment:

(NP) = Firm did not provide requested information.

FIRM: Supervalue Vacations

RES PHONE: 1-800-879-1218

ADDRESS: 361 Greens Road
Houston, TX 77060-1903
PHONE: 713-876-6400
FAX: 713-876-6491
Branch Offices:

CORPORATE INFORMATION

Owner: Stan St. Pierre
Gen Mgr: Bob Gregg
Number of staff: 6
Date originated: 1983
Annual sales: $10 - 25 million
Bond coverage: (NP)
Accredited: ARC & IATAN
Escrow: No
Security: (NP)

DESTINATIONS

EUROPE, MID EAST,
ORIENT, AFRICA,
LATIN AMERICA,
SOUTH PACIFIC,
NORTH AMERICA

(For a complete list of the exact cities served within each region, see the Destination Index)

AIRLINES

AF, AR, OS, AM, CX, LY, AZ, NZ, TP, BA, CO, EK, GA, GF, KU, IB, LA, MH, SN, VP, SV, SU, TW, KE, KL, UC, LH, SQ, RG, RJ, UA, SA, TG

Firm books business class: Yes   First class: Yes
Airlines may be contacted for references: Yes
Percentage of sales through scheduled air: 100%

SALES POLICIES

Tickets delivered: One week before departure
Delivered by: *Overnight*   *$6.00*
First class   *no charge*

Fee charged for credit card payment: no charge
Flight confirmed: Two weeks before departure
Is a printed receipt provided? No
Cancellation policy: Varies - some fares $150

Frequent flyer miles offered? Yes
Varies by airline

ORDER BY:
phone letter fax

PAYMENT FORMS ACCEPTED
Credit card
Cash
Personal check

Comment:

(NP) = Firm did not provide requested information.

103

FIRM: TCI Travel & Tours

RES PHONE: 1-800-ASAP-FLY

ADDRESS: 2730 Stemmons Frwy. #W403
Dallas, TX 75207
PHONE: 214-630-3344
FAX: 214-630-3477

Branch Offices:

CORPORATE INFORMATION

Owner:(NP)
Gen Mgr: Dotty Mazidi
Number of staff: 5
Date originated: 1990
Annual sales: Under $1 million
Bond coverage:
Accredited: (NP)
Escrow: No
Security: Travel agents' liability policy
($2 million policy)

DESTINATIONS
EUROPE, MID EAST, ORIENT

(For a complete list of the exact cities served within each region, see the Destination Index)

AIRLINES
AA, BA, CO, AF, DL, LH, KL, TW, UA, TK, NW

(Airline codes defined in Index)

Firm books business class: No   First class: No
Airlines may be contacted for references: No
Percentage of sales through scheduled air: 100%

SALES POLICIES

Tickets delivered: One week after payment
Delivered by:
First class

Fee charged for credit card payment: $20
Flight confirmed: Varies
Is a printed receipt provided? No
Cancellation policy: Subject to each airline; usually
$150

Frequent flyer miles offered? Yes

ORDER BY:
phone letter fax

PAYMENT FORMS ACCEPTED
Credit card
Personal check

Comment:

(NP) = Firm did not provide requested information.

104

FIRM: **Ticketworld/SAF Travel World**

RES PHONE: 1-800-394-8587

ADDRESS: 201-A North 9th Street
Philadelphia, PA 19107
PHONE: 215-440-7200
FAX: 215-440-9602

Branch Offices:

Travel Agent Rating
Overall Average

7.5

(Detailed analysis of results in Ratings Section)

CORPORATE INFORMATION

Owner: S. Fontanilla
Gen Mgr: M. Nable
Number of staff: (NP)
Date originated: 1988
Annual sales: (NP)
Bond coverage: (NP)
Accredited: ARC & IATAN
Escrow: (NP)
Security: (NP)

DESTINATIONS
ORIENT

(For a complete list of the exact cities served within each region, see the Destination Index)

AIRLINES
NW, UA, SQ, KE, GA, PR, TG, ML

(Airline codes defined in Index)

Firm books business class: (NP)   First class: (NP)
Airlines may be contacted for references: (NP)
Percentage of sales through scheduled air: (NP)

SALES POLICIES

Tickets delivered: (NP)
Delivered by:

Fee charged for credit card payment:
Flight confirmed: (NP)
Is a printed receipt provided? (NP)
Cancellation policy: (NP)

Frequent flyer miles offered? (NP)

ORDER BY:

PAYMENT FORMS ACCEPTED

Comment:

(NP) = Firm did not provide requested information.

FIRM: Travac Tours & Charters

RES PHONE: 1-800-TRAV-800

ADDRESS: 989 6th Ave.
New York, NY 10018
PHONE: 212-563-3303
FAX: 212-563-3631

Branch Offices:
2601 E. Jefferson St.
Orlando, FL 32803
407-896-0014

Travel Agent Rating
Overall Average

7.52

(Detailed analysis of results in Ratings Section)

CORPORATE INFORMATION

Owner: John Deacon/Sindy Calay
Gen Mgr: Surinder Calay
Number of staff: 30
Date originated: 1979
Annual sales: Over $25 million
Bond coverage: No
Accredited: ARC & IATAN
Escrow: No
Security: Credit cards and reputation

DESTINATIONS
EUROPE, MID EAST, AFRICA

(For a complete list of the exact cities served within each region, see the Destination Index)

AIRLINES
AI, AF, AY, BA, DL, CO, LH, LT, US, TW, SR, SK, UA, BD, OS, SN, WO, VS

(Airline codes defined in Index)

Firm books business class: No   First class: No
Airlines may be contacted for references: Yes
Percentage of sales through scheduled air: 95%

SALES POLICIES

Tickets delivered: Upon payment
Delivered by: *Overnight*   *$15.00*

Two day delivery $7.00

Fee charged for credit card payment: no charge
Flight confirmed: At booking
Is a printed receipt provided? Yes
Cancellation policy: Varies by airline

Frequent flyer miles offered? Yes
Varies by airline

ORDER BY:
phone letter fax

PAYMENT FORMS ACCEPTED
Credit card
Personal check

Comment:

(NP) = Firm did not provide requested information.

FIRM: Travel Associates

RES PHONE: 1-800-992-7388

ADDRESS: 5550 Wilshire Blvd. #201
Los Angeles, CA 90036
PHONE: 213-933-7388
FAX: 213-933-5563

Branch Offices:
104 E. 40th St., Ste. 702
New York, NY 10016
212-922-0599

CORPORATE INFORMATION

Owner: Leonard Jesupason
Gen Mgr: Sonya Pereira
Number of staff: 12
Date originated: April 1964
Annual sales: $10 - 25 million
Bond coverage: $70,000
Accredited: ARC & IATAN
Escrow: (NP)
Security: (NP)

DESTINATIONS
EUROPE, MID EAST

(For a complete list of the exact cities served within each region, see the Destination Index)

AIRLINES
(NP)

(Airline codes defined in Index)

Firm books business class: (NP)   First class: Yes
Airlines may be contacted for references: Yes
Percentage of sales through scheduled air: 100%

SALES POLICIES

Tickets delivered: Two days following payment
Delivered by: *Overnight*   *$10.00*

Fee charged for credit card payment:
Flight confirmed: At booking
Is a printed receipt provided? Yes
Cancellation policy: Varies on type of ticket

Frequent flyer miles offered? Yes
Varies by airline

ORDER BY:
phone   *fax*

PAYMENT FORMS ACCEPTED
Credit card
Cash
COD

Comment:

(NP) = Firm did not provide requested information.

FIRM: Travel Bargains

RES PHONE: 1-800-247-3273

ADDRESS: 2250 Butler Pike Suite 130
Plymouth Meeting, PA 19462
PHONE: 610-834-8150
FAX: 610-834-8713
Branch Offices:

Travel Agent Rating
Overall Average
6.17
(Detailed analysis of results in Ratings Section)

CORPORATE INFORMATION

Owner: Bahir Browsh
Gen Mgr: Bert Stevenson
Number of staff: 250
Date originated: 1991
Annual sales: Over $25 million
Bond coverage: Yes
Accredited: ARC & IATAN
Escrow: (NP)
Security: (NP)

DESTINATIONS

EUROPE, MID EAST, ORIENT, MEXICO, LATIN AMERICA

(For a complete list of the exact cities served within each region, see the Destination Index)

AIRLINES
Most major airlines

(Airline codes defined in Index)

Firm books business class: No   First class: No
Airlines may be contacted for references: Yes
Percentage of sales through scheduled air: 100%

SALES POLICIES

Tickets delivered: Seven days before departure
Delivered by: *Overnight*   *$7.95*

Fee charged for credit card payment:
Flight confirmed: At booking
Is a printed receipt provided? No
Cancellation policy: Varies by airline

Frequent flyer miles offered? Yes
Varies by airline

ORDER BY:

phone

PAYMENT FORMS ACCEPTED

Credit card
Money order

Comment:

(NP) = Firm did not provide requested information.

FIRM: Travel Center

RES PHONE: 1-800-419-0960

ADDRESS: 373 5th Ave. 2nd Floor
New York, NY 10016
PHONE: 212-545-7474
FAX: 212-545-7698

Branch Offices:

CORPORATE INFORMATION

Owner: Ved P. Gulati
Gen Mgr: Navim Mathun
Number of staff: 8
Date originated: 1976
Annual sales: $5 - 10 million
Bond coverage: Yes
Accredited: ARC & IATAN
Escrow: Yes
Security: (NP)

DESTINATIONS

ORIENT, AFRICA, LATIN AMERICA, NORTH AMERICA

(For a complete list of the exact cities served within each region, see the Destination Index)

AIRLINES

AI, AR, PR, BA, DL, UA, SQ, KE, KU, AA, AF, KL, VN, NW, TG

(Airline codes defined in Index)

Firm books business class: Yes   First class: Yes
Airlines may be contacted for references: Yes
Percentage of sales through scheduled air: 95%

SALES POLICIES

Tickets delivered: 24 - 48 hours after payment
Delivered by: *Overnight*
First class

Fee charged for credit card payment: (NP)
Flight confirmed: Varies
Is a printed receipt provided? (NP)
Cancellation policy: Determined on case-by-case
basis

Frequent flyer miles offered? Yes
Varies by airline

ORDER BY:

phone letter fax

PAYMENT FORMS ACCEPTED

*Credit card
Cash*

Comment:

(NP) = Firm did not provide requested information.

FIRM: Travel Expressions, Inc.

RES PHONE: 1-800-724-6274

ADDRESS: 141 East 44 Street, Suite 309
New York, NY 10017-4006
PHONE: 212-338-9730
FAX: 212-338-9730
Branch Offices:

Travel Agent Rating
Overall Average
4.67
(Detailed analysis of results in Ratings Section)

CORPORATE INFORMATION

Owner: Sam Morjaria
Gen Mgr: Sam Morjaria
Number of staff: 2
Date originated: 1990
Annual sales: Under $1 million
Bond coverage: (NP)
Accredited: IATAN
Escrow: (NP)
Security: Accredited agency - Dunn & Bradstreet; BBB

DESTINATIONS
EUROPE, MID EAST, ORIENT, AFRICA, SOUTH PACIFIC

(For a complete list of the exact cities served within each region, see the Destination Index)

AIRLINES
BA, AF, KL, LH, UA, AA, CO, NW, DL, SA, AI, KQ, SN, TW

(Airline codes defined in Index)

Firm books business class: Yes   First class: Yes
Airlines may be contacted for references: Yes
Percentage of sales through scheduled air: 90%

SALES POLICIES

Tickets delivered: 15 days before departure
Delivered by: *Overnight*   *Varies*
First class   *no charge*

Fee charged for credit card payment: Varies
Flight confirmed: 21days before departure/varies
Is a printed receipt provided? Yes
Cancellation policy: $50, plus airline charges

Frequent flyer miles offered? Yes
Varies by airline

ORDER BY:
phone letter fax

PAYMENT FORMS ACCEPTED
Credit card
Personal check

Comment:

(NP) = Firm did not provide requested information.

FIRM: Tread Lightly LTD.

RES PHONE: 1-800-643-0060

ADDRESS: One Titus Road
Washington Depot, CT 06794
PHONE: 203-868-1710
FAX: 203-868-1718
Branch Offices:

Travel Agent Rating
Overall Average
9
(Detailed analysis of results in Ratings Section)

CORPORATE INFORMATION

Owner: Audrey & James Patterson
Gen Mgr: Audrey Patterson
Number of staff: NP
Date originated: 1992
Annual sales: $1 - 4 million
Bond coverage: Yes
Accredited: ARC & IATAN
Escrow: No
Security: (NP)

DESTINATIONS
LATIN AMERICA

(For a complete list of the exact cities served within each region, see the Destination Index)

AIRLINES
Continental, American

(Airline codes defined in Index)

Firm books business class: No   First class: No
Airlines may be contacted for references: Yes
Percentage of sales through scheduled air: 100%

SALES POLICIES

Tickets delivered: Days before departure
Delivered by: *Overnight*   *$10.00*
First class

Fee charged for credit card payment:
Flight confirmed: Days before departure
Is a printed receipt provided? (NP)
Cancellation policy: (NP)

Frequent flyer miles offered? Yes
Varies by airline

ORDER BY:
phone letter fax

PAYMENT FORMS ACCEPTED
*Credit card
Cash
Personal check*

Comment:

(NP) = Firm did not provide requested information.

FIRM: **Tulips Travel**

RES PHONE: 1-800-882-3383

ADDRESS: 420 Lexington Ave., Ste. 2738
New York, NY 10170
PHONE: 212-490-3388
FAX: 212-490-3580
Branch Offices:

CORPORATE INFORMATION

Owner: Marianne Yee
Gen Mgr: Mary Stirland
Number of staff: 5
Date originated: 1990
Annual sales: $1 - 4 million
Bond coverage: (NP)
Accredited: ARC & IATAN
Escrow: (NP)
Security: (NP)

DESTINATIONS
EUROPE, ORIENT

(For a complete list of the exact cities served within each region, see the Destination Index)

AIRLINES
(NP)

(Airline codes defined in Index)

Firm books business class: (NP)   First class: No
Airlines may be contacted for references: Yes
Percentage of sales through scheduled air: 90%

SALES POLICIES

Tickets delivered: One/two weeks before
   Delivered by: *Overnight*   *$10.00*
                 First class   *no charge*

Fee charged for credit card payment: (NP)
Flight confirmed: Two weeks before departure
Is a printed receipt provided? Yes
Cancellation policy: $200 - $500; some fare non-
                     refundable
Frequent flyer miles offered? Yes
                 Varies by airline

ORDER BY:
phone   *fax*

PAYMENT FORMS ACCEPTED
Credit card
Personal check

Comment:

(NP) = Firm did not provide requested information.

FIRM: Unlimited World Travel

RES PHONE: 1-800-322-3557

ADDRESS: 7851 W. Ogden Ave. PO Box 306
Lyons, IL 60534
PHONE: 708-442-7715
FAX: 708-442-7759

Branch Offices:

Travel Agent Rating
Overall Average
8
(Detailed analysis of results in Ratings Section)

CORPORATE INFORMATION

Owner: Walter Veselinovic
Gen Mgr: Walter Veselinovic
Number of staff: 12
Date originated: (NP)
Annual sales: $5 - 10 million
Bond coverage: $75,000
Accredited: ARC & IATAN
Escrow: (NP)
Security: (NP)

DESTINATIONS
EUROPE

(For a complete list of the exact cities served within each region, see the Destination Index)

AIRLINES
KLM, SU, LH, SN,OK, GU, RJ, MA, 3D, RO

(Airline codes defined in Index)

Firm books business class: (NP)   First class: (NP)
Airlines may be contacted for references: Yes
Percentage of sales through scheduled air: 90%

SALES POLICIES

Tickets delivered: (NP)
Delivered by: *Overnight*   *$10.00*
First class   *no charge*

Fee charged for credit card payment:
Flight confirmed: At booking
Is a printed receipt provided? (NP)
Cancellation policy: (NP)

Frequent flyer miles offered? (NP)

ORDER BY:

PAYMENT FORMS ACCEPTED

Comment:

(NP) = Firm did not provide requested information.

FIRM: Up & Away Travel

RES PHONE: 1-800-275-8001

ADDRESS: 347 Fifth Ave.
NY, NY 10016
PHONE: 212-889-2345
FAX: 212-889-2350

Branch Offices:
918 16 St. NW #304
Washington, D.C. 20006
202-466-8900

Travel Agent Rating
Overall Average

7

(Detailed analysis of results in Ratings Section)

CORPORATE INFORMATION

Owner: Terence Mascarenhas
Gen Mgr: Abbas Raja
Number of staff: 12
Date originated: 1984
Annual sales: Over $25 million
Bond coverage: $100,000
Accredited: ARC & IATAN
Escrow: (NP)
Security: (NP)

DESTINATIONS

EUROPE, MID EAST, ORIENT, AFRICA, LATIN AMERICA, SOUTH PACIFIC, NORTH AMERICA

(For a complete list of the exact cities served within each region, see the Destination Index)

AIRLINES
All IATA airlines

(Airline codes defined in Index)

Firm books business class: (NP)   First class: (NP)
Airlines may be contacted for references: Yes
Percentage of sales through scheduled air: 100%

SALES POLICIES

Tickets delivered: Upon payment
Delivered by: *Overnight*   *$10.00*
                    First class

Fee charged for credit card payment:
Flight confirmed: Subject to availability
Is a printed receipt provided? Yes
Cancellation policy: Varies

Frequent flyer miles offered? Yes
                    Varies by airline

ORDER BY:

PAYMENT FORMS ACCEPTED

Comment:

(NP) = Firm did not provide requested information.

114

FIRM: Value Holidays

RES PHONE: 1-800-558-6850

ADDRESS: 10224 N. Port Washington Rd.
Mequon, WI 53092
PHONE: 414-241-6373
FAX: 414-241-6373

Branch Offices:

Travel Agent Rating
Overall Average
7
(Detailed analysis of results in Ratings Section)

CORPORATE INFORMATION

Owner: Kenneth T. Spitz
Gen Mgr: Joerg Kramer
Number of staff: 8
Date originated: 1971
Annual sales: $1 - 4 million
Bond coverage: (NP)
Accredited: ARC & IATAN
Escrow: (NP)
Security: (NP)

DESTINATIONS
EUROPE

(For a complete list of the exact cities served within each region, see the Destination Index)

AIRLINES
KL, LH, AF, BA

(Airline codes defined in Index)

Firm books business class: No   First class: No
Airlines may be contacted for references: Yes
Percentage of sales through scheduled air: 100%

SALES POLICIES

Tickets delivered: Two weeks before departure
Delivered by: *Overnight $15.00*
              First class   no charge

Fee charged for credit card payment: 4%
Flight confirmed: At booking
Is a printed receipt provided? (NP)
Cancellation policy: Non-refundable once issued

Frequent flyer miles offered? No

ORDER BY:
phone letter fax

PAYMENT FORMS ACCEPTED
Credit card
Personal check

Comment:

(NP) = Firm did not provide requested information.

FIRM: Winggate Travel

RES PHONE: 1-800-

ADDRESS: 11822 Quivera
Overland Park, Kansas 55210
PHONE: 913-451-9200
FAX: 913-451-9680
Branch Offices:

CORPORATE INFORMATION

Owner: Young Sexton
Gen Mgr: Young Sexton
Number of staff: 2
Date originated: 1992
Annual sales: Under $1 million
Bond coverage: $50,000
Accredited: ARC & IATAN
Escrow: (NP)
Security: (NP)

DESTINATIONS
ORIENT

(For a complete list of the exact cities served within each region, see the Destination Index)

AIRLINES
KE

(Airline codes defined in Index)

Firm books business class: (NP)   First class: (NP)
Airlines may be contacted for references: Yes
Percentage of sales through scheduled air: (NP)

SALES POLICIES

Tickets delivered: (NP)
Delivered by: *Overnight*   *$10.00*
First class   *no charge*

Fee charged for credit card payment:
Flight confirmed: (NP)
Is a printed receipt provided? (NP)
Cancellation policy: (NP)

Frequent flyer miles offered? (NP)

ORDER BY:

PAYMENT FORMS ACCEPTED

Comment:

(NP) = Firm did not provide requested information.

116

FIRM: Worldvision Travel

RES PHONE: 1-800-545-7118

ADDRESS: 110 Forest Hill Rd.
W. Orange, NJ 07052
PHONE: 201-736-8210
FAX: 201-736-9659

Branch Offices:

CORPORATE INFORMATION

Owner: Robert R. Hervian
Gen Mgr: Lili Hervian
Number of staff: 4
Date originated: 1987
Annual sales: $1 - 4 million
Bond coverage: No
Accredited: (NP)
Escrow: No
Security: (NP)

DESTINATIONS

EUROPE, MID EAST, ORIENT, AFRICA, SOUTH PACIFIC, NORTH AMERICA

(For a complete list of the exact cities served within each region, see the Destination Index)

AIRLINES

UA, CO, LH, KL, AF, DL, TW, BA, SN, FI, AI, RJ, KU, LY, SR, ET, AZ, FF, RK, UM

(Airline codes defined in Index)

Firm books business class: Yes   First class: Yes
Airlines may be contacted for references: Yes
Percentage of sales through scheduled air: 100%

SALES POLICIES

Tickets delivered: Two days after payment
Delivered by: *Overnight $7.00*
First class

Fee charged for credit card payment: (NP)
Flight confirmed: At booking
Is a printed receipt provided? Yes
Cancellation policy: After ticketing - $250; before
ticketing - $0

Frequent flyer miles offered? Yes
Varies by airline

ORDER BY:

phone letter fax

PAYMENT FORMS ACCEPTED

*Credit card
Cash
Personal check*

Comment:

(NP) = Firm did not provide requested information.

FIRM: Worldwide Travel

RES PHONE: 1-800-343-0038

ADDRESS: 1026 - 16th St. NW
Washington, DC 20036
PHONE: 202-659-6430
FAX: 703-820-4500

Branch Offices:

1026 16th St., NW	441 Lexington Ave.	3606 Forest Dr.
Washington, D.C.	New York, NY 10117	Alexandria, VA 22032
1-800-343-0038	212-682-6313	703-820-9700

CORPORATE INFORMATION

Owner: Laxmi Chand
Gen Mgr: Usha Chand
Number of staff: 20
Date originated: 1975
Annual sales: $10 - 25 million
Bond coverage: $70,000
Accredited: ARC & IATAN
Escrow: (NP)
Security: (NP)

DESTINATIONS

EUROPE, MID EAST, ORIENT, AFRICA

(For a complete list of the exact cities served within each region, see the Destination Index)

AIRLINES
BA, KL, UA, LH, GF, RK, SN, KE

(Airline codes defined in Index)

Firm books business class: (NP)   First class: (NP)
Airlines may be contacted for references: Yes
Percentage of sales through scheduled air: 100%

SALES POLICIES

Tickets delivered: Upon payment
Delivered by: *Overnight*   *$9.00*

Fee charged for credit card payment: 5%
Flight confirmed: (NP)
Is a printed receipt provided? Yes
Cancellation policy: (NP)

Frequent flyer miles offered? No

ORDER BY:

PAYMENT FORMS
ACCEPTED

Comment:

(NP) = Firm did not provide requested information.

FIRM: Zig Zag International Travel

RES PHONE: 1-800-226-9383

ADDRESS: 2705 W. Wendarm Ct.
Peoria, IL 61604
PHONE: 309-637-9647
FAX: 309-637-9663

Branch Offices:

CORPORATE INFORMATION

Owner: Michael Garza
Gen Mgr: Michael Garza
Number of staff: 2
Date originated: 1991
Annual sales: Under $1 million
Bond coverage: (NP)
Accredited: ARC
Escrow: N/A
Security: N/A

DESTINATIONS

**ORIENT, AFRICA,
LATIN AMERICA,
SOUTH PACIFIC**

*(For a complete list of the exact
cities served within each region, see
the Destination Index)*

AIRLINES
KE, MH, CI, BR, JL, TG, UA, RG, UM, HM, MK, GF, VL, RA, KQ

(Airline codes defined in Index)

Firm books business class: Yes   First class: No
Airlines may be contacted for references: Yes
Percentage of sales through scheduled air: 100%

SALES POLICIES

Tickets delivered: One day before - six months
Delivered by: *Overnight*   *$10.00*
First class   *no charge*
Two day UPS   *$6.00*

Fee charged for credit card payment: 4%
Flight confirmed: Up to 11 months
Is a printed receipt provided? Yes
Cancellation policy: Varies by airline

Frequent flyer miles offered? (NP)

ORDER BY:
phone   fax

**PAYMENT FORMS
ACCEPTED**

*Credit card
Personal check*

Comment: *We specialize in custom itineraries Round-the-World, Circle-Pacific, and
Circle-Atlantic.*

(NP) = Firm did not provide requested information.

FIRM: Zig Zag Travel

RES PHONE: 1-800-726-0249

ADDRESS: 229 Broadway
Lynbrook, NY 11563
PHONE: 516-887-0776
FAX: 516-887-3682

Branch Offices:

CORPORATE INFORMATION

Owner: Mr. B. Bershitski
Gen Mgr: Elliot Berger
Number of staff: 10
Date originated: 1987
Annual sales: $1 - 4 million
Bond coverage: $75,000
Accredited: ARC & IATAN
Escrow: (NP)
Security: (NP)

DESTINATIONS
EASTERN EUROPE, ISRAEL

(For a complete list of the exact cities served within each region, see the Destination Index)

AIRLINES
DL, LH, AF, SK, SU, GU, KL, TW, FF, LY

(Airline codes defined in Index)

Firm books business class: Yes   First class: Yes
Airlines may be contacted for references: Yes
Percentage of sales through scheduled air: 80%

SALES POLICIES

Tickets delivered: Varies
Delivered by: *Overnight*   *Cost varies*
First class   *no charge*

Fee charged for credit card payment: (NP)
Flight confirmed: Varies
Is a printed receipt provided? Yes
Cancellation policy: Varies

Frequent flyer miles offered? Yes
Varies by airline

ORDER BY:
phone letter fax

PAYMENT FORMS ACCEPTED
Credit card
Cash
Personal check

Comment:

(NP) = Firm did not provide requested information.

120

Profiles of Firms that Sell Only Through Travel Agents

FIRM: 4th Dimension Tours

RES PHONE: 1-800-343-0020

ADDRESS: 1150 NW 72 Ave, Ste. 333
Miami, FL 33126
PHONE: 305-279-0014
FAX: 305-273-9777

Branch Offices:

Travel Agent Rating
Overall Average
7.83
(Detailed analysis of results in Ratings Section)

CORPORATE INFORMATION

Owner: Jaime Alvarez
Gen Mgr: Tony Latour
Number of staff: 25
Date originated: 1989
Annual sales: $10 - 25 million
Bond coverage: (NP)
Accredited: ARC
Escrow: (NP)
Security: (NP)

DESTINATIONS
EUROPE, LATIN AMERICA

(For a complete list of the exact cities served within each region, see the Destination Index)

AIRLINES
American Airlines, Ladeco, Saeta, Aero Costa Rica

(Airline codes defined in Index)

Firm books business class: (NP)   First class: (NP)
Airlines may be contacted for references: Yes
Percentage of sales through scheduled air: 50%

SALES POLICIES

Tickets delivered: 3 to 7 days before departure
Delivered by: *Overnight   varies*

Fee charged for credit card payment: (NP)
Flight confirmed: Two weeks before departure
Is a printed receipt provided? (NP)
Cancellation policy: (NP)

Frequent flyer miles offered? (NP)

TRAVEL AGENCY
orders accepted by:
phone letter fax

PAYMENT FORMS ACCEPTED
AGENCY CHECK

Comment:

(NP) = Firm did not provide requested information.

FIRM: AIT Anderson International

RES PHONE: 1-800-365-1929

ADDRESS: 1308 Michigan Ave.
East Lansing, MI 48823-4099
PHONE: 517-337-1300
FAX: 517-337-8561

Branch Offices:

Travel Agent Rating
Overall Average
9.07
(Detailed analysis of results in Ratings Section)

CORPORATE INFORMATION

Owner: R. Sorum, R. Barnes, R. Anderson
Gen Mgr: Bob Sorum
Number of staff: 15
Date originated: 1976
Annual sales: $5 - 10 million
Bond coverage: $70,000
Accredited: ARC & IATAN
Escrow: (NP)
Security: (NP)

DESTINATIONS

EUROPE, AFRICA, LATIN AMERICA, SOUTH PACIFIC

(For a complete list of the exact cities served within each region, see the Destination Index)

AIRLINES
NW, KL, AY, BA, RG, SN, UM, GA, AF

(Airline codes defined in Index)

Firm books business class: No   First class: No
Airlines may be contacted for references: Yes
Percentage of sales through scheduled air: 100%

SALES POLICIES

Tickets delivered: Varies
Delivered by: *Overnight*   *$16.00*
First class
Second day   *$11.00*
Fee charged for credit card payment: (NP)
Flight confirmed: At booking
Is a printed receipt provided? Yes
Cancellation policy: 50%

Frequent flyer miles offered? Yes
Only on NW and KL

TRAVEL AGENCY
orders accepted by:
phone

PAYMENT FORMS
ACCEPTED
CREDIT CARD
AGENCY CHECK

Comment:

(NP) = Firm did not provide requested information.

FIRM: APC/American Passenger Con

RES PHONE: 1-800-526-2447

ADDRESS: 41 East 42nd Street
New York, NY 10022
PHONE: 212-972-1558
FAX: 212-949-8776

Branch Offices:
120 Montgomery St.
San Francisco, CA 94104
800-959-8540

Travel Agent Rating
Overall Average
8
*(Detailed analysis of
results in Ratings
Section)*

CORPORATE INFORMATION
Owner: M. Shmilzadeh
Gen Mgr: S. Nokiani
Number of staff: 12
Date originated: 1982
Annual sales: $5 - 10 million
Bond coverage: $100,000
Accredited: ARC & IATAN
Escrow: (NP)
Security: (NP)

DESTINATIONS
**EUROPE, MID EAST,
NORTH AMERICA**

*(For a complete list of the exact
cities served within each region, see
the Destination Index)*

AIRLINES
All U.S. International airlines

(Airline codes defined in Index)

Firm books business class: (NP)   First class: (NP)
Airlines may be contacted for references: (NP)
Percentage of sales through scheduled air: (NP)

SALES POLICIES

Tickets delivered: Days before departure
Delivered by: *Overnight*   *$12.00*
First class   *varies*

Fee charged for credit card payment: (NP)
Flight confirmed: One day before departure
Is a printed receipt provided? (NP)
Cancellation policy: (NP)

Frequent flyer miles offered? (NP)

TRAVEL AGENCY
orders accepted by:
phone   letter   fax

PAYMENT FORMS
ACCEPTED
*AGENCY CHECK
COD*

Comment:

(NP) = Firm did not provide requested information.

FIRM: Abratours

RES PHONE: 1-800-227-2887

ADDRESS: 175 Main St., Ste. 508
White Plains, NY 10601
PHONE: 914-949-3300
FAX: 914-949-4154

Branch Offices:

Travel Agent Rating
Overall Average
8
(Detailed analysis of results in Ratings Section)

CORPORATE INFORMATION
Owner: Yaacov Amit
Gen Mgr: Dalia Arkan
Number of staff: 5
Date originated: 1933
Annual sales: $1 - 4 million
Bond coverage: (NP)
Accredited: ARC
Escrow: (NP)
Security: (NP)

DESTINATIONS
MID EAST

(For a complete list of the exact cities served within each region, see the Destination Index)

AIRLINES
all scheduled airlines

(Airline codes defined in Index)

Firm books business class: (NP)   First class: (NP)
Airlines may be contacted for references: Yes
Percentage of sales through scheduled air: 100%

SALES POLICIES

Tickets delivered: Seven days before departure
Delivered by:

Fee charged for credit card payment: (NP)
Flight confirmed: 24 hours
Is a printed receipt provided? (NP)
Cancellation policy: (NP)

Frequent flyer miles offered? No

TRAVEL AGENCY
orders accepted by:
fax

PAYMENT FORMS ACCEPTED
CREDIT CARD
AGENCY CHECK

Comment:

(NP) = Firm did not provide requested information.

FIRM: The Africa Desk

RES PHONE: 1-800-284-8796

ADDRESS: 516 Danbury Rd., Route 7
New Milford, CT 06776
PHONE: 203-354-9344
FAX: 203-354-9345

Branch Offices:

Travel Agent Rating
Overall Average

7

(Detailed analysis of results in Ratings Section)

CORPORATE INFORMATION

Owner: Christine Tyson
Gen Mgr: Gail DePietro
Number of staff: 6
Date originated: 1991
Annual sales: $1 - 4 million
Bond coverage: $70,000
Accredited: ARC & IATAN
Escrow: (NP)
Security: (NP)

DESTINATIONS
EUROPE, MID EAST, AFRICA

(For a complete list of the exact cities served within each region, see the Destination Index)

AIRLINES
South African Airways, Air Afrique, Sabena

(Airline codes defined in Index)

Firm books business class: (NP)   First class: (NP)
Airlines may be contacted for references: Yes
Percentage of sales through scheduled air: 100%

SALES POLICIES

Tickets delivered: (NP)
   Delivered by: *Overnight*   *$11.00*

Fee charged for credit card payment: (NP)
Flight confirmed: (NP)
Is a printed receipt provided? (NP)
Cancellation policy: (NP)

Frequent flyer miles offered? (NP)

TRAVEL AGENCY
orders accepted by:
phone   letter   fax

PAYMENT FORMS ACCEPTED
AGENCY CHECK CASH

Comment:

(NP) = Firm did not provide requested information.

FIRM: Agents Advantage

RES PHONE: 1-800-816-2211

ADDRESS: P.O. Box 7100
West Orange, NJ 07052-7100
PHONE: 908-355-2222
FAX: 201-857-4661

Branch Offices:

Travel Agent Rating
Overall Average
9
(Detailed analysis of results in Ratings Section)

CORPORATE INFORMATION

Owner: Mark Shapiro
Gen Mgr: Mark Shapiro
Number of staff: 3
Date originated: 1994
Annual sales: $5 - 10 million
Bond coverage: (NP)
Accredited: (NP)
Escrow: Yes
Security: Payments may be placed in escrow account

DESTINATIONS

EUROPE, MID EAST, ORIENT, LATIN AMERICA

(For a complete list of the exact cities served within each region, see the Destination Index)

AIRLINES

AF, AA, OZ, OS, BA, CO, AY, GF, IB, KL, BF, TW, LH, OA, RJ, SN, SA, TP, UA, US, AR, AZ, AI, KU, LA, RG, UC, KE, MH, JL

(Airline codes defined in Index)

Firm books business class: Yes   First class: (NP)
Airlines may be contacted for references: Yes
Percentage of sales through scheduled air: 100%

SALES POLICIES

Tickets delivered: ASAP
    Delivered by: *Overnight   no charge*

Fee charged for credit card payment: Yes
Flight confirmed: ASAP
Is a printed receipt provided? Yes
Cancellation policy: After ticketing, penalty varies by airline
Frequent flyer miles offered? No

TRAVEL AGENCY
orders accepted by:
phone   letter   fax

PAYMENT FORMS ACCEPTED
CREDIT CARD
AGENCY CHECK

Comment: *The first consolidator specifically formed to service the travel professional*

(NP) = Firm did not provide requested information.

FIRM: **AirFax Airline Marketing Assoc**

RES PHONE: 1-800-

ADDRESS: 3455 Peachtree Indstrl Blvd., Ste.305
Duluth, GA 30136-2657
PHONE: 404-662-0885
FAX: 404-662-0906

Branch Offices:

CORPORATE INFORMATION
Owner: Carol Shimkus Leone
Gen Mgr: (NP)
Number of staff: 2
Date originated: 1988
Annual sales: $1 - 4 million
Bond coverage: (NP)
Accredited: (NP)
Escrow: Yes
Security: DOT approved escrow account

DESTINATIONS
WORLDWIDE

(For a complete list of the exact cities served within each region, see the Destination Index)

AIRLINES
Strictly chartered carriers

(Airline codes defined in Index)

Firm books business class: No   First class: (NP)
Airlines may be contacted for references: Yes
Percentage of sales through scheduled air: 0%

SALES POLICIES

Tickets delivered: (NP)
Delivered by: *Overnight*   *no charge*
First class   *no charge*

Fee charged for credit card payment: (NP)
Flight confirmed: (NP)
Is a printed receipt provided? N/A
Cancellation policy: (NP)

Frequent flyer miles offered? No

TRAVEL AGENCY
orders accepted by:
phone   letter   fax

PAYMENT FORMS ACCEPTED
AGENCY CHECK
CASH

Comment: *We are air charter brokers for large group travel - domestic and international. This is based on a full utilization of the aircraft. We do not do individual ticketing.*

(NP) = Firm did not provide requested information.

FIRM: Airplan

RES PHONE: 1-800-866-7526

ADDRESS: 2600 Boyce Plaza Road Ste. 130
Pittsburgh, PA 15241
PHONE: 412-257-3199
FAX: 412-257-8421

Branch Offices:

Travel Agent Rating
Overall Average
8.14
(Detailed analysis of results in Ratings Section)

CORPORATE INFORMATION

Owner: John Latimer
Gen Mgr: Patricia Lucido
Number of staff: 15
Date originated: 1989
Annual sales: $10 - 25 million
Bond coverage: $95,000
Accredited: ARC & IATAN
Escrow: No
Security: (NP)

DESTINATIONS
EUROPE, ORIENT, AFRICA, LATIN AMERICA

(For a complete list of the exact cities served within each region, see the Destination Index)

AIRLINES
BA, AA, US, TW, KE, TR, AR

(Airline codes defined in Index)

Firm books business class: Varies   First class: Varies
Airlines may be contacted for references: Yes
Percentage of sales through scheduled air: 100%

SALES POLICIES

Tickets delivered: Upon payment
    Delivered by: *Overnight   no charge*

                UPS   no charge
Fee charged for credit card payment: 3%
Flight confirmed: Any time
Is a printed receipt provided? Yes
Cancellation policy: Varies by airline

Frequent flyer miles offered? Yes
              Varies by airline

TRAVEL AGENCY
orders accepted by:
phone   fax

PAYMENT FORMS ACCEPTED
CREDIT CARD
AGENCY CHECK
NET 10 DAYS

Comment: *All airlines used are by direct contract between airplane and the carrier.
Also, we offer tours to Britain commissionable at 12%.*

(NP) = Firm did not provide requested information.

130

FIRM: American Intl. Consolidators

RES PHONE: 1-800-888-5774

ADDRESS: 152 South Sawmill River Rd.
Elmsford, NY 10523
PHONE: 914-592-0206
FAX: 914-592-2889

Branch Offices:

Travel Agent Rating
Overall Average
7.81
(Detailed analysis of results in Ratings Section)

CORPORATE INFORMATION
Owner: Christopher Horne
Gen Mgr: Christopher Horne
Number of staff: 4
Date originated: 1990
Annual sales: $1 - 4 million
Bond coverage: (NP)
Accredited: ARC & IATAN
Escrow: Yes
Security: (NP)

DESTINATIONS
EUROPE, AFRICA, NORTH AMERICA

(For a complete list of the exact cities served within each region, see the Destination Index)

AIRLINES
TW, AF, BA, CO, AA, KLM, UA

(Airline codes defined in Index)

Firm books business class: No   First class: (NP)
Airlines may be contacted for references: Yes
Percentage of sales through scheduled air: 100%

SALES POLICIES

Tickets delivered: ASAP
        Delivered by: *Overnight*   *no charge*

Fee charged for credit card payment: (NP)
Flight confirmed: ASAP
Is a printed receipt provided? (NP)
Cancellation policy: (NP)

Frequent flyer miles offered? Yes
                Varies by airline

TRAVEL AGENCY orders accepted by:
phone   letter   fax

PAYMENT FORMS ACCEPTED
CREDIT CARD
AGENCY CHECK

Comment: *ASTA member*

(NP) = Firm did not provide requested information.

FIRM: American Travel Abroad Inc

RES PHONE: 1-800-228-0877

ADDRESS: 250 West 57 Street
New York, NY 10107
PHONE: 212-586-5230
FAX: 212-581-7925

Branch Offices:

Travel Agent Rating
Overall Average
6.58
(Detailed analysis of results in Ratings Section)

CORPORATE INFORMATION

Owner: Zbigniew Wegiel
Gen Mgr: Rose Pascoe
Number of staff: 35
Date originated: 1947
Annual sales: Over $25 million
Bond coverage: $70,000
Accredited: ARC & IATAN
Escrow: (NP)
Security: (NP)

DESTINATIONS
EUROPE

(For a complete list of the exact cities served within each region, see the Destination Index)

AIRLINES
LOT, Delta, Finnair, KLM

(Airline codes defined in Index)

Firm books business class: (NP)   First class: (NP)
Airlines may be contacted for references: Yes
Percentage of sales through scheduled air: 100%

SALES POLICIES

Tickets delivered: Upon payment
Delivered by: *Overnight*
First class   no charge

Fee charged for credit card payment: (NP)
Flight confirmed: At booking
Is a printed receipt provided? (NP)
Cancellation policy: (NP)

Frequent flyer miles offered? (NP)

TRAVEL AGENCY
orders accepted by:
phone letter fax

PAYMENT FORMS
ACCEPTED

CREDIT CARD
AGENCY CHECK
NET 10 DAYS

Comment:

(NP) = Firm did not provide requested information.

FIRM: **Ariel Tours, Inc.**

RES PHONE: 1-800-262-1818

ADDRESS: 4311 - 18th Ave
Brooklyn, NY 11218
PHONE: 718-633-7900
FAX: 718-972-0518

Branch Offices:

Travel Agent Rating
Overall Average
9.33
(Detailed analysis of results in Ratings Section)

CORPORATE INFORMATION

Owner: (NP)
Gen Mgr: Meir Weingarten
Number of staff: 9
Date originated: 1985
Annual sales: $5 - 10 million
Bond coverage: $65,000
Accredited: ARC & IATAN
Escrow: No
Security: (NP)

DESTINATIONS
MID EAST, AFRICA

(For a complete list of the exact cities served within each region, see the Destination Index)

AIRLINES
LY, TWA

(Airline codes defined in Index)

Firm books business class: (NP)   First class: (NP)
Airlines may be contacted for references: Yes
Percentage of sales through scheduled air: 100%

SALES POLICIES

Tickets delivered: Upon payment
     Delivered by: *Overnight $15.50*
                          First class

Fee charged for credit card payment: (NP)
Flight confirmed: (NP)
Is a printed receipt provided? (NP)
Cancellation policy: (NP)

Frequent flyer miles offered? Yes
                    Varies by airline

TRAVEL AGENCY
orders accepted by:
phone   letter   fax

PAYMENT FORMS ACCEPTED
CREDIT CARD
AGENCY CHECK

Comment:

(NP) = Firm did not provide requested information.

FIRM: **Balkan Holidays**

RES PHONE: 1-800-852-0944

ADDRESS: 41 E. 42nd St.
New York, NY 10017
PHONE: 212-573-5530
FAX: 212-573-5538

Branch Offices:

Travel Agent Rating
Overall Average
7
(Detailed analysis of results in Ratings Section)

CORPORATE INFORMATION

Owner: Maxim Starkov
Gen Mgr: (NP)
Number of staff: 10
Date originated: 1985
Annual sales: $5 - 10 million
Bond coverage: (NP)
Accredited: ARC & IATAN
Escrow: (NP)
Security: (NP)

DESTINATIONS
EUROPE, MID EAST, AFRICA

(For a complete list of the exact cities served within each region, see the Destination Index)

AIRLINES
Balkan Airlines, Austria Airlines, Czechoslovak Airlines, British Airways

(Airline codes defined in Index)

Firm books business class: (NP)   First class: (NP)
Airlines may be contacted for references: Yes
Percentage of sales through scheduled air: (NP)

SALES POLICIES

Tickets delivered: ASAP
Delivered by: *Overnight* $12.00 - 15.00
First class

Fee charged for credit card payment: (NP)
Flight confirmed: One day before departure
Is a printed receipt provided? (NP)
Cancellation policy: (NP)

Frequent flyer miles offered? (NP)

TRAVEL AGENCY
orders accepted by:
phone   letter   fax

PAYMENT FORMS ACCEPTED
CREDIT CARD
AGENCY CHECK

Comment:

(NP) = Firm did not provide requested information.

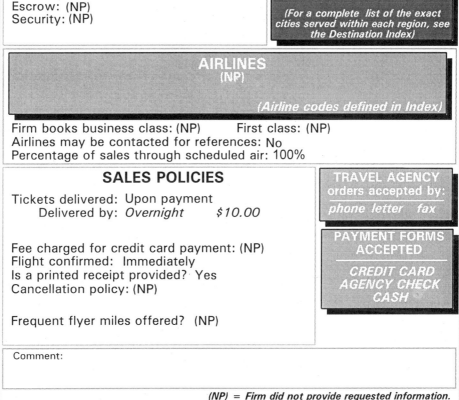

FIRM: Bon Voyage

RES PHONE: 1-800-826-8500

ADDRESS: 246 South Robertson
Beverly Hills, CA 90211
PHONE: 310-854-8585
FAX: 310-657-2348

Branch Offices:

Travel Agent Rating
Overall Average
5.71
(Detailed analysis of results in Ratings Section)

CORPORATE INFORMATION

Owner: (NP)
Gen Mgr: David Rezaieh
Number of staff: (NP)
Date originated: 1934
Annual sales: Over $25 million
Bond coverage: (NP)
Accredited: ARC & IATAN
Escrow: (NP)
Security: (NP)

DESTINATIONS

EUROPE, MID EAST,
ORIENT, AFRICA,
LATIN AMERICA,
SOUTH PACIFIC,
NORTH AMERICA

(For a complete list of the exact cities served within each region, see the Destination Index)

AIRLINES
(NP)

(Airline codes defined in Index)

Firm books business class: (NP)   First class: (NP)
Airlines may be contacted for references: No
Percentage of sales through scheduled air: 100%

SALES POLICIES

Tickets delivered: Upon payment
    Delivered by: *Overnight*   *$10.00*

Fee charged for credit card payment: (NP)
Flight confirmed: Immediately
Is a printed receipt provided? Yes
Cancellation policy: (NP)

Frequent flyer miles offered? (NP)

TRAVEL AGENCY
orders accepted by:
phone letter fax

PAYMENT FORMS ACCEPTED

*CREDIT CARD
AGENCY CHECK
CASH*

Comment:

(NP) = Firm did not provide requested information.

FIRM: **Brendan Air**

RES PHONE: 1-800-491-9633

ADDRESS: 15137 Califa St.
　　　　　Van Nuys, CA 91411
　　PHONE: 800-491-9633
　　FAX: 818-901-2685

Branch Offices:

Travel Agent Rating
Overall Average

7.5

(Detailed analysis of results in Ratings Section)

CORPORATE INFORMATION

Owner: James Murphy
Gen Mgr: Diane Hatwell - VP
Number of staff: 15
Date originated: 1993
Annual sales: $10 - 25 million
Bond coverage: $1,000,000
Accredited: ARC & IATAN
Escrow: Yes
Security: USTOA member; $1 million
　　　　　security plan

DESTINATIONS

EUROPE, ORIENT, AFRICA, LATIN AMERICA, SOUTH PACIFIC

(For a complete list of the exact cities served within each region, see the Destination Index)

AIRLINES

AA, NW, TW, IB, NZ, JL, OZ, CI, NH, UA, QF, FJ, GA, SA, KQ, UY, KL, VP, RG, AR, LA

(Airline codes defined in Index)

Firm books business class: Yes　　　First class: Yes
Airlines may be contacted for references: Yes
Percentage of sales through scheduled air: 95%

SALES POLICIES

Tickets delivered: Upon payment
　　Delivered by: *Overnight*　　*$10.00*

　　　　　　　　UPS　　　　*$3.00*
Fee charged for credit card payment: $15.00
Flight confirmed: At booking
Is a printed receipt provided? No
Cancellation policy: (NP)

Frequent flyer miles offered? Yes
　　　　　　　Varies by airline

TRAVEL AGENCY
orders accepted by:
phone letter fax

PAYMENT FORMS ACCEPTED

*CREDIT CARD
AGENCY CHECK*

Comment:

(NP) = Firm did not provide requested information.

136

FIRM: CL Thomson Express Int'l

RES PHONE: 1-800-

ADDRESS: 900 Wilshire Blvd. #938
Los Angeles, CA 90017
PHONE: 213-628-9550
FAX: 213-689-0261

Branch Offices:

Travel Agent Rating
Overall Average
7.37
(Detailed analysis of results in Ratings Section)

CORPORATE INFORMATION

Owner: (NP)
Gen Mgr: Robin Chen
Number of staff: 12
Date originated: 1978
Annual sales: (NP)
Bond coverage: (NP)
Accredited: ARC & IATAN
Escrow: (NP)
Security: (NP)

DESTINATIONS

EUROPE, MID EAST, ORIENT, AFRICA, LATIN AMERICA, SOUTH PACIFIC, NORTH AMERICA

(For a complete list of the exact cities served within each region, see the Destination Index)

AIRLINES
(NP)

(Airline codes defined in Index)

Firm books business class: (NP)   First class: (NP)
Airlines may be contacted for references: (NP)
Percentage of sales through scheduled air: (NP)

SALES POLICIES

Tickets delivered: (NP)
Delivered by: *Overnight*   *varies*
First class   *no charge*

Fee charged for credit card payment: (NP)
Flight confirmed: Yes
Is a printed receipt provided? (NP)
Cancellation policy: (NP)

Frequent flyer miles offered? (NP)

TRAVEL AGENCY
orders accepted by:
phone   letter   fax

PAYMENT FORMS ACCEPTED
CREDIT CARD
AGENCY CHECK
CASH

Comment:

(NP) = Firm did not provide requested information.

137

FIRM: Central Holidays

RES PHONE: 1-800-935-5000

ADDRESS: 206 Central Avenue
　　　　　Jersey City, NJ 07307
　PHONE:
　FAX: 201-963-0966
Branch Offices:

Travel Agent Rating
Overall Average
7.21
(Detailed analysis of results in Ratings Section)

CORPORATE INFORMATION

Owner: Joe and Fred Berardo
Gen Mgr: (NP)
Number of staff: 100
Date originated: 1972
Annual sales: Over $25 million
Bond coverage: USTOA
Accredited: ARC
Escrow: (NP)
Security: (NP)

DESTINATIONS
EUROPE

(For a complete list of the exact cities served within each region, see the Destination Index)

AIRLINES
AZ, TW, AF, UA, IB, CO

(Airline codes defined in Index)

Firm books business class: (NP)　　First class: (NP)
Airlines may be contacted for references: Yes
Percentage of sales through scheduled air: (NP)

SALES POLICIES

Tickets delivered: Normal time frame
　Delivered by: *Overnight　　$16.00 -25.00*
　　　　　　　　First class　　no charge
　　　　　　　　UPS two days $10.00
Fee charged for credit card payment: (NP)
Flight confirmed: At time of booking
Is a printed receipt provided? (NP)
Cancellation policy: (NP)

Frequent flyer miles offered? (NP)

TRAVEL AGENCY
orders accepted by:
phone

PAYMENT FORMS ACCEPTED
CREDIT CARD
AGENCY CHECK

Comment:

(NP) = Firm did not provide requested information.

138

FIRM: Centrav, Inc.

RES PHONE: 1-800-874-2033

ADDRESS: 9725 Garfield Avenue, S.
Minneapolis, MN 55420-4240
PHONE: 612-948-8400
FAX: 612-948-8444

Branch Offices:

Travel Agent Rating
Overall Average
8.71
*(Detailed analysis of
results in Ratings
Section)*

CORPORATE INFORMATION

Owner: Tim Skoog/Ron Weeks
Gen Mgr: Tim Skoog
Number of staff: 25
Date originated: 1988
Annual sales: $10 - 25 million
Bond coverage: maximum
Accredited: ARC & IATAN
Escrow: (NP)
Security: (NP)

DESTINATIONS

**EUROPE, MID EAST,
ORIENT, AFRICA,
LATIN AMERICA,
SOUTH PACIFIC**

*(For a complete list of the exact
cities served within each region, see
the Destination Index)*

AIRLINES
AIRLINES NOT LISTED BY REQUEST OF AIRLINES

(Airline codes defined in Index)

Firm books business class: No   First class: (NP)
Airlines may be contacted for references: Yes
Percentage of sales through scheduled air: 100%

SALES POLICIES

Tickets delivered: Upon payment
    Delivered by: *Overnight*   *$15.00*

            Teleticket: *$5.00*
Fee charged for credit card payment: (NP)
Flight confirmed: Immediately
Is a printed receipt provided? No
Cancellation policy: (NP)

Frequent flyer miles offered? Yes
                Varies by airline

TRAVEL AGENCY
orders accepted by:
phone   letter   fax

PAYMENT FORMS
ACCEPTED

*CREDIT CARD
AGENCY CHECK*

Comment:

(NP) = Firm did not provide requested information.

FIRM: **Charterways**

RES PHONE: 1-800-869-2344

ADDRESS: P.O. 9586
San Jose, CA 95157
PHONE: 408-257-2652
FAX: 408-257-2664

Branch Offices:

Travel Agent Rating
Overall Average
8.7
(Detailed analysis of results in Ratings Section)

CORPORATE INFORMATION

Owner: Tony & Audrey Cooper
Gen Mgr: (NP)
Number of staff: 8
Date originated: 1967
Annual sales: $5 - 10 million
Bond coverage: $70,000
Accredited: ARC & IATAN
Escrow: (NP)
Security: Money put in trust account.

DESTINATIONS

EUROPE, MID EAST, ORIENT, AFRICA, LATIN AMERICA, SOUTH PACIFIC

(For a complete list of the exact cities served within each region, see the Destination Index)

AIRLINES

BA, AA, KL, QF, CX, OZ, AF, LH, UA, NW, BD, UK, TW, DL, CP, AC, GA

(Airline codes defined in Index)

Firm books business class: (NP)   First class: (NP)
Airlines may be contacted for references: Yes
Percentage of sales through scheduled air: 100%

SALES POLICIES

Tickets delivered: Upon payment
Delivered by: *Overnight*   *$11.00*

Fee charged for credit card payment: (NP)
Flight confirmed: At booking
Is a printed receipt provided? No
Cancellation policy: Varies by airline

Frequent flyer miles offered? Yes
Varies by airline

TRAVEL AGENCY
orders accepted by:
phone   letter   fax

PAYMENT FORMS ACCEPTED
CREDIT CARD
AGENCY CHECK

Comment: *Charterways sells land products (accommodations, tours, car rentals) and rail Europe products and Britrail passes.*

(NP) = Firm did not provide requested information.

FIRM: City Tours

RES PHONE: 1-800-238-2489

ADDRESS: 26A Oak St.
            E Rutherford, NJ 07073
PHONE: 201-939-6572
FAX: 201-939-2545

Branch Offices:

Travel Agent Rating
Overall Average
7.5
(Detailed analysis of results in Ratings Section)

CORPORATE INFORMATION

Owner: Ray Thomas
Gen Mgr: Eric Thomas
Number of staff: 40
Date originated: 1978
Annual sales: $10 - 25 million
Bond coverage: $50,000
Accredited: ARC & IATAN
Escrow: (NP)
Security: (NP)

DESTINATIONS

ORIENT, LATIN AMERICA, SOUTH PACIFIC

(For a complete list of the exact cities served within each region, see the Destination Index)

AIRLINES
UA, KE, AR

(Airline codes defined in Index)

Firm books business class: (NP)   First class: (NP)
Airlines may be contacted for references: Yes
Percentage of sales through scheduled air: 100%

SALES POLICIES

Tickets delivered: Two weeks before departure
    Delivered by: *Overnight*   *$10.00*
                  First class   *no charge*

Fee charged for credit card payment: (NP)
Flight confirmed: Two weeks before departure
Is a printed receipt provided? (NP)
Cancellation policy: (NP)

Frequent flyer miles offered? (NP)

TRAVEL AGENCY
orders accepted by:
phone   *fax*

PAYMENT FORMS ACCEPTED
CREDIT CARD
AGENCY CHECK

Comment:

(NP) = Firm did not provide requested information.

FIRM: Consolidated Tours, Inc.

RES PHONE: 1-800-228-0877

ADDRESS: 250 W. 57th Street
New York, NY 10107
PHONE: 212-586-5230
FAX: 212-581-7925

Branch Offices:

Travel Agent Rating
Overall Average
7.75
(Detailed analysis of results in Ratings Section)

CORPORATE INFORMATION

Owner: Zbigniew Wegiel
Gen Mgr: Rose Pascoe
Number of staff: 35
Date originated: 1947
Annual sales: Over $25 million
Bond coverage: $70,000
Accredited: ARC
Escrow: (NP)
Security: (NP)

DESTINATIONS
EUROPE

(For a complete list of the exact cities served within each region, see the Destination Index)

AIRLINES
LOT, Delta, Finnair, Lufthansa

(Airline codes defined in Index)

Firm books business class: Yes   First class: Yes
Airlines may be contacted for references: (NP)
Percentage of sales through scheduled air: 99%

SALES POLICIES

Tickets delivered: Five days after payment
Delivered by:

Regular mail
Fee charged for credit card payment: (NP)
Flight confirmed: At booking
Is a printed receipt provided? (NP)
Cancellation policy: (NP)

Frequent flyer miles offered? (NP)

TRAVEL AGENCY
orders accepted by:

PAYMENT FORMS
ACCEPTED

CREDIT CARD
AGENCY CHECK

Comment:

(NP) = Firm did not provide requested information.

FIRM: Cosmopolitan TVC Ctr

RES PHONE: 1-800-548-7206

ADDRESS: 924 NE 20th Ave
Ft. Lauderdale, FL 33304
PHONE: 305-523-0973
FAX: 305-523-8324

Branch Offices:

Travel Agent Rating
Overall Average
9
(Detailed analysis of results in Ratings Section)

CORPORATE INFORMATION
Owner: S. Mangovski
Gen Mgr: S. Mangovski
Number of staff: 4
Date originated: 1988
Annual sales: $1 - 4 million
Bond coverage: $60,000
Accredited: ARC & IATAN
Escrow: No
Security: (NP)

DESTINATIONS
EUROPE, LATIN AMERICA

(For a complete list of the exact cities served within each region, see the Destination Index)

AIRLINES
AZ, AA, RG, LM

(Airline codes defined in Index)

Firm books business class: Yes   First class: Yes
Airlines may be contacted for references: Yes
Percentage of sales through scheduled air: 99%

SALES POLICIES

Tickets delivered: 15 days before departure
Delivered by: *Overnight*   *$10.00*
First class   *no charge*

Fee charged for credit card payment: (NP)
Flight confirmed: 30 days before departure
Is a printed receipt provided? No
Cancellation policy: $150 penalty

Frequent flyer miles offered? No

TRAVEL AGENCY
orders accepted by:
phone   letter   fax

PAYMENT FORMS
ACCEPTED
*CREDIT CARD
AGENCY CHECK
COD*

Comment:

(NP) = Firm did not provide requested information.

FIRM: Council Charter

RES PHONE: 1-800-800-8222

ADDRESS: 205 East 42nd St.
New York, NY 10017
PHONE: 212-661-0311
FAX: 212-972-0194

Branch Offices:

Travel Agent Rating
Overall Average
6.77
(Detailed analysis of results in Ratings Section)

CORPORATE INFORMATION

Owner: C.I.E.E.
Gen Mgr: (NP)
Number of staff: (NP)
Date originated: 1947
Annual sales: (NP)
Bond coverage: (NP)
Accredited: (NP)
Escrow: (NP)
Security: (NP)

DESTINATIONS
EUROPE, CARIBBEAN

(For a complete list of the exact cities served within each region, see the Destination Index)

AIRLINES
Air France, Sabena, Virgin Atlantic, Tower Air

(Airline codes defined in Index)

Firm books business class: (NP)   First class: (NP)
Airlines may be contacted for references: Yes
Percentage of sales through scheduled air: 98%

SALES POLICIES

Tickets delivered: Upon payment
Delivered by: *Overnight*   *$12.00*

Regular mail
Fee charged for credit card payment: (NP)
Flight confirmed: At booking
Is a printed receipt provided? (NP)
Cancellation policy: (NP)

Frequent flyer miles offered? (NP)

TRAVEL AGENCY
orders accepted by:
phone

PAYMENT FORMS ACCEPTED
CREDIT CARD
AGENCY CHECK

Comment:

(NP) = Firm did not provide requested information.

FIRM: Creative Marketing Management

RES PHONE: 1-800-458-6663

ADDRESS: Greybar Bldg. #347, 420 Lexington Ave
New York, NY 10170
PHONE: 212-557-1530
FAX: 212-818-9501

Branch Offices:

Travel Agent Rating
Overall Average
10
(Detailed analysis of results in Ratings Section)

CORPORATE INFORMATION

Owner: Corporation
Gen Mgr: Leon A. Acriche
Number of staff: 6
Date originated: 1985
Annual sales: $5 - 10 million
Bond coverage: $25,000
Accredited: ARC & IATAN
Escrow: (NP)
Security: (NP)

DESTINATIONS
ORIENT

(For a complete list of the exact cities served within each region, see the Destination Index)

AIRLINES
JL, NW, UA, AA, KE, DL

(Airline codes defined in Index)

Firm books business class: (NP)   First class: (NP)
Airlines may be contacted for references: Yes
Percentage of sales through scheduled air: 100%

SALES POLICIES

Tickets delivered: Varies by airline
    Delivered by: *Overnight*   *$15.00*

Fee charged for credit card payment: (NP)
Flight confirmed: Varies by airline
Is a printed receipt provided? No
Cancellation policy: $25 cancellation policy, per reservation

Frequent flyer miles offered? No

TRAVEL AGENCY
orders accepted by:
phone   *fax*

PAYMENT FORMS ACCEPTED
CREDIT CARD
AGENCY CHECK
COD

Comment: *CMM is a 100% owned subsidiary of Pacifico Creative Service (PCS), the largest Japanese tour operator in the United States.*

(NP) = Firm did not provide requested information.

FIRM: D-FW Tours

RES PHONE: 1-800-527-2589

ADDRESS: 7616 LBJ Freeway Ste. 524
Dallas, TX 75251
PHONE: 214-980-4540
FAX: 214-386-3802

Branch Offices:

Travel Agent Rating
Overall Average
8.69
(Detailed analysis of results in Ratings Section)

CORPORATE INFORMATION

Owner: John Przywar
Gen Mgr: Jan Woodside
Number of staff: 40
Date originated: 1978
Annual sales: Over $25 million
Bond coverage: yes
Accredited: ARC
Escrow: (NP)
Security: (NP)

DESTINATIONS

EUROPE, MID EAST, ORIENT, AFRICA, LATIN AMERICA

(For a complete list of the exact cities served within each region, see the Destination Index)

AIRLINES

BA, AA, CO, DL, UA, OS, Thai, Cathay Pacific, Aeroflot, Air France, Lufthansa, Malaysia, Air Canada

(Airline codes defined in Index)

Firm books business class: Yes   First class: Yes
Airlines may be contacted for references: Yes
Percentage of sales through scheduled air: 100%

SALES POLICIES

Tickets delivered: ASAP or 14 days after booking
    Delivered by: *Overnight*   *$10.00*
                  First class   *no charge*

Fee charged for credit card payment: 3%
Flight confirmed: At booking
Is a printed receipt provided? No
Cancellation policy: Varies

Frequent flyer miles offered? Yes
                  Varies by airline

TRAVEL AGENCY
orders accepted by:
phone   letter   fax

PAYMENT FORMS ACCEPTED
CREDIT CARD
AGENCY CHECK

Comment:

(NP) = Firm did not provide requested information.

FIRM: Diplomat Tours

RES PHONE: 1-800-727-8687

ADDRESS: 3174 Arden
Sacramento, CA 95825
PHONE: 916-972-1500
FAX: 916-481-4728

Branch Offices:

Travel Agent Rating
Overall Average
7.97
(Detailed analysis of results in Ratings Section)

CORPORATE INFORMATION

Owner: Darlene Rippon
Gen Mgr: Larry Young
Number of staff: 38
Date originated: 1985
Annual sales: Over $25 million
Bond coverage: yes
Accredited: ARC & IATAN
Escrow: (NP)
Security: (NP)

DESTINATIONS

EUROPE, MID EAST, ORIENT, AFRICA, LATIN AMERICA, SOUTH PACIFIC, NORTH AMERICA

(For a complete list of the exact cities served within each region, see the Destination Index)

AIRLINES

Asiana Airlines, Air Canada, Air France, Air Inter, British Midland

(Airline codes defined in Index)

Firm books business class: (NP)   First class: (NP)
Airlines may be contacted for references: Yes
Percentage of sales through scheduled air: 100%

SALES POLICIES

Tickets delivered: Five days after payment rcd.
Delivered by: *Overnight   no charge*

Fee charged for credit card payment: (NP)
Flight confirmed: At booking
Is a printed receipt provided? (NP)
Cancellation policy: (NP)

Frequent flyer miles offered? (NP)

TRAVEL AGENCY orders accepted by:
phone   letter   fax

PAYMENT FORMS ACCEPTED
*CREDIT CARD
AGENCY CHECK*

Comment:

(NP) = Firm did not provide requested information.

FIRM: Eastern European Travel Center

RES PHONE: 1-800-

ADDRESS: 1324 E 15 Street
Brooklyn, NY 11230
PHONE: 718-339-1100
FAX: 718-339-1376

Branch Offices:

Travel Agent Rating
Overall Average
8.75
(Detailed analysis of results in Ratings Section)

CORPORATE INFORMATION

Owner: Alex Gorn
Gen Mgr: Alex Gorn
Number of staff: 5
Date originated: 1986
Annual sales: $5 - 10 million
Bond coverage: (NP)
Accredited: (NP)
Escrow: (NP)
Security: (NP)

DESTINATIONS
EUROPE

(For a complete list of the exact cities served within each region, see the Destination Index)

AIRLINES
SU, AY, OK, LO, SN, OS

(Airline codes defined in Index)

Firm books business class: (NP)   First class: (NP)
Airlines may be contacted for references: Yes
Percentage of sales through scheduled air: 100%

SALES POLICIES

Tickets delivered: Yes
Delivered by: *Overnight*   *$15.00*
First class   *no charge*

Fee charged for credit card payment: (NP)
Flight confirmed: Yes
Is a printed receipt provided? (NP)
Cancellation policy: (NP)

Frequent flyer miles offered? (NP)

TRAVEL AGENCY
orders accepted by:
phone   letter   fax

PAYMENT FORMS ACCEPTED
CREDIT CARD
AGENCY CHECK

Comment:

(NP) = Firm did not provide requested information.

FIRM: The Egyptian Connection

RES PHONE: 1-800-334-4477

ADDRESS: P.O. Box 6777
Fresh Meadows, NY 11365
PHONE: 718-762-3838
FAX: 718-762-4171

Branch Offices:

Travel Agent Rating
Overall Average
6
(Detailed analysis of results in Ratings Section)

CORPORATE INFORMATION

Owner: (NP)
Gen Mgr: Mounir Hanna
Number of staff: 5
Date originated: 1987
Annual sales: Under $1 million
Bond coverage: (NP)
Accredited: (NP)
Escrow: (NP)
Security: (NP)

DESTINATIONS

MID EAST, ORIENT, AFRICA

(For a complete list of the exact cities served within each region, see the Destination Index)

AIRLINES

Egyptair, Royal Jordanian, BA, Air France, KLM, Alitalia, Lufthansa, TWA

(Airline codes defined in Index)

Firm books business class: Yes   First class: (NP)
Airlines may be contacted for references: Yes
Percentage of sales through scheduled air: 100%

SALES POLICIES

Tickets delivered: (NP)
    Delivered by: *Overnight*   *$10.00*
                  First class   *no charge*

Fee charged for credit card payment: (NP)
Flight confirmed: (NP)
Is a printed receipt provided? (NP)
Cancellation policy: (NP)

Frequent flyer miles offered? Yes
                  Varies by airline

TRAVEL AGENCY
orders accepted by:
phone   *fax*

PAYMENT FORMS
ACCEPTED

CREDIT CARD
AGENCY CHECK

Comment: *During low season, stand-by rates available.*

(NP) = Firm did not provide requested information.

FIRM: Fantastiques Tours

RES PHONE: 1-800-

ADDRESS: 13470 Washington Blvd., Ste. 301
Marina del Rey, CA 90292
PHONE: 310-577-6711
FAX: 310-577-6707

Branch Offices:

CORPORATE INFORMATION

Owner: (NP)
Gen Mgr: (NP)
Number of staff: 11
Date originated: 1994
Annual sales: $1 - 4 million
Bond coverage: $20,000
Accredited: ARC & IATAN
Escrow: (NP)
Security: Trust account for passengers'
funds

DESTINATIONS

EUROPE, LATIN AMERICA

(For a complete list of the exact cities served within each region, see the Destination Index)

AIRLINES

CO, TW, AF, IW, SS, CO, TW, VP, VG, DL, UA, AA, IB, LH

(Airline codes defined in Index)

Firm books business class: Yes   First class: Yes
Airlines may be contacted for references: Yes
Percentage of sales through scheduled air: 90%

SALES POLICIES

Tickets delivered: Up to 60 days before
Delivered by: *Overnight*   *$7.00*

LA county   no charge
Fee charged for credit card payment: (NP)
Flight confirmed: At booking
Is a printed receipt provided? Yes
Cancellation policy: (NP)

Frequent flyer miles offered? Yes

TRAVEL AGENCY
orders accepted by:
phone letter   fax

PAYMENT FORMS ACCEPTED
AGENCY CHECK

Comment:

(NP) = Firm did not provide requested information.

150

FIRM: Festival of Asia

RES PHONE: 1-800-533-9953

ADDRESS: 155 Montgomery St., Ste. 508
San Francisco, CA 94104
PHONE: 415-693-0880
FAX: 415-693-0884

Branch Offices:

Travel Agent Rating
Overall Average
8.43
(Detailed analysis of results in Ratings Section)

CORPORATE INFORMATION

Owner: Luis Cuadros
Gen Mgr: Luis Cuadros
Number of staff: 6
Date originated: 1988
Annual sales: $5 - 10 million
Bond coverage: (NP)
Accredited: ARC
Escrow: (NP)
Security: Secured account for air ticket
payments

DESTINATIONS

ORIENT, SOUTH PACIFIC

(For a complete list of the exact cities served within each region, see the Destination Index)

AIRLINES
BA, BR, CI, CX, GA, KL, MH, MK, OZ, PX, PR, SQ, TG

(Airline codes defined in Index)

Firm books business class: (NP)   First class: (NP)
Airlines may be contacted for references: Yes
Percentage of sales through scheduled air: 100%

SALES POLICIES

Tickets delivered: (NP)
Delivered by: *Overnight*   *$9.00*

Fee charged for credit card payment: (NP)
Flight confirmed: N/A
Is a printed receipt provided? No
Cancellation policy: Varies by airline

Frequent flyer miles offered? Yes
Varies by airline

TRAVEL AGENCY
orders accepted by:
phone   fax

PAYMENT FORMS ACCEPTED
CREDIT CARD
AGENCY CHECK

Comment:

(NP) = Firm did not provide requested information.

151

FIRM: G. G. Tours

RES PHONE: 1-800-

ADDRESS: 2180 Yonge St.
Toronto, ON M4S 2B9
PHONE: 416-487-1146
FAX: 416-487-2749

Branch Offices:

Travel Agent Rating
Overall Average
8
(Detailed analysis of results in Ratings Section)

CORPORATE INFORMATION

Owner: (NP)
Gen Mgr: George Gideon
Number of staff: 9
Date originated: 1989
Annual sales: $1 - 4 million
Bond coverage: (NP)
Accredited: IATAN
Escrow: (NP)
Security: (NP)

DESTINATIONS
CARIBBEAN

(For a complete list of the exact cities served within each region, see the Destination Index)

AIRLINES
Air Canada

(Airline codes defined in Index)

Firm books business class: (NP)   First class: (NP)
Airlines may be contacted for references: No
Percentage of sales through scheduled air: (NP)

SALES POLICIES

Tickets delivered: Yes
      Delivered by: *Overnight*   *no charge*
                          First class   *no charge*

Fee charged for credit card payment: (NP)
Flight confirmed: Yes
Is a printed receipt provided? (NP)
Cancellation policy: Payments non-refundable

Frequent flyer miles offered? (NP)

TRAVEL AGENCY
orders accepted by:
phone   letter   fax

PAYMENT FORMS ACCEPTED
CREDIT CARD
AGENCY CHECK

Comment:

(NP) = Firm did not provide requested information.

152

FIRM: Gate 1

RES PHONE: 1-800-682-3333

ADDRESS: 101 Limekiln Pike
Glenside, PA 19038
PHONE: 215-572-7676
FAX: 215-886-2228

Branch Offices:

Travel Agent Rating
Overall Average
6
(Detailed analysis of results in Ratings Section)

CORPORATE INFORMATION

Owner: Dani Pipano
Gen Mgr: (NP)
Number of staff: 60
Date originated: 1981
Annual sales: Over $25 million
Bond coverage: (NP)
Accredited: ARC & IATAN
Escrow: (NP)
Security: $1,000,000 Consumer
Protection Plan

DESTINATIONS
EUROPE, MID EAST

(For a complete list of the exact cities served within each region, see the Destination Index)

AIRLINES
US, AA, BA, TW, LY, LH, OA, TK, AY

(Airline codes defined in Index)

Firm books business class: (NP)   First class: (NP)
Airlines may be contacted for references: Yes
Percentage of sales through scheduled air: 100%

SALES POLICIES

Tickets delivered: Upon payment
Delivered by: *Overnight*   *no charge*

Fee charged for credit card payment: Yes
Flight confirmed: At booking
Is a printed receipt provided? Yes
Cancellation policy: Dependent upon program

Frequent flyer miles offered? Yes
Varies by airline

TRAVEL AGENCY
orders accepted by:
phone letter fax

PAYMENT FORMS ACCEPTED
CREDIT CARD
AGENCY CHECK

Comment:

(NP) = Firm did not provide requested information.

FIRM: **Gateway Express Ltd.**

RES PHONE: **1-800-334-1188**

ADDRESS: 25 SW Jefferson St
Portland, OR 97201
PHONE: 503-242-0088
FAX: 503-227-7564

Branch Offices:

Travel Agent Rating
Overall Average
8.67
(Detailed analysis of results in Ratings Section)

CORPORATE INFORMATION

Owner: Ester/Gordan Yeh
Gen Mgr: Ester/Gordan Yeh
Number of staff: 15
Date originated: 1982
Annual sales: Over $25 million
Bond coverage: (NP)
Accredited: ARC & IATAN
Escrow: (NP)
Security: (NP)

DESTINATIONS

EUROPE, MID EAST, ORIENT, AFRICA, LATIN AMERICA, SOUTH PACIFIC

(For a complete list of the exact cities served within each region, see the Destination Index)

AIRLINES

UA, LH, CX, QF, TG, JL, RG, MH, SQ, AI, BR, OZ, and Japan rail passes - 7, 14, and 21 days

(Airline codes defined in Index)

Firm books business class: Yes   First class: (NP)
Airlines may be contacted for references: Yes
Percentage of sales through scheduled air: 90%

SALES POLICIES

Tickets delivered: Immediately upon payment
Delivered by: *Overnight*   *varies*
First class   *varies*

Fee charged for credit card payment: Varies
Flight confirmed: At booking
Is a printed receipt provided? (NP)
Cancellation policy: Varies by airline

Frequent flyer miles offered? Yes
Varies by airline

TRAVEL AGENCY
orders accepted by:
phone   letter   fax

PAYMENT FORMS
ACCEPTED
CREDIT CARD
AGENCY CHECK

Comment: *All calls answered promptly - very little on-hold time.*

(NP) = Firm did not provide requested information.

154

FIRM: **Global Travel Consolidators**

RES PHONE: 1-800-366-3544

ADDRESS: 2950 31st St.
Santa Monica, CA 90405
PHONE: 310-581-5610
FAX: 310-581-5621

Branch Offices:

Travel Agent Rating
Overall Average
5.5
(Detailed analysis of results in Ratings Section)

CORPORATE INFORMATION

Owner: Mr. Jake Piha
Gen Mgr: Fred Pandidan
Number of staff: 7
Date originated: 1984
Annual sales: $10 - 25 million
Bond coverage: $70,000 ARC
Accredited: ARC & IATAN
Escrow: (NP)
Security: (NP)

DESTINATIONS

EUROPE, MID EAST, ORIENT, AFRICA, LATIN AMERICA, SOUTH PACIFIC

(For a complete list of the exact cities served within each region, see the Destination Index)

AIRLINES

BA, AA, IB, OK, VP, EK, AY, FJ, SD, NZ, CO, BD, KE, OZ, QF, SV, TK, TW, US

(Airline codes defined in Index)

Firm books business class: Yes   First class: Yes
Airlines may be contacted for references: Yes
Percentage of sales through scheduled air: 100%

SALES POLICIES

Tickets delivered: Possibly at booking
Delivered by: *Overnight*   *$6.00*

Fee charged for credit card payment: (NP)
Flight confirmed: No advance
Is a printed receipt provided? Yes
Cancellation policy: If refundable, $25 - $200;
also varies by airline

Frequent flyer miles offered? Yes
Varies by airline

TRAVEL AGENCY
orders accepted by:
phone   letter   fax

PAYMENT FORMS
ACCEPTED

*CREDIT CARD
AGENCY CHECK**

Comment: *We are located in LA area. Delivery in LA county will be free.*
*AGENCY CHECK: give us at least seven days to clear.

(NP) = Firm did not provide requested information.

155

FIRM: Golden Pacific #1 Travel

RES PHONE: 1-800-500-8021

ADDRESS: 210-P S. Kings Ave.
Brandon, FL 33511
PHONE: 813-684-6365
FAX: 813-689-2731

Branch Offices:

Travel Agent Rating
Overall Average
7
(Detailed analysis of results in Ratings Section)

CORPORATE INFORMATION

Owner: David Chen
Gen Mgr: James Lin
Number of staff: 7
Date originated: 1989
Annual sales: $1 - 4 million
Bond coverage: $25,000
Accredited: ARC & IATAN
Escrow: Yes
Security: (NP)

DESTINATIONS
ORIENT, SOUTH PACIFIC

(For a complete list of the exact cities served within each region, see the Destination Index)

AIRLINES
CI, CX, SQ, KE, CA

(Airline codes defined in Index)

Firm books business class: Yes   First class: No
Airlines may be contacted for references: Yes
Percentage of sales through scheduled air: 95%

SALES POLICIES

Tickets delivered: Varies
Delivered by: *Overnight*   *$10.00*
First class   *no charge*

Fee charged for credit card payment: (NP)
Flight confirmed: Seven days before departure
Is a printed receipt provided? No
Cancellation policy: According to airline policy

Frequent flyer miles offered? Yes
Only on UA and NW

TRAVEL AGENCY
orders accepted by:
phone letter fax

PAYMENT FORMS ACCEPTED
CREDIT CARD
AGENCY CHECK
CASH

Comment:

(NP) = Firm did not provide requested information.

FIRM: HTI Tours

RES PHONE: 1-800-441-4411

ADDRESS: 1819 JFK Boulevard, Ste. 480
Philadelphia, PA 19103
PHONE: 215-563-8484
FAX: 215-563-4411

Branch Offices:

Travel Agent Rating
Overall Average
6.86
(Detailed analysis of results in Ratings Section)

CORPORATE INFORMATION

Owner: Rita Hirschhorn
Gen Mgr: Rita Hirschhorn
Number of staff: 9
Date originated: 1982
Annual sales: $5 - 10 million
Bond coverage: (NP)
Accredited: ARC & IATAN
Escrow: Yes
Security: Escrow bank account

DESTINATIONS

EUROPE, MID EAST, ORIENT, AFRICA, LATIN AMERICA, SOUTH PACIFIC

(For a complete list of the exact cities served within each region, see the Destination Index)

AIRLINES

AA, AF, BA, CX, EK, AY, GA, KE, LH, MH, OA, QF, RJ, SN, TG, TR, TW, SQ, RG, UA

(Airline codes defined in Index)

Firm books business class: (NP)   First class: (NP)
Airlines may be contacted for references: Yes
Percentage of sales through scheduled air: 100%

SALES POLICIES

Tickets delivered: Two days after payment
Delivered by: *Overnight $10.00*

Fee charged for credit card payment: varies
Flight confirmed: One to 365 days before
Is a printed receipt provided? Yes
Cancellation policy: Varies by airline

Frequent flyer miles offered? Yes
Varies by airline

TRAVEL AGENCY
orders accepted by:
phone   letter   fax

PAYMENT FORMS
ACCEPTED
*CREDIT CARD
AGENCY CHECK*

Comment: *HTI only sells airlines that we have a contract with directly; we are never subagents.*

(NP) = Firm did not provide requested information.

FIRM: Happy Tours

RES PHONE: 1-800-877-5262

ADDRESS: #1 Victor Square, Ste. B
Scotts Valley, CA 95066
PHONE: 408-461-0150
FAX: 408-461-0150

Branch Offices:

Travel Agent Rating
Overall Average
8.57
(Detailed analysis of results in Ratings Section)

CORPORATE INFORMATION

Owner: (NP)
Gen Mgr: (NP)
Number of staff: (NP)
Date originated: 1969
Annual sales: (NP)
Bond coverage: (NP)
Accredited: ARC & IATAN
Escrow: (NP)
Security: (NP)

DESTINATIONS
NORTH AMERICA

(For a complete list of the exact cities served within each region, see the Destination Index)

AIRLINES
UA, NW, AQ

(Airline codes defined in Index)

Firm books business class: (NP)   First class: (NP)
Airlines may be contacted for references: No
Percentage of sales through scheduled air: (NP)

SALES POLICIES

Tickets delivered: Three weeks before departure
Delivered by: *Overnight*   *$15.00*

UPS
Fee charged for credit card payment: (NP)
Flight confirmed: At booking
Is a printed receipt provided? (NP)
Cancellation policy: (NP)

Frequent flyer miles offered? (NP)

TRAVEL AGENCY orders accepted by:
phone   letter   fax

PAYMENT FORMS ACCEPTED
CREDIT CARD
AGENCY CHECK

Comment:

(NP) = Firm did not provide requested information.

FIRM: J & O Air

RES PHONE: 1-800-877-8111

ADDRESS: 3131 Caminio Del Rio No,
San Diego, CA 92108
PHONE: 619-282-4124
FAX: 619-282-4164

Branch Offices:

Travel Agent Rating
Overall Average
8.59
(Detailed analysis of results in Ratings Section)

CORPORATE INFORMATION

Owner: Tyler Tanaka
Gen Mgr: Stephen Lepisto
Number of staff: 14
Date originated: 1991
Annual sales: (NP)
Bond coverage: $150,000
Accredited: ARC & IATAN
Escrow: (NP)
Security: (NP)

DESTINATIONS

EUROPE, ORIENT, AFRICA, LATIN AMERICA, SOUTH PACIFIC

(For a complete list of the exact cities served within each region, see the Destination Index)

AIRLINES

UA, KE, CX, NH, MH, GA, TG, VP, AA, NW, QF, AF, RG, LR, AV, LA, IW, AZ, BA

(Airline codes defined in Index)

Firm books business class: (NP)   First class: (NP)
Airlines may be contacted for references: Yes
Percentage of sales through scheduled air: 100%

SALES POLICIES

Tickets delivered: UPS
Delivered by:

UPS   no charge
Fee charged for credit card payment: (NP)
Flight confirmed: At booking
Is a printed receipt provided? (NP)
Cancellation policy: (NP)

Frequent flyer miles offered? (NP)

TRAVEL AGENCY
orders accepted by:
phone   fax

PAYMENT FORMS ACCEPTED
CREDIT CARD
AGENCY CHECK

Comment:

(NP) = Firm did not provide requested information.

FIRM: Jetset Tours Inc.

RES PHONE: 1-800-638-3273

ADDRESS: 122 S. Michigan Ave., Ste. 1290
Chicago, IL 60603
PHONE: 312-362-9960
FAX: 312-362-9119

Branch Offices:

5120 W. Goldleaf Circle, #310	17 E. 45th St., Ste. 601	53rd St., Ste. 1014
Los Angeles, CA 90056	New York, NY 10017	San Francisco, CA 94103
800-453-8738	212-818-9848	415-546-6200

Travel Agent Rating
Overall Average
8.15
(Detailed analysis of results in Ratings Section)

CORPORATE INFORMATION

Owner: Jetset Travel Holdings
Gen Mgr: Ross Webster
Number of staff: 112
Date originated: 1978
Annual sales: Over $25 million
Bond coverage: USTOA
Accredited: ARC & IATAN
Escrow: (NP)
Security: (NP)

DESTINATIONS

EUROPE, MID EAST, ORIENT, AFRICA, LATIN AMERICA, SOUTH PACIFIC

(For a complete list of the exact cities served within each region, see the Destination Index)

AIRLINES

QF, NZ, CO, UA, BA , LH, CP, MH, CX, VASP, Asiana, Air Pacific, AN
SA, GA

(Airline codes defined in Index)

Firm books business class: (NP)   First class: (NP)
Airlines may be contacted for references: Yes
Percentage of sales through scheduled air: 100%

SALES POLICIES

Tickets delivered: immediately after payment
Delivered by: *Overnight*   *$15.00*
First class   *no charge*
UPS   *no charge*
Fee charged for credit card payment: (NP)
Flight confirmed: At booking
Is a printed receipt provided? (NP)
Cancellation policy: (NP)

Frequent flyer miles offered? (NP)

TRAVEL AGENCY
orders accepted by:
phone letter

PAYMENT FORMS ACCEPTED
CREDIT CARD
AGENCY CHECK
CASH

Comment: *Offices: Los Angeles, San Francisco, Seattle, Chicago, New York, Houston, Orlando, San Diego, Washington D.C., Portland, Vancouver & Toronto - call 1-800-NETFARE.*

(NP) = Firm did not provide requested information.

FIRM: Leisure Resources

RES PHONE: 1-800-729-9051

ADDRESS: 344 West Main St.
Milford, CT 06460
PHONE: 203-874-4965
FAX: 203-878-0665

Branch Offices:

Travel Agent Rating
Overall Average
5.25
(Detailed analysis of results in Ratings Section)

CORPORATE INFORMATION

Owner: Corporation
Gen Mgr: Bruce Reichert
Number of staff: 15
Date originated: (NP)
Annual sales: $1 - 4 million
Bond coverage: $70,000
Accredited: ARC & IATAN
Escrow: (NP)
Security: (NP)

DESTINATIONS
EUROPE, AFRICA

(For a complete list of the exact cities served within each region, see the Destination Index)

AIRLINES
AA, AI, SN, MS, KQ, TW, IB, LH, UK, SK, AY

(Airline codes defined in Index)

Firm books business class: (NP)   First class: (NP)
Airlines may be contacted for references: Yes
Percentage of sales through scheduled air: 100%

SALES POLICIES

Tickets delivered: Upon payment
    Delivered by: *Overnight*   *$7.00*
                  First class

Fee charged for credit card payment: (NP)
Flight confirmed: At booking
Is a printed receipt provided? (NP)
Cancellation policy: (NP)

Frequent flyer miles offered? (NP)

TRAVEL AGENCY
orders accepted by:
phone   letter   fax

PAYMENT FORMS ACCEPTED
AGENCY CHECK

Comment:

(NP) = Firm did not provide requested information.

FIRM: MLT Vacations

RES PHONE: 1-800-328-0025

ADDRESS: 5130 Hwy. 101
Minnetonka, MN 55345
PHONE: 612-474-2540
FAX: 612-474-9730

Branch Offices:

Travel Agent Rating
Overall Average
8.56
*(Detailed analysis of
results in Ratings
Section)*

CORPORATE INFORMATION

Owner: NWA, Inc.
Gen Mgr: (NP)
Number of staff: 800
Date originated: 1969
Annual sales: (NP)
Bond coverage: Yes
Accredited: ARC
Escrow: (NP)
Security: (NP)

DESTINATIONS

ORIENT, NORTH AMERICA, CARIBBEAN

*(For a complete list of the exact
cities served within each region, see
the Destination Index)*

AIRLINES
Sun Country, Northwest Airlines

(Airline codes defined in Index)

Firm books business class: (NP)   First class: (NP)
Airlines may be contacted for references: Yes
Percentage of sales through scheduled air: (NP)

SALES POLICIES

Tickets delivered: Three weeks before departure
Delivered by: *Overnight $11.00*
First class   no charge

Fee charged for credit card payment: (NP)
Flight confirmed: At booking
Is a printed receipt provided? (NP)
Cancellation policy: (NP)

Frequent flyer miles offered? (NP)

TRAVEL AGENCY orders accepted by:
phone

PAYMENT FORMS ACCEPTED
*CREDIT CARD
AGENCY CHECK*

Comment:

(NP) = Firm did not provide requested information.

FIRM: MT&T

RES PHONE: 1-800-

ADDRESS: 1600 Hwy. 10 NE
Minneapolis, MN 55432
PHONE: 612-784-3226
FAX: 612-784-2934

Branch Offices:

Travel Agent Rating
Overall Average
7.6
(Detailed analysis of results in Ratings Section)

CORPORATE INFORMATION

Owner: Bennet Cyrus
Gen Mgr: Diane Cyrus
Number of staff: 28
Date originated: 1982
Annual sales: $10 - 25 million
Bond coverage: $70,000
Accredited: ARC & IATAN
Escrow: None
Security: (NP)

DESTINATIONS
EUROPE, ORIENT, SOUTH PACIFIC

(For a complete list of the exact cities served within each region, see the Destination Index)

AIRLINES
NW, MH, NZ, KU, GF, PR, CI, TW, OZ, BR

(Airline codes defined in Index)

Firm books business class: Yes   First class: Yes
Airlines may be contacted for references: Yes
Percentage of sales through scheduled air: 100%

SALES POLICIES

Tickets delivered: Upon payment
    Delivered by: *Overnight $10.00*
            First class   no charge

Fee charged for credit card payment: (NP)
Flight confirmed: Upon payment
Is a printed receipt provided? Yes
Cancellation policy: $100 per ticket; other
                charges vary by airline.

Frequent flyer miles offered? Yes
            Varies by airline

TRAVEL AGENCY
orders accepted by:
phone letter fax

PAYMENT FORMS ACCEPTED
AGENCY CHECK

Comment: *We are an American Express travel affiliate and an ASTA member.*

(NP) = Firm did not provide requested information.

FIRM: Marnella Tours Inc.

RES PHONE: 1-800-937-6999

ADDRESS: Ste. 117 33 Walt Whitman Rd.
Huntington Station, NY 11746
PHONE: 516-271-6969
FAX: 516-271-8593

Branch Offices:

CORPORATE INFORMATION
Owner: Martha Tavera
Gen Mgr: John Tavera
Number of staff: 8
Date originated: 1981
Annual sales: $1 - 4 million
Bond coverage: (NP)
Accredited: ARC & IATAN
Escrow: (NP)
Security: (NP)

DESTINATIONS
LATIN AMERICA, NORTH AMERICA

(For a complete list of the exact cities served within each region, see the Destination Index)

AIRLINES
AA, AR, ML, UA, LR, PL, GU, GY, CM, TA, LA, EH, TR, RG, VP

(Airline codes defined in Index)

Firm books business class: (NP)　　　First class: (NP)
Airlines may be contacted for references: Yes
Percentage of sales through scheduled air: 100%

SALES POLICIES

Tickets delivered: Two weeks before departure
　　Delivered by: *Overnight*　　*$12.00*
　　　　　　　　First class　　*no charge*

Fee charged for credit card payment: (NP)
Flight confirmed: Immediately
Is a printed receipt provided? (NP)
Cancellation policy: (NP)

Frequent flyer miles offered? No

TRAVEL AGENCY
orders accepted by:
phone letter fax

PAYMENT FORMS ACCEPTED
*CREDIT CARD
AGENCY CHECK
NET 10 DAYS*

Comment:

(NP) = Firm did not provide requested information.

FIRM: Northwest World Vacations

RES PHONE: 1-800-727-1111

ADDRESS: 5130 Highway 101
Minnetonka, MN 55345
PHONE: 612-474-2540
FAX: 612-474-9730

Branch Offices:

Travel Agent Rating
Overall Average
8.73
(Detailed analysis of results in Ratings Section)

CORPORATE INFORMATION

Owner: NWA, Inc.
Gen Mgr: (NP)
Number of staff: 800
Date originated: 1969
Annual sales: (NP)
Bond coverage: Yes
Accredited: ARC
Escrow: (NP)
Security: (NP)

DESTINATIONS

ORIENT, NORTH AMERICA, CARIBBEAN

(For a complete list of the exact cities served within each region, see the Destination Index)

AIRLINES
Northwest Airlines

(Airline codes defined in Index)

Firm books business class: (NP)   First class: (NP)
Airlines may be contacted for references: (NP)
Percentage of sales through scheduled air: (NP)

SALES POLICIES

Tickets delivered: (NP)
Delivered by: *Overnight*   *$11.00*
First class   *no charge*

Fee charged for credit card payment: (NP)
Flight confirmed: At booking, guaranteed
Is a printed receipt provided? (NP)
Cancellation policy: (NP)

Frequent flyer miles offered? (NP)

TRAVEL AGENCY
orders accepted by:
phone

PAYMENT FORMS ACCEPTED
CREDIT CARD
AGENCY CHECK

Comment:

(NP) = Firm did not provide requested information.

FIRM: Orbis Polish Travel, Inc.

RES PHONE: 1-800-87-Orbis

ADDRESS: 342 Madison Ave, Ste.1512
New York, NY 10173
PHONE: 212-867-5011
FAX: 212-682-4715

Branch Offices:

Travel Agent Rating
Overall Average
7.44
(Detailed analysis of results in Ratings Section)

CORPORATE INFORMATION
Owner: (NP)
Gen Mgr: Tomasz Cuprys
Number of staff: 14
Date originated: 1937
Annual sales: $5 - 10 million
Bond coverage: Yes
Accredited: ARC & IATAN
Escrow: (NP)
Security: (NP)

DESTINATIONS
EUROPE

(For a complete list of the exact cities served within each region, see the Destination Index)

AIRLINES
Lot Polish Airlines, etc.

(Airline codes defined in Index)

Firm books business class: Yes   First class: (NP)
Airlines may be contacted for references: No
Percentage of sales through scheduled air: 90%

SALES POLICIES
Tickets delivered: Upon payment
Delivered by: *Overnight*   *varies*
First class   *varies*

Fee charged for credit card payment: (NP)
Flight confirmed: At booking
Is a printed receipt provided? (NP)
Cancellation policy: Varies

Frequent flyer miles offered? No

TRAVEL AGENCY orders accepted by:

PAYMENT FORMS ACCEPTED
CREDIT CARD
AGENCY CHECK

Comment:

(NP) = Firm did not provide requested information.

FIRM: PCS

RES PHONE: 1-800-367-8833

ADDRESS: 700 S. Flower Street, 10th floor
Los Angeles, CA 90017
PHONE: 213-239-2424
FAX: 213-239-2410

Branch Offices:

Travel Agent Rating
Overall Average
9.33
(Detailed analysis of results in Ratings Section)

CORPORATE INFORMATION

Owner: (NP)
Gen Mgr: Eddie Fujimori
Number of staff: 19
Date originated: 1976
Annual sales: $10 - 25 million
Bond coverage: (NP)
Accredited: ARC & IATAN
Escrow: (NP)
Security: (NP)

DESTINATIONS
ORIENT, LATIN AMERICA

(For a complete list of the exact cities served within each region, see the Destination Index)

AIRLINES
JL, VA, AA, NW, DL, OZ, MH

(Airline codes defined in Index)

Firm books business class: Yes   First class: (NP)
Airlines may be contacted for references: Yes
Percentage of sales through scheduled air: (NP)

SALES POLICIES

Tickets delivered: Varies
    Delivered by: *Overnight*

    Certified
Fee charged for credit card payment: (NP)
Flight confirmed: At booking
Is a printed receipt provided? Yes
Cancellation policy: Varies by airline

Frequent flyer miles offered? Yes
        Varies by airline

TRAVEL AGENCY orders accepted by:
phone   letter   fax

PAYMENT FORMS ACCEPTED
*CREDIT CARD
CASH
COD*

Comment:

(NP) = Firm did not provide requested information.

FIRM: Panorama Tours

RES PHONE: 1-800-527-4888

ADDRESS: 139 E South Temple Ste. 230
Salt Lake City, UT 84111
PHONE: 801-328-5390
FAX: 801-524-8405

Branch Offices:

Travel Agent Rating
Overall Average
8.67
(Detailed analysis of results in Ratings Section)

CORPORATE INFORMATION

Owner: Murdock Corporation
Gen Mgr: Carlos L. Fida, CTC
Number of staff: 18
Date originated: 1985
Annual sales: $5 - 10 million
Bond coverage: (NP)
Accredited: ARC & IATAN
Escrow: (NP)
Security: (NP)

DESTINATIONS
LATIN AMERICA

(For a complete list of the exact cities served within each region, see the Destination Index)

AIRLINES
RG, AR, LA, AA, UA, TW, UC, PL, CF, PZ, TA, LR, GU, CM, GY, TR

(Airline codes defined in Index)

Firm books business class: (NP)   First class: (NP)
Airlines may be contacted for references: Yes
Percentage of sales through scheduled air: 100%

SALES POLICIES

Tickets delivered: Upon payment
    Delivered by: *Overnight $15.00*
                  First class   no charge
                  Second day $10.00
Fee charged for credit card payment: 2%
Flight confirmed: At booking
Is a printed receipt provided? No
Cancellation policy: Varies by airline and fare
                     basis

Frequent flyer miles offered? Yes
            Available on most fares

TRAVEL AGENCY
orders accepted by:
phone letter fax

PAYMENT FORMS ACCEPTED
CREDIT CARD
AGENCY CHECK

Comment: *We specialize in customized FIT and group tours.*

(NP) = Firm did not provide requested information.

FIRM: Passport Travel Mgmt Group

RES PHONE: 1-800-950-5864

ADDRESS: 1503 W. Busch Blvd. Ste. A
Tampa, FL 33612
PHONE: 813-931-3166
FAX: 813-933-1670

Branch Offices:

Travel Agent Rating
Overall Average
9
(Detailed analysis of results in Ratings Section)

CORPORATE INFORMATION

Owner: Ernie Azucena
Gen Mgr: Ron Plummer
Number of staff: 9
Date originated: 1990
Annual sales: $1 - 4 million
Bond coverage: $37,000
Accredited: ARC & IATAN
Escrow: (NP)
Security: (NP)

DESTINATIONS
ORIENT, SOUTH PACIFIC

(For a complete list of the exact cities served within each region, see the Destination Index)

AIRLINES
MH, TG, PR, KE, CX, GA

(Airline codes defined in Index)

Firm books business class: (NP)   First class: (NP)
Airlines may be contacted for references: Yes
Percentage of sales through scheduled air: 100%

SALES POLICIES

Tickets delivered: ASAP
    Delivered by: *Overnight*   *$10.00*

Fee charged for credit card payment: (NP)
Flight confirmed: ASAP
Is a printed receipt provided? (NP)
Cancellation policy: (NP)

Frequent flyer miles offered? (NP)

TRAVEL AGENCY
orders accepted by:
phone   *fax*

PAYMENT FORMS ACCEPTED
AGENCY CHECK

Comment:

(NP) = Firm did not provide requested information.

FIRM: **Pleasure Break Vacations, Inc.**

RES PHONE: 1-800-777-1566

ADDRESS: 3701 Algonquin Rd., Ste. 900
Rolling Meadows, IL 60008
PHONE: 708-670-6300
FAX: 708-670-7682
Branch Offices:

Travel Agent Rating
Overall Average
8.39
(Detailed analysis of results in Ratings Section)

CORPORATE INFORMATION

Owner: Engelbert Saile
Gen Mgr: Ralph Saile
Number of staff: 75
Date originated: 1973
Annual sales: Over $25 million
Bond coverage: (NP)
Accredited: ARC & IATAN
Escrow: Yes
Security: Escrow for charter flights; NTA and ASTA protection plans

DESTINATIONS

EUROPE, MID EAST, LATIN AMERICA

(For a complete list of the exact cities served within each region, see the Destination Index)

AIRLINES

AA, AF, BA, CO, KL, LH, NW, SN, SR, TW, UA, Rich International, American Trans Air

(Airline codes defined in Index)

Firm books business class: Yes   First class: Yes
Airlines may be contacted for references: Yes
Percentage of sales through scheduled air: 80%

SALES POLICIES

Tickets delivered: 21 days or sooner
Delivered by: *Overnight* $14.00
First class no charge

Fee charged for credit card payment: $20
Flight confirmed: At booking
Is a printed receipt provided? Yes
Cancellation policy: Varies by airline

Frequent flyer miles offered? Yes
Varies by airline

TRAVEL AGENCY
orders accepted by:
phone   *fax*

PAYMENT FORMS ACCEPTED
CREDIT CARD
AGENCY CHECK

Comment: *We will be adding a 24-hour capability for certain reservations services in mid-1995. (Automated line)*

(NP) = Firm did not provide requested information.

FIRM: Plus Ultra Tours

RES PHONE: 1-800- FOR-SPAIN

ADDRESS: 174 - 7th Ave.
New York, NY 10011
PHONE: 212-242-0393
FAX: 212-633-6652

Branch Offices:

Travel Agent Rating
Overall Average
3
(Detailed analysis of results in Ratings Section)

CORPORATE INFORMATION

Owner: Aniceto Perez
Gen Mgr: Bob Perez
Number of staff: 12
Date originated: 1980
Annual sales: $5 - 10 million
Bond coverage: $70,000
Accredited: ARC & IATAN
Escrow: Yes
Security: (NP)

DESTINATIONS
EUROPE

(For a complete list of the exact cities served within each region, see the Destination Index)

AIRLINES
Spanair, Air Europa

(Airline codes defined in Index)

Firm books business class: (NP)   First class: (NP)
Airlines may be contacted for references: Yes
Percentage of sales through scheduled air: 70%

SALES POLICIES

Tickets delivered: At travel agent's request
Delivered by: *Overnight $7.00*
First class

Fee charged for credit card payment: (NP)
Flight confirmed: At booking
Is a printed receipt provided? Yes
Cancellation policy: (NP)

Frequent flyer miles offered? Yes
Varies by airline

TRAVEL AGENCY
orders accepted by:
phone letter fax

PAYMENT FORMS ACCEPTED
*CREDIT CARD
AGENCY CHECK
COD*

Comment: *Largest tour operator to Spain in the U.S.*

(NP) = Firm did not provide requested information.

FIRM: Queue Travel

RES PHONE: 1-800-356-4871

ADDRESS: 1530 W. Lewis St.
San Diego, CA 92103
PHONE: 619-260-8577
FAX: 619-260-0832

Branch Offices:
1530 West Lewis St.
San Diego, CA 92103
800-356-4871

Travel Agent Rating
Overall Average
6
(Detailed analysis of results in Ratings Section)

CORPORATE INFORMATION

Owner: Queue Travel, Inc.
Gen Mgr: Thomas N. Cermola
Number of staff: 20
Date originated: 1987
Annual sales: $5 - 10 million
Bond coverage: $155,000
Accredited: ARC & IATAN
Escrow: $25,000
Security: (NP)

DESTINATIONS

EUROPE, MID EAST, ORIENT, AFRICA, LATIN AMERICA, NORTH AMERICA

(For a complete list of the exact cities served within each region, see the Destination Index)

AIRLINES

AA, AR, CO, CP, CX, GA, IB, KE, LH, LR, LA, MH, NW, OZ, OF, RG, SU, TA, LA, TW, AY, GU

(Airline codes defined in Index)

Firm books business class: Yes   First class: Yes
Airlines may be contacted for references: Yes
Percentage of sales through scheduled air: 100%

SALES POLICIES

Tickets delivered: Three days after payment
Delivered by: *Overnight* $15.00

UPS   *no charge*
Fee charged for credit card payment: 4%
Flight confirmed: At booking
Is a printed receipt provided? Yes
Cancellation policy: $50 for cancellation/re-issue

Frequent flyer miles offered? Yes
Varies by airline

TRAVEL AGENCY orders accepted by:
phone letter fax

PAYMENT FORMS ACCEPTED
CREDIT CARD
AGENCY CHECK

Comment: *Queue Travel Fare Quote Program; FastFare -- Available to Travel Agents includes free updates of over 50,000 fares VIA 800-598-1880*

(NP) = Firm did not provide requested information.

FIRM: Rahim Tours

RES PHONE: 1-800-556-5305

ADDRESS: 12 South Dixie Highway
Lake Worth, FL 33460
PHONE: 407-585-5305
FAX: 407-582-1353

Branch Offices:

Travel Agent Rating
Overall Average
7.2
(Detailed analysis of results in Ratings Section)

CORPORATE INFORMATION

Owner: VAO "INTOURIST" Russia
Gen Mgr: Alexey N. Mesiatsev
Number of staff: 11
Date originated: 1983
Annual sales: $5 - 10 million
Bond coverage: $1,000,000
Accredited: IATA
Escrow: No
Security: (NP)

DESTINATIONS

EASTERN & CENTRAL EUROPE, RUSSIA, CHINA, MONGOLIA, C.I.S., SCANDINAVIA

(For a complete list of the exact cities served within each region, see the Destination Index)

AIRLINES
AY, SK, SU, OS, all major US and C.I.S. carriers

(Airline codes defined in Index)

Firm books business class: Yes   First class: Yes
Airlines may be contacted for references: Yes
Percentage of sales through scheduled air: (NP)

SALES POLICIES

Tickets delivered: Five days before departure
Delivered by: *Overnight*   *$20.00*

Fee charged for credit card payment: (NP)
Flight confirmed: Two days
Is a printed receipt provided? (NP)
Cancellation policy: $150 to $200 after ticket is issued

Frequent flyer miles offered? Yes
Varies by airline

TRAVEL AGENCY orders accepted by:
phone letter fax

PAYMENT FORMS ACCEPTED
AGENCY CHECK

Comment: *Accepts money orders, certified checks, and bank wires.*

(NP) = Firm did not provide requested information.

FIRM: STA Travel

RES PHONE: 1-800-825-3001

ADDRESS: 5900 Wilshire Blvd., Suite 2110
Los Angeles, CA 90036
PHONE: 213-937-9274
FAX: 213-937-9572

Branch Offices:

Travel Agent Rating
Overall Average
9.18
(Detailed analysis of results in Ratings Section)

CORPORATE INFORMATION

Owner: STA Travel, Inc.
Gen Mgr: Bill Gale, Director
Number of staff: 9
Date originated: 1970
Annual sales: Over $25 million
Bond coverage: (NP)
Accredited: ARC & IATAN
Escrow: (NP)
Security: (NP)

DESTINATIONS

EUROPE, MID EAST, ORIENT, AFRICA, LATIN AMERICA, SOUTH PACIFIC, NORTH AMERICA

(For a complete list of the exact cities served within each region, see the Destination Index)

AIRLINES

AF, CO, NZ, SK, BD, KL, BA, NW, QF, VS, TG, DL, UA, RG, LR, CX

(Airline codes defined in Index)

Firm books business class: (NP)   First class: (NP)
Airlines may be contacted for references: No
Percentage of sales through scheduled air: 100%

SALES POLICIES

Tickets delivered: Days before departure
Delivered by: *Overnight*   *$15.00*
First class

Fee charged for credit card payment: (NP)
Flight confirmed: (NP)
Is a printed receipt provided? (NP)
Cancellation policy: (NP)

Frequent flyer miles offered? (NP)

TRAVEL AGENCY
orders accepted by:
letter

PAYMENT FORMS
ACCEPTED
AGENCY CHECK

Comment:

(NP) = Firm did not provide requested information.

FIRM: STT Worldwide Travel, Inc.

RES PHONE: 1-800-348-0886

ADDRESS: 9880 S.W. Beaverton Hillsdale Hwy.
Beaverton, OR 97005
PHONE: 503-671-0494
FAX: 503-641-2171

Branch Offices:
350 Figuerda St. Ste. 170
Los Angeles, CA 90071
213-625-5851

2033 6th Ave., Ste. 1007
Seattle, WA 98121
206-441-4028

Travel Agent Rating
Overall Average
8.8
(Detailed analysis of results in Ratings Section)

CORPORATE INFORMATION

Owner: S.B. Kim
Gen Mgr: Tracy Singer
Number of staff: 28
Date originated: (NP)
Annual sales: Over $25 million
Bond coverage: $70,000
Accredited: ARC & IATAN
Escrow: (NP)
Security: (NP)

DESTINATIONS

EUROPE, ORIENT, AFRICA, LATIN AMERICA, SOUTH PACIFIC, NORTH AMERICA

(For a complete list of the exact cities served within each region, see the Destination Index)

AIRLINES

AM, AA, PL, CP, AC, CX, MU, CD, DL, MS, BR, KO, BF, MX, PR, VA, VP, RG, TG

(Airline codes defined in Index)

Firm books business class: Yes   First class: Yes
Airlines may be contacted for references: Yes
Percentage of sales through scheduled air: 95%

SALES POLICIES

Tickets delivered: Upon payment
Delivered by: *Overnight*   *$10.00*

Fee charged for credit card payment: $25
Flight confirmed: At booking
Is a printed receipt provided? Yes
Cancellation policy: Varies; $175 - change, $225 - cancel.

Frequent flyer miles offered? No
Varies by airline

TRAVEL AGENCY
orders accepted by:
phone letter fax

PAYMENT FORMS ACCEPTED
CREDIT CARD AGENCY CHECK CASH

Comment:

(NP) = Firm did not provide requested information.

FIRM: Skylink Travel

RES PHONE: 1-800-247-6659

ADDRESS: 265 Madison Ave., 5th Floor
New York, NY 10016
PHONE: 212-573-8980
FAX: 212-573-8878

Branch Offices:

Travel Agent Rating
Overall Average
7.33
(Detailed analysis of results in Ratings Section)

CORPORATE INFORMATION

Owner: Fernando Virgolino
Gen Mgr: Mr. Gajinder S. Pujji
Number of staff: 20
Date originated: 1983
Annual sales: $10 - 25 million
Bond coverage: $70,000
Accredited: ARC & IATAN
Escrow: (NP)
Security: (NP)

DESTINATIONS

EUROPE, ORIENT, AFRICA

(For a complete list of the exact cities served within each region, see the Destination Index)

AIRLINES

KLM, Delta, Lufthansa, AA, Air India, Royal Jordanian, Austrian, Taro Airlines

(Airline codes defined in Index)

Firm books business class: (NP)   First class: (NP)
Airlines may be contacted for references: Yes
Percentage of sales through scheduled air: (NP)

SALES POLICIES

Tickets delivered: One day before departure
    Delivered by: *Overnight*
        First class   *no charge*

Fee charged for credit card payment: (NP)
Flight confirmed: At booking/or in 1 week if WL
Is a printed receipt provided? (NP)
Cancellation policy: (NP)

Frequent flyer miles offered? (NP)

TRAVEL AGENCY
orders accepted by:
phone   *fax*

PAYMENT FORMS ACCEPTED
CREDIT CARD
AGENCY CHECK

Comment:

(NP) = Firm did not provide requested information.

176

FIRM: Solar Tours

RES PHONE: 1-800-388-7652

ADDRESS: 1629 K St. N.W., Ste. 604
Washington, DC 20006
PHONE: 202-861-6864
FAX: 202-452-0905

Branch Offices:
8460 South Tamiami Trail
Sarasota, FL 34238
800-727-7652

Travel Agent Rating
Overall Average
8.29
(Detailed analysis of results in Ratings Section)

CORPORATE INFORMATION

Owner: Maria Checa
Gen Mgr: Maria Checa
Number of staff: 29
Date originated: 1984
Annual sales: $10 - 25 million
Bond coverage: (NP)
Accredited: ARC & IATAN
Escrow: Yes
Security: (NP)

DESTINATIONS
EUROPE, LATIN AMERICA, NORTH AMERICA

(For a complete list of the exact cities served within each region, see the Destination Index)

AIRLINES
AA, AR, AV, CF, CM, CO, EH, IB, LA, LH, LR, ML, NW, PL, RG, TA, TR, UA, UC, VA

(Airline codes defined in Index)

Firm books business class: (NP)   First class: (NP)
Airlines may be contacted for references: Yes
Percentage of sales through scheduled air: 100%

SALES POLICIES

Tickets delivered: Immediately
Delivered by: *Overnight*   *no charge*
First class

Fee charged for credit card payment: (NP)
Flight confirmed: At booking
Is a printed receipt provided? Yes
Cancellation policy: $25 30 days before; $175
once ticket is issued.

Frequent flyer miles offered? No

TRAVEL AGENCY
orders accepted by:
phone   letter   fax

PAYMENT FORMS ACCEPTED
*CREDIT CARD
AGENCY CHECK
COD*

Comment:

(NP) = Firm did not provide requested information.

FIRM: Sunny Land Tours

RES PHONE: 1-800-783-7839

ADDRESS: 166 Main Street
Hackensack, NJ 07601
PHONE: 201-487-2150
FAX: 201-487-1546

Branch Offices:

Travel Agent Rating
Overall Average
7
(Detailed analysis of results in Ratings Section)

CORPORATE INFORMATION

Owner: Elie Sidawi/President
Gen Mgr: Lori Sidawi
Number of staff: 22
Date originated: 1964
Annual sales: $10 - 25 million
Bond coverage: $1,000,000
Accredited: ARC & IATAN
Escrow: Yes
Security: $1,000,000 - USTOA Member

DESTINATIONS

EUROPE, MID EAST, AFRICA, LATIN AMERICA

(For a complete list of the exact cities served within each region, see the Destination Index)

AIRLINES

Egypt Air, Royal Jordanian, Olympic, Finnair, Air Europa, Lacsa, UA, Viasa, Avensa, Saeta

(Airline codes defined in Index)

Firm books business class: Yes   First class: Yes
Airlines may be contacted for references: Yes
Percentage of sales through scheduled air: 80%

SALES POLICIES

Tickets delivered: Two weeks before departure
    Delivered by:
                First class

Fee charged for credit card payment: (NP)
Flight confirmed: At booking
Is a printed receipt provided? No
Cancellation policy: Varies by airline

Frequent flyer miles offered? No

TRAVEL AGENCY
orders accepted by:
phone letter fax

PAYMENT FORMS ACCEPTED
AGENCY CHECK

Comment:

(NP) = Firm did not provide requested information.

FIRM: TFI Tours Intl. Ltd.

RES PHONE: 1-800-745-8000

ADDRESS: 34 W 32nd St
New York, NY 10001
PHONE: 212-736-1140
FAX: 212-564-4081
Branch Offices:

Travel Agent Rating
Overall Average
4.97
(Detailed analysis of results in Ratings Section)

CORPORATE INFORMATION

Owner: Eric Schoenberger
Gen Mgr: Rita Anthony
Number of staff: 35
Date originated: 1981
Annual sales: Over $25 million
Bond coverage: (NP)
Accredited: ARC & IATAN
Escrow: (NP)
Security: (NP)

DESTINATIONS

EUROPE, MID EAST, ORIENT, AFRICA, LATIN AMERICA, SOUTH PACIFIC, NORTH AMERICA

(For a complete list of the exact cities served within each region, see the Destination Index)

AIRLINES

Air France, United, Continental, TWA, American, Northwest, Sabena, South African

(Airline codes defined in Index)

Firm books business class: (NP)   First class: (NP)
Airlines may be contacted for references: (NP)
Percentage of sales through scheduled air: 100%

SALES POLICIES

Tickets delivered: Overnight
Delivered by: *Overnight*   *$12.00*
First class   *no charge*

Fee charged for credit card payment: (NP)
Flight confirmed: At booking
Is a printed receipt provided? (NP)
Cancellation policy: (NP)

Frequent flyer miles offered? (NP)

TRAVEL AGENCY
orders accepted by:
phone letter

PAYMENT FORMS ACCEPTED
CREDIT CARD
AGENCY CHECK

Comment:

(NP) = Firm did not provide requested information.

FIRM: Thrifty Air

RES PHONE: 1-800-423-4488

ADDRESS: 5757 W. Century Blvd., Ste. 514
Los Angeles, CA 90045
PHONE: 310-337-9982
FAX: 800-423-4424

Branch Offices:

Travel Agent Rating
Overall Average
8
(Detailed analysis of results in Ratings Section)

CORPORATE INFORMATION

Owner: Vision Expedition, Inc.
Gen Mgr: Manolo Relova
Number of staff: 50
Date originated: 1989
Annual sales: Over $25 million
Bond coverage: Varies
Accredited: ARC & IATAN
Escrow: No
Security: ARC bonded; tickets guaranteed by airlines involved.

DESTINATIONS

EUROPE, ORIENT, SOUTH PACIFIC, LATIN AMERICA, NORTH AMERICA

(For a complete list of the exact cities served within each region, see the Destination Index)

AIRLINES
KE, SQ, NW, CX, MU, PR, OZ, TG, VP, PL, IB, BR, KW

(Airline codes defined in Index)

Firm books business class: Yes   First class: (NP)
Airlines may be contacted for references: Yes
Percentage of sales through scheduled air: 100%

SALES POLICIES

Tickets delivered: ASAP
Delivered by: *Overnight*   *$10.00*
First class   *no charge*

Fee charged for credit card payment: (NP)
Flight confirmed: ASAP
Is a printed receipt provided? Yes
Cancellation policy: Varies by airline

Frequent flyer miles offered? Yes
Varies by airline

TRAVEL AGENCY
orders accepted by:
phone letter fax

PAYMENT FORMS ACCEPTED
CREDIT CARD
AGENCY CHECK

Comment: *The consolidator offering "China domestic air" tickets. Member of PATA and ASTA.*

(NP) = Firm did not provide requested information.

FIRM: Time Travel

RES PHONE: 1-800-847-7026

ADDRESS: 1000 Tower Lane, Ste. 135
Bensenville, IL 60106
PHONE: 708-595-8463
FAX: 708-595-8597

Branch Offices:

CORPORATE INFORMATION

Owner: Nippon Express Travel
Gen Mgr: Simon Shimomura
Number of staff: 3
Date originated: 1992
Annual sales: $1 - 4 million
Bond coverage: (NP)
Accredited: ARC & IATAN
Escrow: (NP)
Security: (NP)

DESTINATIONS

EUROPE, ORIENT, LATIN AMERICA, SOUTH PACIFIC

(For a complete list of the exact cities served within each region, see the Destination Index)

AIRLINES

United, Japan Northwest, Delta, Asiana, American

(Airline codes defined in Index)

Firm books business class: (NP)   First class: (NP)
Airlines may be contacted for references: Yes
Percentage of sales through scheduled air: 100%

SALES POLICIES

Tickets delivered: Upon payment
Delivered by: *Overnight*   *$10.00*

Certified
Fee charged for credit card payment: (NP)
Flight confirmed: (NP)
Is a printed receipt provided? (NP)
Cancellation policy: (NP)

Frequent flyer miles offered? (NP)

TRAVEL AGENCY orders accepted by:
phone letter   fax

PAYMENT FORMS ACCEPTED
*CREDIT CARD
AGENCY CHECK
COD*

Comment:

(NP) = Firm did not provide requested information.

FIRM: Tourlite International Inc.

RES PHONE: 1-800-272-7600

ADDRESS: 551 Fifth Avenue Ste. 1001
New York, NY 10176
PHONE: 212-599-2727
FAX: 212-370-0913

Branch Offices:

Travel Agent Rating
Overall Average
8.2
(Detailed analysis of results in Ratings Section)

CORPORATE INFORMATION

Owner: Nicholas Athans
Gen Mgr: Valerie Athans
Number of staff: 30
Date originated: 1970
Annual sales: (NP)
Bond coverage: (NP)
Accredited: ARC
Escrow: (NP)
Security: (NP)

DESTINATIONS
MID EAST, LATIN AMERICA

(For a complete list of the exact cities served within each region, see the Destination Index)

AIRLINES
AF, AZ, OA, UA, DL, MS, RG

(Airline codes defined in Index)

Firm books business class: (NP)   First class: (NP)
Airlines may be contacted for references: Yes
Percentage of sales through scheduled air: (NP)

SALES POLICIES

Tickets delivered: Two weeks before departure
Delivered by:

Two day air $5. per bk
Fee charged for credit card payment: (NP)
Flight confirmed: At booking
Is a printed receipt provided? (NP)
Cancellation policy: (NP)

Frequent flyer miles offered? (NP)

TRAVEL AGENCY
orders accepted by:

PAYMENT FORMS ACCEPTED
CREDIT CARD
AGENCY CHECK

Comment: *also serving Chile.*

(NP) = Firm did not provide requested information.

FIRM: Tours International Inc.

RES PHONE: 1-800-247-7965

ADDRESS: 14855 Memorial Drive, Ste. 811
Houston, TX 77079
PHONE: 713-293-0809
FAX: 713-584-0870

Branch Offices:

Travel Agent Rating
Overall Average
8
(Detailed analysis of results in Ratings Section)

CORPORATE INFORMATION

Owner: Josefa Grana
Gen Mgr: Josefa Grana
Number of staff: 2
Date originated: 1991
Annual sales: Under $1 million
Bond coverage: Yes
Accredited: (NP)
Escrow: (NP)
Security: (NP)

DESTINATIONS
LATIN AMERICA

(For a complete list of the exact cities served within each region, see the Destination Index)

AIRLINES
PL, CF, RG, VA, LA, AR, LB, EH

(Airline codes defined in Index)

Firm books business class: (NP)   First class: (NP)
Airlines may be contacted for references: No
Percentage of sales through scheduled air: 99%

SALES POLICIES

Tickets delivered: Depends on order & pymnt
Delivered by: *Overnight*   *$15.00*
First class   *no charge*

Fee charged for credit card payment: $10.00
Flight confirmed: Dependent upon day of request
Is a printed receipt provided? No
Cancellation policy: Varies by airline

Frequent flyer miles offered? No

TRAVEL AGENCY
orders accepted by:
phone   letter   fax

PAYMENT FORMS ACCEPTED
CREDIT CARD
AGENCY CHECK
NET 10 DAYS

Comment:

(NP) = Firm did not provide requested information.

FIRM: Trans Am Travel

RES PHONE: 1-800-822-7600

ADDRESS: 3101 Park Center Drive
Alexandria, VA 22302
PHONE: 703-998-7676
FAX: 703-824-8190

Branch Offices:
25 W. 45th St., Ste. 1409
New York, NY 10036
212-730-4980

Travel Agent Rating
Overall Average
8.09
(Detailed analysis of results in Ratings Section)

CORPORATE INFORMATION
Owner: S. Paul Kapoor
Gen Mgr: James Clampet
Number of staff: 26
Date originated: 1979
Annual sales: Over $25 million
Bond coverage: $500,000
Accredited: ARC & IATAN
Escrow: (NP)
Security: (NP)

DESTINATIONS
EUROPE, MID EAST, ORIENT, AFRICA, LATIN AMERICA, SOUTH PACIFIC

(For a complete list of the exact cities served within each region, see the Destination Index)

AIRLINES
UA, NW, US, AA, FI, EK, GF, AR, BD, CO, KE, SQ, TG, CI, BR, MH, OZ

(Airline codes defined in Index)

Firm books business class: Yes   First class: (NP)
Airlines may be contacted for references: Yes
Percentage of sales through scheduled air: 100%

SALES POLICIES
Tickets delivered: Upon payment
    Delivered by: *Overnight   no charge*

Fee charged for credit card payment: Varies
Flight confirmed: At booking
Is a printed receipt provided? No
Cancellation policy: Varies by airline

Frequent flyer miles offered? Yes
                Varies by airline

TRAVEL AGENCY
orders accepted by:
phone letter fax

PAYMENT FORMS ACCEPTED
CREDIT CARD
AGENCY CHECK

Comment:

(NP) = Firm did not provide requested information.

FIRM: Travel Beyond

RES PHONE: 1-800-876-3131

ADDRESS: 214 South Minnetonka Ave.
Wayzata, MN 55391
PHONE: 612-475-2565
FAX: 612-475-1029

Branch Offices:

Travel Agent Rating
Overall Average
7.5
(Detailed analysis of results in Ratings Section)

CORPORATE INFORMATION

Owner: David & Audrey Beal
Gen Mgr: Julie Sopoci, CTC
Number of staff: 20
Date originated: 1975
Annual sales: $10 - 25 million
Bond coverage: Maximum
Accredited: ARC
Escrow: (NP)
Security: (NP)

DESTINATIONS
AFRICA

(For a complete list of the exact cities served within each region, see the Destination Index)

AIRLINES
South African Airways

(Airline codes defined in Index)

Firm books business class: (NP)   First class: (NP)
Airlines may be contacted for references: (NP)
Percentage of sales through scheduled air: (NP)

SALES POLICIES

Tickets delivered: Varies
Delivered by:

Fee charged for credit card payment: (NP)
Flight confirmed: Varies
Is a printed receipt provided? (NP)
Cancellation policy: (NP)

Frequent flyer miles offered? (NP)

TRAVEL AGENCY
orders accepted by:

PAYMENT FORMS
ACCEPTED

AGENCY CHECK

Comment:

(NP) = Firm did not provide requested information.

FIRM: **The Travel Group**

RES PHONE: 1-800-836-6269

ADDRESS: 24165 I.H. 10 West, Ste. 121
San Antonio, TX 78257
PHONE: 210-698-0100
FAX: 210-698-0199

Branch Offices:

CORPORATE INFORMATION
Owner: Barrie Duggan/John Asmus
Gen Mgr: Eileen Dillard
Number of staff: 15
Date originated: 1989
Annual sales: $10 - 25 million
Bond coverage: $20,000
Accredited: ARC & IATAN
Escrow: Yes
Security: (NP)

DESTINATIONS
EUROPE, ORIENT, AFRICA, SOUTH PACIFIC

(For a complete list of the exact cities served within each region, see the Destination Index)

AIRLINES
CP, LH, IB

(Airline codes defined in Index)

Firm books business class: (NP)   First class: (NP)
Airlines may be contacted for references: Yes
Percentage of sales through scheduled air: 100%

SALES POLICIES

Tickets delivered: Upon payment
Delivered by: *Overnight*   *Varies*
First class   *no charge*

Fee charged for credit card payment: 4%
Flight confirmed: At booking
Is a printed receipt provided? Yes
Cancellation policy: $50 plus applicable airline
charge

Frequent flyer miles offered? Yes
Varies by airline

TRAVEL AGENCY
orders accepted by:
phone   *fax*

PAYMENT FORMS ACCEPTED
CREDIT CARD
AGENCY CHECK

Comment:

(NP) = Firm did not provide requested information.

FIRM: Travel Leaders, Inc.

RES PHONE: 1-800-323-3218

ADDRESS: 1701 Ponce de Leon Blvd, PO 149005
Coral Gables, FL 33124-9005
PHONE: 305-443-7755
FAX: 305-443-7742

Branch Offices:

Travel Agent Rating
Overall Average
7.25
*(Detailed analysis of
results in Ratings
Section)*

CORPORATE INFORMATION

Owner: Simon Hassine
Gen Mgr: Ed Pitman
Number of staff: 8
Date originated: 1986
Annual sales: $10 - 25 million
Bond coverage: (NP)
Accredited: ARC & IATAN
Escrow: (NP)
Security: (NP)

DESTINATIONS

**EUROPE, MID EAST,
ORIENT, AFRICA,
LATIN AMERICA**

*(For a complete list of the exact
cities served within each region, see
the Destination Index)*

AIRLINES

United, American, British, Lufthansa, Air France, Alitalia, KLM, Varig,
most major scheduled airlines

(Airline codes defined in Index)

Firm books business class: (NP)   First class: (NP)
Airlines may be contacted for references: Yes
Percentage of sales through scheduled air: 100%

SALES POLICIES

Tickets delivered: (NP)
Delivered by: *Overnight*   *$7.50*

Fee charged for credit card payment: (NP)
Flight confirmed: Varies
Is a printed receipt provided? (NP)
Cancellation policy: (NP)

Frequent flyer miles offered? (NP)

TRAVEL AGENCY
orders accepted by:
phone   letter   fax

**PAYMENT FORMS
ACCEPTED**

*CREDIT CARD
AGENCY CHECK
CASH*

Comment:

(NP) = Firm did not provide requested information.

FIRM: Travel N Tours

RES PHONE: 1-800-854-5400

ADDRESS: PO Box 390 200A Main St.
Beacon, NY 12508
PHONE: 914-838-2600
FAX: 914-831-4160

Branch Offices:

Travel Agent Rating
Overall Average

7.75

(Detailed analysis of results in Ratings Section)

CORPORATE INFORMATION

Owner: Corporation
Gen Mgr: Gour Saha
Number of staff: 10
Date originated: 1978
Annual sales: $5 - 10 million
Bond coverage: $70,000
Accredited: ARC & IATAN
Escrow: Yes
Security: (NP)

DESTINATIONS

EUROPE, ORIENT, AFRICA, LATIN AMERICA

(For a complete list of the exact cities served within each region, see the Destination Index)

AIRLINES

NW, KL, KU, KE, AR, VP, LH, AY, SN, KQ, UM, CI, BR, IB, SU, SA

(Airline codes defined in Index)

Firm books business class: (NP)   First class: (NP)
Airlines may be contacted for references: Yes
Percentage of sales through scheduled air: 100%

SALES POLICIES

Tickets delivered: Within 28 days
Delivered by: *Overnight*   *$7.00*

Fee charged for credit card payment: 2%
Flight confirmed: At booking
Is a printed receipt provided? No
Cancellation policy: Varies by airline

Frequent flyer miles offered? Yes
Varies by airline

TRAVEL AGENCY
orders accepted by:

phone   *fax*

PAYMENT FORMS ACCEPTED

CREDIT CARD
AGENCY CHECK

Comment:

(NP) = Firm did not provide requested information.

FIRM: Travel Wholesalers

RES PHONE: 1-800-487-8944

ADDRESS: 3401 Circle Office Park, Ste. 101
Fairfax, VA 22031
PHONE: 703-359-8855
FAX: 703-359-8895
Branch Offices:

Travel Agent Rating
Overall Average
8.6
(Detailed analysis of results in Ratings Section)

CORPORATE INFORMATION

Owner: Gloria Bohan
Gen Mgr: Jackie Clarke
Number of staff: 9
Date originated: 1978
Annual sales: $1 - 4 million
Bond coverage: (NP)
Accredited: ARC & IATAN
Escrow: (NP)
Security: Subsidiary Omega World Travel

DESTINATIONS

EUROPE, MID EAST, ORIENT, LATIN AMERICA

(For a complete list of the exact cities served within each region, see the Destination Index)

AIRLINES
UA, DL, TW, NW, FI, AY, SU, FQ, FF, LH

(Airline codes defined in Index)

Firm books business class: Yes First class: Yes
Airlines may be contacted for references: Yes
Percentage of sales through scheduled air: 100%

SALES POLICIES

Tickets delivered: Immediately after payment
Delivered by: *Overnight* $6.00

Fee charged for credit card payment: (NP)
Flight confirmed: At booking
Is a printed receipt provided? Yes
Cancellation policy: Varies by airline

Frequent flyer miles offered? Yes
Varies by airline

TRAVEL AGENCY
orders accepted by:
phone letter fax

PAYMENT FORMS ACCEPTED
CREDIT CARD
AGENCY CHECK

Comment:

(NP) = Firm did not provide requested information.

FIRM: Travelogue, Inc.

RES PHONE: 1-800-542-9446

ADDRESS: 4000 A Spring Garden St.
Greensboro, NC 27407
PHONE: 910-855-1735
FAX: 910-852-3571

Branch Offices:

CORPORATE INFORMATION

Owner: Mr. Osman Siddique
Gen Mgr: Mr. Vinod Manchhani
Number of staff: 10
Date originated: 1976
Annual sales: $10 - 25 million
Bond coverage: ARC
Accredited: ARC & IATAN
Escrow: (NP)
Security: (NP)

DESTINATIONS
EUROPE, ORIENT, AFRICA

(For a complete list of the exact cities served within each region, see the Destination Index)

AIRLINES
KE, MH, GF, SQ, CX, TG, EK, AA, OZ

(Airline codes defined in Index)

Firm books business class: Yes   First class: Yes
Airlines may be contacted for references: Yes
Percentage of sales through scheduled air: 100%

SALES POLICIES

Tickets delivered: Upon payment
        Delivered by: *Overnight*   *$8.00*

Fee charged for credit card payment: 4%
Flight confirmed: At booking
Is a printed receipt provided? Yes
Cancellation policy: Varies by airline

Frequent flyer miles offered? Yes
                Varies by airline

TRAVEL AGENCY
orders accepted by:
phone   letter   fax

PAYMENT FORMS ACCEPTED
CREDIT CARD
AGENCY CHECK

Comment:

(NP) = Firm did not provide requested information.

190

FIRM: Travnet Inc.

RES PHONE: 1-800-359-6388

ADDRESS: 230 N. Michigan Ave. #2005
Chicago, IL 60601
PHONE: 312-759-9200
FAX: 312-759-9234
Branch Offices:

Travel Agent Rating
Overall Average
8.65
(Detailed analysis of results in Ratings Section)

CORPORATE INFORMATION

Owner: Randy Lynch
Gen Mgr: (NP)
Number of staff: 15
Date originated: 1989
Annual sales: $10 - 25 million
Bond coverage: $70,000
Accredited: ARC & IATAN
Escrow: No
Security: All tickets Fedexed to agents 48 hrs. after payment

DESTINATIONS

ORIENT, SOUTH PACIFIC

(For a complete list of the exact cities served within each region, see the Destination Index)

AIRLINES

Cathay Pacific Airways, Korean Air, Garuda Indonesia, Malaysia Airlines, Japan Airlines, Thai Airways, United Airlines, Air New Zealan

(Airline codes defined in Index)

Firm books business class: Yes   First class: (NP)
Airlines may be contacted for references: Yes
Percentage of sales through scheduled air: 100%

SALES POLICIES

Tickets delivered: 48 hrs after payment
Delivered by: *Overnight   no charge*

Fee charged for credit card payment: $30
Flight confirmed: Immediately
Is a printed receipt provided? Yes
Cancellation policy: (NP)

Frequent flyer miles offered? Yes
Varies by airline

TRAVEL AGENCY
orders accepted by:
phone   letter   fax

PAYMENT FORMS ACCEPTED

CREDIT CARD
AGENCY CHECK

Comment:

(NP) = Firm did not provide requested information.

FIRM: US Inf Tours

RES PHONE: 1-800- 262-0456

ADDRESS: 71 Old Camplain Rd
     Somerville, NJ 08876
 PHONE: 908-526-0085
   FAX: 908-526-5855

Branch Offices:

CORPORATE INFORMATION

Owner: Abby Elkholy
Gen Mgr: Sam Elkholy
Number of staff: 4
Date originated: 1985
Annual sales: $1 - 4 million
Bond coverage: (NP)
Accredited: ARC & IATAN
Escrow: (NP)
Security: (NP)

DESTINATIONS
MID EAST, AFRICA

(For a complete list of the exact cities served within each region, see the Destination Index)

AIRLINES
(NP)

(Airline codes defined in Index)

Firm books business class: (NP) First class: (NP)
Airlines may be contacted for references: Yes
Percentage of sales through scheduled air: (NP)

SALES POLICIES

Tickets delivered: (NP)
  Delivered by: *Overnight*
        First class

Fee charged for credit card payment: (NP)
Flight confirmed: (NP)
Is a printed receipt provided? (NP)
Cancellation policy: (NP)

Frequent flyer miles offered? (NP)

TRAVEL AGENCY
orders accepted by:
fax

PAYMENT FORMS
ACCEPTED
AGENCY CHECK
COD

Comment:

(NP) = Firm did not provide requested information.

FIRM: United Tours Corp

RES PHONE: 1-800-245-0203

ADDRESS: 235 West 48th Street Ste. 42C
New York, NY 10036
PHONE: 212-245-1100
FAX: 212-245-0292

Branch Offices:

Travel Agent Rating
Overall Average
6.5
(Detailed analysis of results in Ratings Section)

CORPORATE INFORMATION

Owner: Y. Korogodsky
Gen Mgr: (NP)
Number of staff: 10
Date originated: 1987
Annual sales: $5 - 10 million
Bond coverage: (NP)
Accredited: ARC & IATAN
Escrow: (NP)
Security: (NP)

DESTINATIONS
EUROPE

(For a complete list of the exact cities served within each region, see the Destination Index)

AIRLINES
HY, KK, OK, AY, IB, LH, Aeroflot-USA, Air Ukraine, Austrian Airlines

(Airline codes defined in Index)

Firm books business class: Yes First class: (NP)
Airlines may be contacted for references: Yes
Percentage of sales through scheduled air: (NP)

SALES POLICIES

Tickets delivered: (NP)
Delivered by: *Overnight* *$10.00*
First class

Fee charged for credit card payment: (NP)
Flight confirmed: (NP)
Is a printed receipt provided? (NP)
Cancellation policy: Varies

Frequent flyer miles offered? No

TRAVEL AGENCY
orders accepted by:
phone *fax*

PAYMENT FORMS ACCEPTED
AGENCY CHECK
COD

Comment:

(NP) = Firm did not provide requested information.

FIRM: **Unitravel**

RES PHONE: 1-800-325-2222

ADDRESS: 1177 N Warson Road
St. Louis, MO 63132
PHONE: 314-569-0900
FAX: 314-569-2503

Branch Offices:

Travel Agent Rating
Overall Average
7.62
(Detailed analysis of results in Ratings Section)

CORPORATE INFORMATION

Owner: David Harris
Gen Mgr: Sophia Desherlia
Number of staff: (NP)
Date originated: 1968
Annual sales: (NP)
Bond coverage: (NP)
Accredited: ARC & IATAN
Escrow: (NP)
Security: (NP)

DESTINATIONS

EUROPE, ORIENT, AFRICA, LATIN AMERICA, NORTH AMERICA

(For a complete list of the exact cities served within each region, see the Destination Index)

AIRLINES

AA, AC, AF, AI, AY, BA, CO, DL, IB, KL, LH, JI, NW, SK, SN, TW, UA, US, OS

(Airline codes defined in Index)

Firm books business class: (NP)   First class: (NP)
Airlines may be contacted for references: Yes
Percentage of sales through scheduled air: 100%

SALES POLICIES

Tickets delivered: FEDEX
Delivered by: *Overnight*
First class

Fee charged for credit card payment: (NP)
Flight confirmed: At booking
Is a printed receipt provided? (NP)
Cancellation policy: (NP)

Frequent flyer miles offered? (NP)

TRAVEL AGENCY
orders accepted by:
phone   letter   fax

PAYMENT FORMS ACCEPTED
CREDIT CARD
AGENCY CHECK

Comment:

(NP) = Firm did not provide requested information.

FIRM: World Travel & Tours, Inc.

RES PHONE: 1-800-886-4WTT

ADDRESS: 5815 Seminary Rd.
Baileys Crossroads, VA 22041
PHONE: 703-379-6363
FAX: 703-379-6283

Branch Offices:

Travel Agent Rating
Overall Average
6
(Detailed analysis of results in Ratings Section)

CORPORATE INFORMATION

Owner: Mac Bous
Gen Mgr: Afaf Bous
Number of staff: 19
Date originated: 1980
Annual sales: $5 - 10 million
Bond coverage: $70,000
Accredited: ARC & IATAN
Escrow: (NP)
Security: (NP)

DESTINATIONS

EUROPE, MID EAST, ORIENT, AFRICA

(For a complete list of the exact cities served within each region, see the Destination Index).

AIRLINES
AA, AF, BA, KL, LH, FI, TW, UA, NW, SA, LZ, SR, WT, etc.

(Airline codes defined in Index)

Firm books business class: (NP)   First class: (NP)
Airlines may be contacted for references: Yes
Percentage of sales through scheduled air: 100%

SALES POLICIES

Tickets delivered: One day before departure
Delivered by: *Overnight*   *$5.00*

Fee charged for credit card payment: 5%
Flight confirmed: One day before departure
Is a printed receipt provided? Yes
Cancellation policy: 25%

Frequent flyer miles offered? Yes
Varies by airline

TRAVEL AGENCY
orders accepted by:
phone   letter   fax

PAYMENT FORMS ACCEPTED
CREDIT CARD
AGENCY CHECK
NET 10 DAYS

Comment:

(NP) = Firm did not provide requested information.

FIRM: Wright Travel Holidays

RES PHONE: 1-800-877-3240

ADDRESS: 57 E. 77th St., Penthouse
NY, NY 10021
PHONE: 212-570-0969
FAX: 212-570-0981

Branch Offices:

CORPORATE INFORMATION

Owner: Mr. Peter Wright
Gen Mgr: (NP)
Number of staff: 15
Date originated: 1991
Annual sales: $5 - 10 million
Bond coverage: (NP)
Accredited: ARC & IATAN
Escrow: (NP)
Security: (NP)

DESTINATIONS
EUROPE, LATIN AMERICA

(For a complete list of the exact cities served within each region, see the Destination Index)

AIRLINES
VA, IB, OA

(Airline codes defined in Index)

Firm books business class: (NP)   First class: (NP)
Airlines may be contacted for references: Yes
Percentage of sales through scheduled air: 90%

SALES POLICIES

Tickets delivered: Three weeks before departure
    Delivered by: *Overnight*   *$10.00*

Fee charged for credit card payment: (NP)
Flight confirmed: 30 days before departure
Is a printed receipt provided? Yes
Cancellation policy: (NP)

Frequent flyer miles offered? (NP)

TRAVEL AGENCY
orders accepted by:
phone letter   fax

PAYMENT FORMS ACCEPTED
*AGENCY CHECK
COD*

Comment:

(NP) = Firm did not provide requested information.

Part III

The
Travel Agent
Ratings

The Travel Agent Ratings
- *How They Work* -

You aren't the only one who is interested in using consolidators & wholesalers; every travel agent in the industry knows that buying tickets through a good reliable consolidator can save their clients incredible amounts of money on airfare. But before the *Index to Air Travel Consolidators*, the professional edition of *Fly For Less,* there was no effective way for agents to know which companies were reliable, and many didn't want to take an unnecessary risk.

Now, with the *Index*, travel agents are using consolidators & wholesalers more than ever. They are finding the firms that provide outstanding service, as well as the ones that don't, and are very active in reporting these results back to us. We created the Travel Agent Ratings system as a network for our subscribers to share and benefit from their collective experiences. Over 2000 ratings were mailed to us for this edition. The ratings are compiled twice a year and none are more than two years old. Travel agents are as concerned with getting a good deal as you are, so their professional opinions and experience with these companies should be of great value to you.

These ratings are, however, based strictly on opinions and should be used only in conjunction with all the company information provided. Here are four tips to remember when considering a firm's ratings.

*The more ratings a company receives, the more travel agents who have used them, and therefore the more revealing their overall rating may be.

*Always look at the big picture. Don't let the lowest rating received necessarily deter you from using a company. Keep in mind the overall average of the ratings received. Travel agents are only human and can vary in their opinions about service standards. Plus, certain concerns they have may not be pertinent to the general consumer - commissions, etc.

*Companies that have received fewer ratings than the rest may be newer, or smaller, but not necessarily less reliable.

*Company information for a profile listing is requested from every consolidator identified. If a company has been rated, but has not provided their profile information for a free listing , you may want to determine why. All data that we publish is information a consolidator should be happy to provide a potential customer.

THE TRAVEL AGENT RATINGS

Each Firm was evaluated on a scale from 1 to 10, regarding overall customer service. The ratings are based strictly on opinions and should be used with care.

Profiled in book? - Indicates whether the company's full information is provided.
Total # - The total number of ratings received for each firm.
Highest & Lowest Rating - The absolute highest and lowest rating received overall.
Average Rating - The average of all ratings received for the firm.

10 = Excellent, 8-9 = Very Good, 6-7 = Good, 5 = Average, 3-4 = Poor,
2 = Unsatisfactory, 1 = Unresolved Dispute.

firm	profiled in book?	breakdown of ratings received			average rating
4th Dimension Tours	YES	Total # = 6	Highest = 10	Lowest = 6	7.83
AESU	YES	Total # = 11	Highest = 10	Lowest = 3	7.09
AIT Anderson International	YES	Total # = 14	Highest = 10	Lowest = 7	9.07
APC/American Passenger Con	YES	Total # = 3	Highest = 10	Lowest = 6	8
Abratours	YES	Total # = 1	Highest = 8	Lowest = 8	8
Africa Desk	YES	Total # = 2	Highest = 9	Lowest = 5	7
Agents Advantage	YES	Total # = 1	Highest = 9	Lowest = 9	9
Air Brokers Int'l, Inc.	YES	Total # = 6	Highest = 10	Lowest = 4	7.17
Air Travel Discounts, Inc.	YES	Total # = 16	Highest = 10	Lowest = 2	6.25
Airplan	YES	Total # = 14	Highest = 10	Lowest = 2	8.14
All Destinations	YES	Total # = 2	Highest = 9	Lowest = 8	8.5
AmeriCorp Travel Professionals	YES	Total # = 1	Highest = 9	Lowest = 9	9
American Intl. Consolidators	YES	Total # = 16	Highest = 10	Lowest = 2	7.81
American Travel Abroad Inc	YES	Total # = 12	Highest = 10	Lowest = 3	6.58
Ariel Tours, Inc.	YES	Total # = 3	Highest = 10	Lowest = 8	9.33
Asensio Tours & Travel Corp	YES	Total # = 2	Highest = 10	Lowest = 8	9
Auto Europe	NO	Total # = 1	Highest = 8	Lowest = 8	8
Balkan Holidays	YES	Total # = 15	Highest = 10	Lowest = 2	7
Bon Voyage	YES	Total # = 7	Highest = 10	Lowest = 1	5.71
Brazilian Travel Service	NO	Total # = 3	Highest = 10	Lowest = 8	9
Brendan Air	YES	Total # = 10	Highest = 10	Lowest = 5	7.5
British Network, LTD	YES	Total # = 2	Highest = 9	Lowest = 8	8.5

Each Firm was evaluated on a scale from 1 to 10, regarding overall customer service. The ratings are based strictly on opinions and should be used with care.

Profiled in book? - *Indicates whether the company's full information is provided.*
Total # - *The total number of ratings received for each firm.*
Highest & Lowest Rating - *The absolute highest and lowest rating received overall.*
Average Rating - *The average of all ratings received for the firm.*

10 = Excellent, 8-9 = Very Good, 6-7 = Good, 5 = Average, 3-4 = Poor, 2 = Unsatisfactory, 1 = Unresolved Dispute.

firm	profiled in book?	breakdown of ratings received			average rating
CL Thomson Express Int'l	YES	Total # = 30	Highest = 10	Lowest = 2	7.37
CWT/Maharaja	YES	Total # = 1	Highest = 6	Lowest = 6	6
Campus Travel Center/Euroflgts	YES	Total # = 4	Highest = 10	Lowest = 5	8
Cedok Central European Tours	YES	Total # = 10	Highest = 10	Lowest = 3	6.5
Central Holidays	YES	Total # = 21	Highest = 10	Lowest = 3	7.21
Central Tours	YES	Total # = 1	Highest = 8	Lowest = 8	8
Centrav, Inc.	YES	Total # = 21	Highest = 10	Lowest = 5	8.71
Charterways	YES	Total # = 5	Highest = 10	Lowest = 8	8.7
Chartours	YES	Total # = 5	Highest = 9	Lowest = 7	8.4
City Tours	YES	Total # = 4	Highest = 10	Lowest = 6	7.5
Classic Hawaii Custom Vacation	NO	Total # = 1	Highest = 9	Lowest = 9	9
Classical Vacations	NO	Total # = 1	Highest = 10	Lowest = 10	10
Compare Travel	YES	Total # = 4	Highest = 9	Lowest = 5	7.5
Consolidated Tours, Inc.	YES	Total # = 4	Highest = 9	Lowest = 7	7.75
Cosmopolitan	NO	Total # = 1	Highest = 10	Lowest = 10	10
Cosmopolitan TVC Ctr	YES	Total # = 1	Highest = 9	Lowest = 9	9
Costa Azul Travel	YES	Total # = 3	Highest = 7	Lowest = 2	4.67
Council Charter	YES	Total # = 24	Highest = 10	Lowest = 2	6.77
Creative Marketing Management	YES	Total # = 1	Highest = 10	Lowest = 10	10
D-FW Tours	YES	Total # = 32	Highest = 10	Lowest = 5	8.69
DERAIR	YES	Total # = 62	Highest = 10	Lowest = 2	8.13
Destinations Unlimited	YES	Total # = 3	Highest = 10	Lowest = 7	8.33
Dial Europe Inc.	YES	Total # = 6	Highest = 10	Lowest = 6	7.83

Each Firm was evaluated on a scale from 1 to 10, regarding overall customer service. The ratings are based strictly on opinions and should be used with care.

Profiled in book? - *Indicates whether the company's full information is provided.*
Total # - *The total number of ratings received for each firm.*
Highest & Lowest Rating - *The absolute highest and lowest rating received overall.*
Average Rating - *The average of all ratings received for the firm.*

10 = Excellent, 8-9 = Very Good, 6-7 = Good, 5 = Average, 3-4 = Poor, 2 = Unsatisfactory, 1 = Unresolved Dispute.

firm	profiled in book?	breakdown of ratings received			average rating
Diplomat Tours	YES	Total # = 19	Highest = 10	Lowest = 4	7.97
Eastern European Travel Center	YES	Total # = 4	Highest = 10	Lowest = 2	8.75
Egypt Tours & Travel	YES	Total # = 1	Highest = 8	Lowest = 8	8
Egyptian Connection	YES	Total # = 1	Highest = 6	Lowest = 6	6
Euram Tours Inc	YES	Total # = 38	Highest = 10	Lowest = 2	8.05
Everest Travel Inc.	YES	Total # = 7	Highest = 10	Lowest = 2	6.86
Fantasy Holidays	YES	Total # = 3	Highest = 9	Lowest = 7	8.33
Favored Holidays Inc.	YES	Total # = 2	Highest = 10	Lowest = 9	9.5
Festival of Asia	YES	Total # = 7	Highest = 10	Lowest = 7	8.43
Four Seasons Travel	YES	Total # = 1	Highest = 2	Lowest = 2	2
G. G. Tours	YES	Total # = 1	Highest = 8	Lowest = 8	8
GIT Travel	YES	Total # = 4	Highest = 10	Lowest = 5	8.25
GTI Travel Consolidators	NO	Total # = 1	Highest = 10	Lowest = 10	10
Garden State Travel	YES	Total # = 2	Highest = 10	Lowest = 10	10
Gate 1	YES	Total # = 2	Highest = 7	Lowest = 5	6
Gateway Express Ltd.	YES	Total # = 6	Highest = 10	Lowest = 7	8.67
Gateway Travel	NO	Total # = 1	Highest = 10	Lowest = 10	10
General Tours	YES	Total # = 9	Highest = 10	Lowest = 5	7.22
Getaway Travel Intl. Inc.	YES	Total # = 4	Highest = 10	Lowest = 5	7
Global Travel Consolidators	YES	Total # = 4	Highest = 7	Lowest = 1	5.5
Globetrotters - Supercities	NO	Total # = 1	Highest = 9	Lowest = 9	9
Golden Pacific #1 Travel	YES	Total # = 1	Highest = 7	Lowest = 7	7
Guardian Travel Service Inc.	YES	Total # = 1	Highest = 5	Lowest = 5	5

Each Firm was evaluated on a scale from 1 to 10, regarding overall customer service. The ratings are based strictly on opinions and should be used with care.

Profiled in book? - Indicates whether the company's full information is provided.
Total # - The total number of ratings received for each firm.
Highest & Lowest Rating - The absolute highest and lowest rating received overall.
Average Rating - The average of all ratings received for the firm.

10 = Excellent, 8-9 = Very Good, 6-7 = Good, 5 = Average, 3-4 = Poor, 2 = Unsatisfactory, 1 = Unresolved Dispute.

firm	profiled in book?	breakdown of ratings received			average rating
HTI Tours	YES	Total # = 7	Highest = 10	Lowest = 1	6.86
Happy Tours	YES	Total # = 7	Highest = 10	Lowest = 7	8.57
Hari World Travels, Inc.	YES	Total # = 1	Highest = 7	Lowest = 7	7
Holbrook Travel Inc.	YES	Total # = 1	Highest = 9	Lowest = 9	9
Holiday Travel International	YES	Total # = 1	Highest = 8	Lowest = 8	8
Hudson Holidays	YES	Total # = 16	Highest = 10	Lowest = 1	7.38
ITS Tours & Travel	YES	Total # = 5	Highest = 10	Lowest = 7	8.6
Inter Island Tours	YES	Total # = 6	Highest = 8	Lowest = 5	7
International Discount Travel	NO	Total # = 2	Highest = 8	Lowest = 8	8
International Travel Exchange	NO	Total # = 2	Highest = 10	Lowest = 2	6
J & O Air	YES	Total # = 29	Highest = 10	Lowest = 5	8.59
Jenson Baron	NO	Total # = 1	Highest = 9	Lowest = 9	9
Jet Vacations	NO	Total # = 1	Highest = 5	Lowest = 5	5
Jetset Tours Inc.	YES	Total # = 55	Highest = 10	Lowest = 2	8.15
KTS Services	YES	Total # = 1	Highest = 9	Lowest = 9	9
Kambi Travel Intl.	YES	Total # = 2	Highest = 10	Lowest = 8	9
Leisure Resources	YES	Total # = 4	Highest = 10	Lowest = 1	5.25
Lucky Tours	YES	Total # = 1	Highest = 4	Lowest = 4	4
M & H Travel, Inc.	YES	Total # = 7	Highest = 9	Lowest = 5	7.71
MLT Vacations	YES	Total # = 44	Highest = 10	Lowest = 2	8.56
MT&T	YES	Total # = 5	Highest = 9	Lowest = 5	7.6
Magical Holidays, Inc.	YES	Total # = 4	Highest = 10	Lowest = 8	9
Mena Tours & Travel	YES	Total # = 14	Highest = 10	Lowest = 4	7.64

Part III - The Travel Agent Ratings

Each Firm was evaluated on a scale from 1 to 10, regarding overall customer service. The ratings are based strictly on opinions and should be used with care.

Profiled in book? - Indicates whether the company's full information is provided.
Total # - The total number of ratings received for each firm.
Highest & Lowest Rating - The absolute highest and lowest rating received overall.
Average Rating - The average of all ratings received for the firm.

10 = Excellent, 8-9 = Very Good, 6-7 = Good, 5 = Average, 3-4 = Poor, 2 = Unsatisfactory, 1 = Unresolved Dispute.

firm	profiled in book?	breakdown of ratings received			average rating
Midtown Travel Consultants	YES	Total # = 4	Highest = 10	Lowest = 2	7.25
Millrun Tours	YES	Total # = 7	Highest = 9	Lowest = 2	6.43
Northwest World Vacations	YES	Total # = 26	Highest = 10	Lowest = 3	8.73
Orbis Polish Travel, Inc.	YES	Total # = 9	Highest = 10	Lowest = 5	7.44
P & F International Inc.	YES	Total # = 7	Highest = 9	Lowest = 2	6.29
PCS	YES	Total # = 3	Highest = 10	Lowest = 9	9.33
Palm Coast Tours & Travel	YES	Total # = 2	Highest = 8	Lowest = 4	6
Panorama Tours	YES	Total # = 3	Highest = 9	Lowest = 8	8.67
Park Place International	NO	Total # = 1	Highest = 10	Lowest = 10	10
Passport Travel Mgmt Group	YES	Total # = 2	Highest = 9	Lowest = 9	9
Paul Laifer Tours Inc.	YES	Total # = 3	Highest = 9	Lowest = 5	7.33
People Travel Club	NO	Total # = 1	Highest = 7	Lowest = 7	7
Picasso Travel	YES	Total # = 16	Highest = 10	Lowest = 4	7.19
Pino Welcome Travel	YES	Total # = 5	Highest = 10	Lowest = 3	5.2
Pinto Basto USA	YES	Total # = 5	Highest = 10	Lowest = 4	6
Pleasure Break Vacations, Inc.	YES	Total # = 33	Highest = 10	Lowest = 4	8.39
Plus Ultra Tours	YES	Total # = 2	Highest = 4	Lowest = 2	3
Premier Travel Services Inc	YES	Total # = 1	Highest = 10	Lowest = 10	10
Princely Travel	NO	Total # = 1	Highest = 8	Lowest = 8	8
Queue Travel	YES	Total # = 2	Highest = 9	Lowest = 3	6
Rahim Tours	YES	Total # = 10	Highest = 10	Lowest = 4	7.2
STA Travel	YES	Total # = 17	Highest = 10	Lowest = 5	9.18
STT Worldwide Travel, Inc.	YES	Total # = 5	Highest = 10	Lowest = 8	8.8

Each Firm was evaluated on a scale from 1 to 10, regarding overall customer service. The ratings are based strictly on opinions and should be used with care.

Profiled in book? - *Indicates whether the company's full information is provided.*
Total # - *The total number of ratings received for each firm.*
Highest & Lowest Rating - *The absolute highest and lowest rating received overall.*
Average Rating - *The average of all ratings received for the firm.*

10 = Excellent, 8-9 = Very Good, 6-7 = Good, 5 = Average, 3-4 = Poor, 2 = Unsatisfactory, 1 = Unresolved Dispute.

firm	profiled in book?	breakdown of ratings received			average rating
Saga Tours	YES	Total # = 2	Highest = 5	Lowest = 4	4.5
Saltaire Travel	YES	Total # = 2	Highest = 8	Lowest = 2	5
Sega Tours	NO	Total # = 1	Highest = 2	Lowest = 2	2
Sharp Travel Washington	YES	Total # = 1	Highest = 10	Lowest = 10	10
Shedid Travel	NO	Total # = 1	Highest = 2	Lowest = 2	2
Signa Travel	NO	Total # = 1	Highest = 2	Lowest = 2	2
Skylink Travel	YES	Total # = 9	Highest = 10	Lowest = 3	7.33
Solar Tours	YES	Total # = 17	Highest = 10	Lowest = 4	8.29
South American Fiesta	YES	Total # = 3	Highest = 9	Lowest = 7	8
Spanish Heritage Tours	NO	Total # = 1	Highest = 10	Lowest = 10	10
Spector Travel of Boston	YES	Total # = 2	Highest = 5	Lowest = 2	3.5
Sunny Land Tours	YES	Total # = 13	Highest = 9	Lowest = 5	7
Sunrise Tours	YES	Total # = 1	Highest = 6	Lowest = 6	6
TAL Tours Inc.	NO	Total # = 1	Highest = 9	Lowest = 9	9
TFI Tours Intl. Ltd.	YES	Total # = 15	Highest = 8	Lowest = 2	4.97
TT Travel	NO	Total # = 1	Highest = 10	Lowest = 10	10
Thrifty Air	YES	Total # = 2	Highest = 8	Lowest = 8	8
Ticketworld/SAF Travel World	YES	Total # = 1	Highest = 7.5	Lowest = 7.	7.5
Tourlite International Inc.	YES	Total # = 5	Highest = 10	Lowest = 6	8.2
Tours International Inc.	YES	Total # = 1	Highest = 8	Lowest = 8	8
Trans Am Travel	YES	Total # = 23	Highest = 10	Lowest = 2	8.09
Travac Tours & Charters	YES	Total # = 31	Highest = 10	Lowest = 4	7.52
Travel Bargains	YES	Total # = 6	Highest = 9	Lowest = 4	6.17

Each Firm was evaluated on a scale from 1 to 10, regarding overall customer service. The ratings are based strictly on opinions and should be used with care.

Profiled in book? - *Indicates whether the company's full information is provided.*
Total # - *The total number of ratings received for each firm.*
Highest & Lowest Rating - *The absolute highest and lowest rating received overall.*
Average Rating - *The average of all ratings received for the firm.*

10 = Excellent, 8-9 = Very Good, 6-7 = Good, 5 = Average, 3-4 = Poor, 2 = Unsatisfactory, 1 = Unresolved Dispute.

firm	profiled in book?	breakdown of ratings received			average rating
Travel Beyond	YES	Total # = 2	Highest = 8	Lowest = 7	7.5
Travel Expressions, Inc.	YES	Total # = 3	Highest = 8	Lowest = 2	4.67
Travel Leaders, Inc.	YES	Total # = 6	Highest = 10	Lowest = 4	7.25
Travel Link	NO	Total # = 2	Highest = 9	Lowest = 8	8.5
Travel N Tours	YES	Total # = 4	Highest = 9	Lowest = 6	7.75
Travel Wholesalers	YES	Total # = 5	Highest = 10	Lowest = 6	8.6
Travnet Inc.	YES	Total # = 17	Highest = 10	Lowest = 5	8.65
Tread Lightly LTD.	YES	Total # = 2	Highest = 9	Lowest = 9	9
Trilogy Tours	YES	Total # = 1	Highest = 9	Lowest = 9	9
United Tours Corp	YES	Total # = 2	Highest = 9	Lowest = 4	6.5
Unitravel	YES	Total # = 47	Highest = 10	Lowest = 3	7.62
Unlimited World Travel	YES	Total # = 2	Highest = 8	Lowest = 8	8
Up & Away Travel	YES	Total # = 7	Highest = 9	Lowest = 3	7
Value Holidays	YES	Total # = 1	Highest = 7	Lowest = 7	7
Wings Of The World	YES	Total # = 6	Highest = 7	Lowest = 2	4.17
World Connections Travel Srvce	NO	Total # = 2	Highest = 8	Lowest = 2	5
World Travel & Tours, Inc.	YES	Total # = 2	Highest = 10	Lowest = 2	6

Part IV

The Indexes

THE AIRLINE CODES

AA	American Airlines	FC	Chaparral Airlines
AC	Air Canada	FF	Tower Air, Inc.
AD	Exec Express	FI	Icelandair
AF	Air France	FJ	Air Pacific Limited
AI	Air India	FQ	Air Aruba
AL	Alsair S.A.	GA	Garuda Indonesia
AM	Aeromexico	GF	Gulf Air
AN	Ansett Air of Australia	GM	Air America
AP	Aspen Airways	GU	Aviateca S.A.
AQ	Aloha Airlines	GY	Guyana Airways
AR	Aerolineas Argentinas	HA	Hawaiian Airlines
AS	Alaska Airlines	HM	Air Seychelles Ltd.
AT	Royal Air Maroc	HP	America West Airlines
AV	Avianca	HY	Metro Airlines
AY	Finnair	IB	Iberia
AZ	Alitalia	IT	Air Inter
BA	British Airways	IW	Minerve
BD	British Midland	JI	Jet Express
BF	Markair, Inc.	JL	Japan Air Lines
BG	Biman Bangladesh	JM	Air Jamaica
BW	BWIA International	JU	Yugoslav Airlines
CA	CAAC-China	KE	Korean Airlines
CD	Trans-Provincial Airlines Ltd.	KF	OY Air Botnia AB
CF	Compania de Aviacion Faucett	KK	Transportes Aereo Regionais S.A.
CI	China Airlines	KL	KLM Royal Dutch Airlines
CM	Copa	KM	Air Malta
CO	Continental Airlines	KO	Cook Strait Skyferry Ltd.
CP	Canadian International	KQ	Kenya Airways
CX	Cathay Pacific Airways	KU	Kuwait Airlines
CY	Cyprus Airways	LA	Lan Chile
DL	Delta Air Lines	LB	Lloyd Aereo Boliviano
EH	SAETA	LH	Lufthansa German Airlines
EI	Aer Lingus	LM	ALM Antillean Airlines
EK	Emirates Airlines	LO	LOT Polish Airlines
ET	Ethiopian Airlines	LR	LACSA
EU	Ecuatoriana	LT	LTU International Airways

211

The Airline Codes

LY	El Al Israel Airlines	SO	Austrian Air Services
LZ	Balkan - Bulgarian Airlines	SQ	Singapore Airlines
MA	Malev - Hungarian Airlines	SR	Swissair
MD	Air Madagascar	SS	Metro Airlines Northeast, Inc.
MH	Malaysian Airline System	SU	Aeroflot - Soviet Airlines
MK	Air Mauritius	SV	Saudi Arabian Airlines (Saudia)
ML	Midway Airlines	TA	Taca
MS	Egyptair	TE	Air New Zealand
MU	China Eastern Airlines	TG	Thai Airways
MX	Mexicana De Aviacion	TK	Turk Hava Yollari
NH	All Nippon Airways	TP	TAP Air Portugal
NW	Northwest	TR	Transbrasil S/A Linhas Aereas
NZ	Air New Zealand	TW	Trans World Airlines
OA	Olympic Airways	TZ	American Trans Air
OD	Air Transport Schiphol	UA	United Airlines
OK	Czechoslovak Airlines	UC	LADECO - Linea Aerea del Cobre
OS	Austrian Airlines	UE	Air LA
OZ	Asiana Airlines	UK	Air UK
PA	Pan American	UL	Airlanka Ltd.
PK	Pakistan International Airlines	UM	Air Zimbabwe
PL	Aeroperu	US	USAir
PR	Philippine Airlines	UY	Cameroon Airlines
PX	Air Niugini	UZ	Air Resorts Airlines
PZ	LAP Lineas Aereas Paraguayas	VA	Viasa
	(Air Paraguay)	VE	Avensa
QF	Quantas Airways	VG	RFG Regionalflug GMBH
RA	Royal Nepal Airlines	VN	Hang Khong Vietnam
RG	Varig Airlines	VP	VASP
RJ	Royal Jordanian	VS	Virgin Atlantic Airways Ltd.
RK	Air Afrique	VX	Aces
RO	Tarom - Romanian Air Transport	WN	Southwest
SA	South African Airways	WO	Polarwing OY
SD	Sudan Airways	WT	Nigeria Airways Ltd.
SK	Scandinavian Airlines System (SAS)	3D	Edgartown Air, Inc.
SN	Sabena Belgian World		

CONSOLIDATORS & WHOLESALERS BY LOCATION

* - Asterisk indicates firm was contacted, but did not provide information for a free profile listing.

Firm	Phone	Page
California		
Air Brokers Int'l, Inc.	(800)883-3273	17
Alta Tours	(800)338-4191	22
Bon Voyage	(800)826-8500	135
Brendan Air	(800)491-9633	136
C & H International	(800)289-1628	*
CL Thomson Express Int'l	(213)628-9550	137
Cathay Travel	(818)571-6727	29
Charterways	(800)869-2344	140
Chartours	(800)323-4444	32
Continental Travel Shop	(310)453-8655	*
Costa Azul Travel	(800)332-7202	35
DERAIR	(800)717-4247	37
Destinations Unlimited	(800)338-7987	39
Diplomat Tours	(800)727-8687	147
Fantastiques Tours	(310)577-6711	150
Festival of Asia	(800)533-9953	151
Global Access	(800)938-5355	*
Global Travel Consolidators	(800)366-3544	155
Go Way Travel	416-322-1034	*
HTS International, Inc.	(800)387-6888	*
Happy Tours	(800)877-5262	158
J & O Air	(800)877-8111	159
King Tut Travel & Tours	(800)398-1888	69
Latin Air Consolidators	(800)521-6215	*
Picasso Travel	(800)PICASSO	88
Pioneer Tours	(800)228-2107	91
Queue Travel	(800)356-4871	172
Rebel Tours	(800)227-3235	*
STA Travel	(800)825-3001	174
Skytours	(800)246-8687	96
South Pacific Express Trvls	(800)321-7739	98
Specialty Tours Int'l USA	(800)421-3913	99
Supertravel	(310)301-4567	102
Thrifty Air	(800)423-4488	180
Tokyo Travel Service	(800)227-2065	*
Travel Associates	(800)992-7388	107
Colorado		
Overseas Travel	(800)783-7196	82
Connecticut		
The Africa Desk	(800)284-8796	127
All Destinations	(800)228-1510	20
Aquarius Tours & Travel Ltd.	(800)248-4141	*
Leisure Resources	(800)729-9051	161
North Star Tours	(800)431-1511	*
Tread Lightly LTD.	(800)643-0060	111
Florida		
4th Dimension Tours	(800)343-0020	123

Firm	Phone	Page
Florida		
Alek's Travel	(800)929-7768	19
Cosmopolitan TVC Ctr	(800)548-7206	143
Getaway Travel Intl. Inc.	(800)683-6336	53
Golden Pacific #1 Travel	(800)500-8021	156
Guardian Travel Service Inc.	(800)741-3050	55
Holbrook Travel Inc.	(800)451-7111	58
Hostway Tours	(800)327-3207	61
Interworld Travel	(800)468-3796	65
Kompas Travel	(800)233-6422	70
Mega Trvl & Trs of Florida	(954)360-9282	*
Palm Coast Trs & Trvl	(800)444-1560	85
Passport Travel Mgmt Grp	(800)950-5864	169
Rahim Tours	(800)556-5305	173
Travel Leaders, Inc.	(800)323-3218	187
Georgia		
AirFax Airline Mrktng Assoc	(404)662-0885	129
Alpha Travel	(800)793-8424	21
Everest Travel Inc.	(404)231-5222	43
GIT Travel	(800)228-1777	49
Japan Travel Service, Inc.	(800)822-3336	*
Midtown Travel Consultants	(800)548-8904	77
Orient Express Travel	(800)535-6882	*
Hawaii		
Cheap Tickets	(800)377-1000	*
Illinois		
Borgsmiller Travels	(800)228-0585	25
Chisholm Travel, Inc.	(800)631-2824	33
Compare Travel	(312)853-1144	34
Cut Rate Travel	(800)388-0575	36
Egypt Tours & Travel	(800)523-4978	41
FCT International	(800)477-9007	*
Greaves Travel	(312)726-3222	*
Hana Travel Inc.	(800)962-8044	56
Hudson Holidays	(800)323-6855	62
Jetset Tours Inc.	(800)638-3273	160
Mena Tours & Travel	(800)937-6362	76
Millrun Tours	(800)645-5786	78
National Travel Centre	(800)228-6886	79
Overseas Express	(800)343-4873	81
Pleasure Break Vacations	(800)777-1566	170
Time Travel	(800)847-7026	181
Travel Avenue	(800)333-3335	*
Travel Core of America	(800)992-9396	*
Travnet Inc.	(800)359-6388	191
Unlimited World Travel	(800)322-3557	113
Zig Zag International Trvl	(800)226-9383	119

213

*** - Asterisk indicates firm was contacted,
but did not provide information for a free profile listing.**

Firm	Phone	Page
Indiana		
US Int'l Travel & Tours	(800)874-0073	*
Kansas		
Winggate Travel	(913)451-9200	116
Maine		
Auto Europe	(207)828-2525	*
Maryland		
AESU	(800)638-7640	15
Adventure Tours	(410)785-3500	*
Fare Deals Ltd.	(800)347-7006	45
Kambi Travel Intl.	(800)220-2192	66
Massachusetts		
Kutrubes Travel	(800)878-8566	*
Spector Travel of Boston	(800)879-2374	99
Michigan		
AIT Anderson International	(800)365-1929	124
Cosmopolitan	(800)633-4087	*
GTI Travel Consolidators	(800)829-8234	50
Minnesota		
Campus Travel Cntr/Euroflgts	(800)328-3359	28
Centrav, Inc.	(800)874-2033	139
MLT Vacations	(800)328-0025	162
MT&T	(612)784-3226	163
Northwest World Vacations	(800)727-1111	165
Travel Beyond	(800)876-3131	185
Missouri		
Group & Leisure	(800)874-6608	54
Unitravel	(800)325-2222	194
Nebraska		
Lucky Tours	(800)932-6654	72
New Hampshire		
General Tours	(800)221-2216	52
New Jersey		
Agents Advantage	(800)816-2211	128
All Ways Travel	(800)878-0088	*
British Network, LTD	(800)274-8583	26
Central Holidays	(800)935-5000	138
Central Tours	(800)783-9882	31
City Tours	(800)238-2489	141
Garden State Travel	(800)537-2420	51
Littoral Tours	(800)346-0212	*
Marakesh Tourist Company	(800)458-1772	75

Firm	Phone	Page
New Jersey		
Paul Laifer Tours Inc.	(800)346-6314	86
Sunny Land Tours	(800)783-7839	178
US Inf Tours	(800)262-0456	192
Worldvision Travel	(800)545-7118	117
New York		
APC/American Passenger Con	(800)526-2447	125
Abratours	(800)227-2887	126
Aegean Holidays	(800)368-6262	*
Air Travel Discounts, Inc.	(800)888-2621	18
Am-Jet Travels Ltd.	(800)414-4147	*
American Intl. Consolidators	(800)888-5774	131
American Travel Abroad Inc	(800)228-0877	132
Ariel Tours, Inc.	(800)262-1818	133
Asensio Tours & Travel Crp	(800)221-7679	24
Balkan Holidays	(800)852-0944	134
Brazilian Travel Service	(800)342-5746	*
CWT/Maharaja	(800)223-6862	27
Cedok Central European Trs	(800)800-8891	30
Cloud Tours	(800)223-7880	*
Consolidated Tours, Inc.	(800)228-0877	142
Consumer Wholesale Trvl	(800)223-6862	*
Council Charter	(800)800-8222	144
Creative Marketing Mngmnt	(800)458-6663	145
Dial Europe Inc.	(212)758-5310	40
Eastern European Trvl Cntr	(718)339-1100	148
The Egyptian Connection	(800)334-4477	149
Fantasy Holidays	(800)645-2555	44
Favored Holidays Inc.	(718)934-8881	46
Flytime Tours & Travel	(212)760-3737	*
The French Experience	(212)986-3800	48
Hari World Travels, Inc.	(212)957-3000	57
Homeric Tours, Inc.	(800)223-5570	60
Inter Island Tours	(800)245-3434	64
International Travel Exchange	(800)727-7830	*
Jet Vacations	(800)JET-0999	*
KTS Services	(800)531-6677	66
Lotus	(800)998-6116	71
M & H Travel, Inc.	(212)661-7171	73
Magical Holidays, Inc.	(800)433-7773	74
Marnella Tours Inc.	(800)937-6999	164
New Frontiers	(800)366-6387	80
Orbis Polish Travel, Inc.	(800)870RBIS	166
Oxford Travel	(800)851-5290	*
P & F International Inc.	(800)822-3063	83
PCS	(800)367-8833	167
Persvoyage Inc	(800)455-7377	87
Pino Welcome Travel	(800)247-6578	89
Pinto Basto USA	(800)526-8539	90

* - Asterisk indicates firm was contacted, but did not provide information for a free profile listing.

Firm	Phone	Page
New York		
Plus Ultra Tours	(800)FOR-SPAIN	171
Princely Travel	(800)306-6111	*
Saga Tours	(800)683-4200	93
Saltaire Travel	(800)777-8926	94
Sceptre Charters	(800)221-0924	*
Schwaben International	(800)457-0009	*
Skylink Travel	(800)247-6659	176
Sun Island Holidays	(800)824-4653	*
Sunrise Tours	(800)872-3801	101
TFI Tours Intl. Ltd.	(800)745-8000	179
Tourlite International Inc.	(800)272-7600	182
Travac Tours & Charters	(800)TRAV-800	106
Travel Center	(800)419-0960	109
Travel Expressions, Inc.	(800)724-6274	110
Travel N Tours	(800)854-5400	188
Tulips Travel	(800)882-3383	112
United Tours Corp	(800)245-0203	193
Up & Away Travel	(800)275-8001	114
Village Travel	(800)366-2929	*
Viva Tours	(800)445-8482	*
World Trade Tours	(800)732-7386	*
Wright Travel Holidays	(800)877-3240	196
Zig Zag Travel	(800)726-0249	120
Zohny Travel Inc.	(212)953-0077	*
North Carolina		
Four Seasons Travel	(910)292-1887	47
Travelogue, Inc.	(800)542-9446	190
Ohio		
Adventure Int'l Travel Srvce	(800)542-2487	16
Ontario, Canada		
G. G. Tours	(416)487-1146	152
Oregon		
Avanti	(800)634-3837	*
Gateway Express Ltd.	(800)334-1188	154
STT Worldwide Travel, Inc.	(800)348-0886	175
Pennsylvania		
Airplan	(800)866-7526	130
Gate 1	(800)682-3333	153
HTI Tours	(800)441-4411	157
Holiday Travel International	(800)775-7111	59
Premier Travel Srvcs Inc	(800)545-1910	92
Ticketworld/SAF Trvl World	(800)394-8587	105
Travel Bargains	(800)247-3273	108
Texas		
Airfare Busters	(800)232-8783	*

Firm	Phone	Page
Texas		
AmeriCorp Travel Prfssnls	(800)299-LATI	23
Classical Vacations	(800)950-8654	*
D-FW Tours	(800)527-2589	146
Escape Tours	(800)252-0775	*
ITS Tours & Travel	(800)533-8688	63
Katy Van Tours	(800)808-8747	68
PERS Travel, Inc.	(800)583-0909	84
Supervalue Vacations	(800)879-1218	103
TCI Travel & Tours	(800)ASAP-FLY	104
Tours International Inc.	(800)247-7965	183
The Travel Group	(800)836-6269	186
Utah		
Jenson Baron	(800)333-2060	*
Panorama Tours	(800)527-4888	168
Virginia		
International Discount Travel	(800)466-7357	*
Lucky Travel Service	(800)466-5798	*
NOVA	(800)356-6682	*
Sharp Travel Washington	(800)969-7427	95
South American Fiesta	(800)334-3782	97
Trans Am Travel	(800)822-7600	184
Travel Wholesalers	(800)487-8944	189
World Travel & Tours, Inc.	(800)886-4WTT	195
Washington		
Air Makers	(206)216-2837	*
Washington, DC		
Democracy Travel	(800)536-8728	38
Euram Tours Inc	(800)848-6789	42
Solar Tours	(800)388-7652	177
Worldwide Travel	(800)343-0038	118
Wisconsin		
Value Holidays	(800)558-6850	115

THE DESTINATION INDEX
Table of Contents

Table of Contents

Table of Contents

Table of Contents

Firms are listed by region, country, then city, according to the firm's specifications. Firms serving entire region are listed at the beginning of each region section.

Firm name	1-800-phone	Phone	Page
Europe			
4th Dimension Tours	343-0020	305-279-0014	123
AESU	638-7640	410-323-4416	15
AIT Anderson International	365-1929	517-337-1300	124
APC/American Passenger Con	526-2447	212-972-1558	125
Adventure Int'l Travel Service	542-2487	216-228-7171	16
The Africa Desk	284-8796	203-354-9344	127
Agents Advantage	816-2211	908-355-2222	128
Air Travel Discounts, Inc.	888-2621	212-922-1326	18
AirFax Airline Marketing Assoc		404-662-0885	129
Airplan	866-7526	412-257-3199	130
Alek's Travel	929-7768	305-462-6767	19
Alpha Travel	793-8424	770-988-9982	21
American Intl. Consolidators	888-5774	914-592-0206	131
Ariel Tours, Inc.	262-1818	718-633-7900	133
Bon Voyage	826-8500	310-854-8585	135
Brendan Air	491-9633	800-491-9633	136
CL Thomson Express Int'l		213-628-9550	137
CWT/Maharaja	223-6862	212-695-8435	27
Campus Travel Center/Euroflgt	328-3359	612-338-5616	28
Cedok Central European Tour	800-8891	212-689-9720	30
Central Holidays	935-5000		138
Centrav, Inc.	874-2033	612-948-8400	139
Charterways	869-2344	408-257-2652	140
Chartours	323-4444	415-495-8881	32
Cosmopolitan TVC Ctr	548-7206	305-523-0973	143
Costa Azul Travel	332-7202	213-525-3331	35
Council Charter	800-8222	212-661-0311	144
Cut Rate Travel	388-0575	708-405-0587	36
D-FW Tours	527-2589	214-980-4540	146
DERAIR	717-4247	310-479-4411	37
Democracy Travel	536-8728	202-965-7200	38
Dial Europe Inc.		212-758-5310	40
Diplomat Tours	727-8687	916-972-1500	147
Eastern European Travel Cent		718-339-1100	148
Euram Tours Inc	848-6789	202-789-2255	42
Everest Travel Inc.		404-231-5222	43
Fantastiques Tours		310-577-6711	150
Fantasy Holidays	645-2555	516-935-8500	44
Fare Deals Ltd.	347-7006	410-581-8787	45
Favored Holidays Inc.		718-934-8881	46

Firm name	1-800-phone	Phone	Page

Firms are listed by region, country, then city, according to the firm's specifications. Firms serving entire region are listed at the beginning of each region section.

Europe

Firm name	1-800-phone	Phone	Page
Four Seasons Travel		910-292-1887	47
The French Experience		212-986-3800	48
GIT Travel	228-1777	404-399-6404	49
Gate 1	682-3333	215-572-7676	153
Gateway Express Ltd.	334-1188	503-242-0088	154
Global Travel Consolidators	366-3544	310-581-5610	155
Group & Leisure	874-6608	816-224-3717	54
Guardian Travel Service Inc.	741-3050	813-367-5622	55
HTI Tours	441-4411	215-563-8484	157
Hari World Travels, Inc.		212-957-3000	57
Hudson Holidays	323-6855	708-452-0600	62
Interworld Travel	468-3796	305-443-4929	65
J & O Air	877-8111	619-282-4124	159
Jetset Tours Inc.	638-3273	312-362-9960	160
KTS Services	531-6677	718-454-2300	66
Kambi Travel Intl.	220-2192	301-925-9012	67
Katy Van Tours	808-8747	713-492-7032	68
Leisure Resources	729-9051	203-874-4965	161
Lotus	998-6116	212-213-1625	71
M & H Travel, Inc.		212-661-7171	73
MT&T		612-784-3226	163
Magical Holidays, Inc.	433-7773	415-781-1345	74
Marakesh Tourist Company	458-1772	201-435-2800	75
Midtown Travel Consultants	548-8904	404-872-8308	77
Millrun Tours	645-5786	312-641-5914	78
New Frontiers	366-6387	212-779-0600	80
Overseas Express	343-4873		81
Overseas Travel	783-7196	303-337-7196	82
PERS Travel, Inc.	583-0909	214-458-6877	84
Palm Coast Tours & Travel	444-1560	407-433-1558	85
Paul Laifer Tours Inc.	346-6314	201-887-1188	86
Persvoyage Inc	455-7377	212-719-0900	87
Picasso Travel	PICASSO	310-645-4400	88
Pino Welcome Travel	247-6578	212-682-5400	89
Pleasure Break Vacations, Inc.	777-1566	708-670-6300	170
Premier Travel Services Inc	545-1910	215-893-9966	92
Queue Travel	356-4871	619-260-8577	172
STA Travel	825-3001	213-937-9274	174
STT Worldwide Travel, Inc.	348-0886	503-671-0494	175
Saga Tours	683-4200	212-696-5200	93

Firm name	1-800-phone	Phone	Page

Europe

Firms are listed by region, country, then city, according to the firm's specifications. Firms serving entire region are listed at the beginning of each region section.

Firm name	1-800-phone	Phone	Page
Saltaire Travel	777-8926	718-327-4665	94
Skylink Travel	247-6659	212-573-8980	176
Specialty Tours Int'l USA Inc.	421-3913	310-568-8709	99
Sunrise Tours	872-3801	212-947-3617	101
Supertravel		310-301-4567	102
Supervalue Vacations	879-1218	713-876-6400	103
TCI Travel & Tours	ASAP-FLY	214-630-3344	104
TFI Tours Intl. Ltd.	745-8000	212-736-1140	179
Thrifty Air	423-4488	310-337-9982	180
Time Travel	847-7026	708-595-8463	181
Trans Am Travel	822-7600	703-998-7676	184
Travac Tours & Charters	TRAV-800	212-563-3303	106
Travel Bargains	247-3273	610-834-8150	108
Travel Center	419-0960	212-545-7474	109
Travel Expressions, Inc.	724-6274	212-338-9730	110
The Travel Group	836-6269	210-698-0100	186
Travel Leaders, Inc.	323-3218	305-443-7755	187
Travel N Tours	854-5400	914-838-2600	188
Travel Wholesalers	487-8944	703-359-8855	189
United Tours Corp	245-0203	212-245-1100	193
Unitravel	325-2222	314-569-0900	194
Unlimited World Travel	322-3557	708-442-7715	113
Up & Away Travel	275-8001	212-889-2345	114
Value Holidays	558-6850	414-241-6373	115
World Travel & Tours, Inc.	886-4WTT	703-379-6363	195
Worldvision Travel	545-7118	201-736-8210	117
Worldwide Travel	343-0038	202-659-6430	118
Wright Travel Holidays	877-3240	212-570-0969	196

Albania

Tirana

Firm name	1-800-phone	Phone	Page
Balkan Holidays	852-0944	212-573-5530	134
Cosmopolitan TVC Ctr	548-7206	305-523-0973	143
United Tours Corp	245-0203	212-245-1100	193
Value Holidays	558-6850	414-241-6373	115

Austria

Vienna

Firm name	1-800-phone	Phone	Page
AESU	638-7640	410-323-4416	15
Agents Advantage	816-2211	908-355-2222	128
Air Travel Discounts, Inc.	888-2621	212-922-1326	18

Firm name	1-800-phone	Phone	Page

Firms are listed by region, country, then city, according to the firm's specifications. Firms serving entire region are listed at the beginning of each region section.

Europe

Austria

Vienna

Firm name	1-800-phone	Phone	Page
Airplan	866-7526	412-257-3199	130
Alpha Travel	793-8424	770-988-9982	21
American Intl. Consolidators	888-5774	914-592-0206	131
Balkan Holidays	852-0944	212-573-5530	134
Brendan Air	491-9633	800-491-9633	136
Cedok Central European Tour	800-8891	212-689-9720	30
Centrav, Inc.	874-2033	612-948-8400	139
Council Charter	800-8222	212-661-0311	144
Fantastiques Tours		310-577-6711	150
Favored Holidays Inc.		718-934-8881	46
Gate 1	682-3333	215-572-7676	153
Guardian Travel Service Inc.	741-3050	813-367-5622	55
HTI Tours	441-4411	215-563-8484	157
Jetset Tours Inc.	638-3273	312-362-9960	160
Kompas Travel	233-6422	305-771-9200	70
Millrun Tours	645-5786	312-641-5914	78
New Frontiers	366-6387	212-779-0600	80
Persvoyage Inc	455-7377	212-719-0900	87
Picasso Travel	PICASSO	310-645-4400	88
Pleasure Break Vacations, Inc.	777-1566	708-670-6300	170
Skylink Travel	247-6659	212-573-8980	176
Sunrise Tours	872-3801	212-947-3617	101
Supertravel		310-301-4567	102
Travac Tours & Charters	TRAV-800	212-563-3303	106
United Tours Corp	245-0203	212-245-1100	193
Up & Away Travel	275-8001	212-889-2345	114
Value Holidays	558-6850	414-241-6373	115
Worldvision Travel	545-7118	201-736-8210	117

Belarus

Minsk

Firm name	1-800-phone	Phone	Page
Eastern European Travel Cent		718-339-1100	148
Favored Holidays Inc.		718-934-8881	46
United Tours Corp	245-0203	212-245-1100	193

Belgium

Brussels

Firm name	1-800-phone	Phone	Page
4th Dimension Tours	343-0020	305-279-0014	123
AESU	638-7640	410-323-4416	15

Firm name	1-800-phone	Phone	Page

Firms are listed by region, country, then city, according to the firm's specifications. Firms serving entire region are listed at the beginning of each region section.

Europe

Belgium

Brussels

Firm name	1-800-phone	Phone	Page
Agents Advantage	816-2211	908-355-2222	128
Air Travel Discounts, Inc.	888-2621	212-922-1326	18
Airplan	866-7526	412-257-3199	130
Alpha Travel	793-8424	770-988-9982	21
American Intl. Consolidators	888-5774	914-592-0206	131
Brendan Air	491-9633	800-491-9633	136
British Network, LTD	274-8583	201-744-8814	26
Campus Travel Center/Euroflgt	328-3359	612-338-5616	28
Centrav, Inc.	874-2033	612-948-8400	139
Council Charter	800-8222	212-661-0311	144
D-FW Tours	527-2589	214-980-4540	146
Fantasy Holidays	645-2555	516-935-8500	44
Favored Holidays Inc.		718-934-8881	46
HTI Tours	441-4411	215-563-8484	157
Jetset Tours Inc.	638-3273	312-362-9960	160
Millrun Tours	645-5786	312-641-5914	78
New Frontiers	366-6387	212-779-0600	80
Picasso Travel	PICASSO	310-645-4400	88
Pleasure Break Vacations, Inc.	777-1566	708-670-6300	170
Solar Tours	388-7652	202-861-6864	177
Trans Am Travel	822-7600	703-998-7676	184
Travac Tours & Charters	TRAV-800	212-563-3303	106
Tulips Travel	882-3383	212-490-3388	112
Worldvision Travel	545-7118	201-736-8210	117

Britain

Firm name	1-800-phone	Phone	Page
4th Dimension Tours	343-0020	305-279-0014	123
AESU	638-7640	410-323-4416	15
Agents Advantage	816-2211	908-355-2222	128
Air Travel Discounts, Inc.	888-2621	212-922-1326	18
Airplan	866-7526	412-257-3199	130
Alpha Travel	793-8424	770-988-9982	21
American Intl. Consolidators	888-5774	914-592-0206	131
Brendan Air	491-9633	800-491-9633	136
British Network, LTD	274-8583	201-744-8814	26
Campus Travel Center/Euroflgt	328-3359	612-338-5616	28
Fantasy Holidays	645-2555	516-935-8500	44
Favored Holidays Inc.		718-934-8881	46

Firms are listed by region, country, then city, according to the firm's specifications. Firms serving entire region are listed at the beginning of each region section.			
Firm name	*1-800-phone*	*Phone*	*Page*

Europe
Britain

Gate 1	682-3333	215-572-7676	153
Guardian Travel Service Inc.	741-3050	813-367-5622	55
Picasso Travel	PICASSO	310-645-4400	88
Pleasure Break Vacations, Inc.	777-1566	708-670-6300	170
Trans Am Travel	822-7600	703-998-7676	184
Travac Tours & Charters	TRAV-800	212-563-3303	106
Travel Expressions, Inc.	724-6274	212-338-9730	110
United Tours Corp	245-0203	212-245-1100	193
Value Holidays	558-6850	414-241-6373	115
Worldvision Travel	545-7118	201-736-8210	117

Birmingham

Air Travel Discounts, Inc.	888-2621	212-922-1326	18
Airplan	866-7526	412-257-3199	130
Centrav, Inc.	874-2033	612-948-8400	139
Fantasy Holidays	645-2555	516-935-8500	44
New Frontiers	366-6387	212-779-0600	80
Solar Tours	388-7652	202-861-6864	177
Travac Tours & Charters	TRAV-800	212-563-3303	106

Edinburgh

AESU	638-7640	410-323-4416	15
Agents Advantage	816-2211	908-355-2222	128
Alpha Travel	793-8424	770-988-9982	21
D-FW Tours	527-2589	214-980-4540	146
Picasso Travel	PICASSO	310-645-4400	88
Up & Away Travel	275-8001	212-889-2345	114

Glasgow

Agents Advantage	816-2211	908-355-2222	128
Air Travel Discounts, Inc.	888-2621	212-922-1326	18
Airplan	866-7526	412-257-3199	130
Alpha Travel	793-8424	770-988-9982	21
American Intl. Consolidators	888-5774	914-592-0206	131
Brendan Air	491-9633	800-491-9633	136
Guardian Travel Service Inc.	741-3050	813-367-5622	55
Jetset Tours Inc.	638-3273	312-362-9960	160
New Frontiers	366-6387	212-779-0600	80
Picasso Travel	PICASSO	310-645-4400	88
Solar Tours	388-7652	202-861-6864	177

Firm name	1-800-phone	Phone	Page
Europe			
Britain			
Glasgow			
Trans Am Travel	822-7600	703-998-7676	184
Travac Tours & Charters	TRAV-800	212-563-3303	106
Up & Away Travel	275-8001	212-889-2345	114
World Travel & Tours, Inc.	886-4WTT	703-379-6363	195
London			
Agents Advantage	816-2211	908-355-2222	128
Air Travel Discounts, Inc.	888-2621	212-922-1326	18
Airplan	866-7526	412-257-3199	130
Alpha Travel	793-8424	770-988-9982	21
American Intl. Consolidators	888-5774	914-592-0206	131
Brendan Air	491-9633	800-491-9633	136
British Network, LTD	274-8583	201-744-8814	26
Centrav, Inc.	874-2033	612-948-8400	139
Council Charter	800-8222	212-661-0311	144
D-FW Tours	527-2589	214-980-4540	146
DERAIR	717-4247	310-479-4411	37
Fantastiques Tours		310-577-6711	150
Fantasy Holidays	645-2555	516-935-8500	44
Favored Holidays Inc.		718-934-8881	46
Four Seasons Travel		910-292-1887	47
Guardian Travel Service Inc.	741-3050	813-367-5622	55
HTI Tours	441-4411	215-563-8484	157
Hudson Holidays	323-6855	708-452-0600	62
Interworld Travel	468-3796	305-443-4929	65
J & O Air	877-8111	619-282-4124	159
Jetset Tours Inc.	638-3273	312-362-9960	160
Leisure Resources	729-9051	203-874-4965	161
Millrun Tours	645-5786	312-641-5914	78
New Frontiers	366-6387	212-779-0600	80
Persvoyage Inc	455-7377	212-719-0900	87
Picasso Travel	PICASSO	310-645-4400	88
Skylink Travel	247-6659	212-573-8980	176
Skytours	246-8687	415-777-3544	96
Solar Tours	388-7652	202-861-6864	177
Supertravel		310-301-4567	102
Trans Am Travel	822-7600	703-998-7676	184
Travac Tours & Charters	TRAV-800	212-563-3303	106
Travel Associates	992-7388	213-933-7388	107

Firms are listed by region, country, then city, according to the firm's specifications. Firms serving entire region are listed at the beginning of each region section.

Firm name	1-800-phone	Phone	Page
Europe			
Britain			
London			
Travel Center	419-0960	212-545-7474	109
Tulips Travel	882-3383	212-490-3388	112
Up & Away Travel	275-8001	212-889-2345	114
Manchester			
AESU	638-7640	410-323-4416	15
Air Travel Discounts, Inc.	888-2621	212-922-1326	18
Airplan	866-7526	412-257-3199	130
Alpha Travel	793-8424	770-988-9982	21
American Intl. Consolidators	888-5774	914-592-0206	131
Brendan Air	491-9633	800-491-9633	136
Centrav, Inc.	874-2033	612-948-8400	139
D-FW Tours	527-2589	214-980-4540	146
Fantasy Holidays	645-2555	516-935-8500	44
Favored Holidays Inc.		718-934-8881	46
Guardian Travel Service Inc.	741-3050	813-367-5622	55
New Frontiers	366-6387	212-779-0600	80
Picasso Travel	PICASSO	310-645-4400	88
Solar Tours	388-7652	202-861-6864	177
Trans Am Travel	822-7600	703-998-7676	184
Travac Tours & Charters	TRAV-800	212-563-3303	106
Bulgaria			
Sofia			
Adventure Int'l Travel Service	542-2487	216-228-7171	16
Balkan Holidays	852-0944	212-573-5530	134
Cosmopolitan TVC Ctr	548-7206	305-523-0973	143
HTI Tours	441-4411	215-563-8484	157
Kompas Travel	233-6422	305-771-9200	70
Pleasure Break Vacations, Inc.	777-1566	708-670-6300	170
United Tours Corp	245-0203	212-245-1100	193
Worldvision Travel	545-7118	201-736-8210	117
Croatia			
Zagreb			
Adventure Int'l Travel Service	542-2487	216-228-7171	16
Cyprus			
Larnaca			
Cyprus Airways	333-2977	212-714-2190	

228

Firms are listed by region, country, then city, according to the firm's specifications. Firms serving entire region are listed at the beginning of each region section.

Firm name	1-800-phone	Phone	Page
	Europe		
	Cyprus		
	Larnaca		
Adventure Int'l Travel Service	542-2487	216-228-7171	16
Air Travel Discounts, Inc.	888-2621	212-922-1326	18
D-FW Tours	527-2589	214-980-4540	146
Homeric Tours, Inc.	223-5570	212-753-1100	60
Lotus	998-6116	212-213-1625	71
Sunny Land Tours	783-7839	201-487-2150	178
Tourlite International Inc.	272-7600	212-599-2727	182
Up & Away Travel	275-8001	212-889-2345	114
	Czech Republic		
	Prague		
AESU	638-7640	410-323-4416	15
Adventure Int'l Travel Service	542-2487	216-228-7171	16
Agents Advantage	816-2211	908-355-2222	128
Air Travel Discounts, Inc.	888-2621	212-922-1326	18
Alpha Travel	793-8424	770-988-9982	21
American Intl. Consolidators	888-5774	914-592-0206	131
Brendan Air	491-9633	800-491-9633	136
Cedok Central European Tour	800-8891	212-689-9720	30
Centrav, Inc.	874-2033	612-948-8400	139
D-FW Tours	527-2589	214-980-4540	146
Eastern European Travel Cent		718-339-1100	148
Favored Holidays Inc.		718-934-8881	46
GTI Travel Consolidators	829-8234	616-396-1234	50
HTI Tours	441-4411	215-563-8484	157
J & O Air	877-8111	619-282-4124	159
Kompas Travel	233-6422	305-771-9200	70
Millrun Tours	645-5786	312-641-5914	78
Orbis Polish Travel, Inc.	87-Orbis	212-867-5011	166
Picasso Travel	PICASSO	310-645-4400	88
Skylink Travel	247-6659	212-573-8980	176
Sunrise Tours	872-3801	212-947-3617	101
Trans Am Travel	822-7600	703-998-7676	184
United Tours Corp	245-0203	212-245-1100	193
Up & Away Travel	275-8001	212-889-2345	114
Value Holidays	558-6850	414-241-6373	115
Worldvision Travel	545-7118	201-736-8210	117

Firms are listed by region, country, then city, according to the firm's specifications. Firms serving entire region are listed at the beginning of each region section.			
Firm name	1-800-phone	Phone	Page

Europe

Denmark

Copenhagen

Firm name	1-800-phone	Phone	Page
AESU	638-7640	410-323-4416	15
Agents Advantage	816-2211	908-355-2222	128
Air Travel Discounts, Inc.	888-2621	212-922-1326	18
Alpha Travel	793-8424	770-988-9982	21
Brendan Air	491-9633	800-491-9633	136
Centrav, Inc.	874-2033	612-948-8400	139
D-FW Tours	527-2589	214-980-4540	146
Favored Holidays Inc.		718-934-8881	46
HTI Tours	441-4411	215-563-8484	157
Jetset Tours Inc.	638-3273	312-362-9960	160
Picasso Travel	PICASSO	310-645-4400	88
Pleasure Break Vacations, Inc.	777-1566	708-670-6300	170
Skylink Travel	247-6659	212-573-8980	176
Skytours	246-8687	415-777-3544	96
Travac Tours & Charters	TRAV-800	212-563-3303	106
Value Holidays	558-6850	414-241-6373	115
Worldvision Travel	545-7118	201-736-8210	117

Estonia

Tallinn

Firm name	1-800-phone	Phone	Page
Air Travel Discounts, Inc.	888-2621	212-922-1326	18
Eastern European Travel Cent		718-339-1100	148
Favored Holidays Inc.		718-934-8881	46
Millrun Tours	645-5786	312-641-5914	78
Palm Coast Tours & Travel	444-1560	407-433-1558	85
Rahim Tours	556-5305	407-585-5305	173

Finland

Helsinki

Firm name	1-800-phone	Phone	Page
AESU	638-7640	410-323-4416	15
Agents Advantage	816-2211	908-355-2222	128
Air Travel Discounts, Inc.	888-2621	212-922-1326	18
Alpha Travel	793-8424	770-988-9982	21
Brendan Air	491-9633	800-491-9633	136
Centrav, Inc.	874-2033	612-948-8400	139
D-FW Tours	527-2589	214-980-4540	146
Eastern European Travel Cent		718-339-1100	148
Favored Holidays Inc.		718-934-8881	46
HTI Tours	441-4411	215-563-8484	157

Firms are listed by region, country, then city, according to the firm's specifications. Firms serving entire region are listed at the beginning of each region section.			
Firm name	1-800-phone	Phone	Page

Europe
Finland
Helsinki

Jetset Tours Inc.	638-3273	312-362-9960	160
Millrun Tours	645-5786	312-641-5914	78
Palm Coast Tours & Travel	444-1560	407-433-1558	85
Picasso Travel	PICASSO	310-645-4400	88
Pleasure Break Vacations, Inc.	777-1566	708-670-6300	170
Rahim Tours	556-5305	407-585-5305	173
Skytours	246-8687	415-777-3544	96
Sunny Land Tours	783-7839	201-487-2150	178
Sunrise Tours	872-3801	212-947-3617	101
Travac Tours & Charters	TRAV-800	212-563-3303	106
United Tours Corp	245-0203	212-245-1100	193
Up & Away Travel	275-8001	212-889-2345	114
Worldvision Travel	545-7118	201-736-8210	117

France

4th Dimension Tours	343-0020	305-279-0014	123
AESU	638-7640	410-323-4416	15
Air Travel Discounts, Inc.	888-2621	212-922-1326	18
Airplan	866-7526	412-257-3199	130
Alpha Travel	793-8424	770-988-9982	21
American Intl. Consolidators	888-5774	914-592-0206	131
Brendan Air	491-9633	800-491-9633	136
Campus Travel Center/Euroflgt	328-3359	612-338-5616	28
Central Holidays	935-5000		138
Council Charter	800-8222	212-661-0311	144
Gate 1	682-3333	215-572-7676	153
Guardian Travel Service Inc.	741-3050	813-367-5622	55
Millrun Tours	645-5786	312-641-5914	78
Picasso Travel	PICASSO	310-645-4400	88
Pleasure Break Vacations, Inc.	777-1566	708-670-6300	170
Travac Tours & Charters	TRAV-800	212-563-3303	106
Value Holidays	558-6850	414-241-6373	115
Worldvision Travel	545-7118	201-736-8210	117

Bordeaux

AESU	638-7640	410-323-4416	15
Travac Tours & Charters	TRAV-800	212-563-3303	106
Up & Away Travel	275-8001	212-889-2345	114

Firms are listed by region, country, then city, according to the firm's specifications. Firms serving entire region are listed at the beginning of each region section.			
Firm name	1-800-phone	Phone	Page

Europe
France
Lyon

AESU	638-7640	410-323-4416	15
Air Travel Discounts, Inc.	888-2621	212-922-1326	18
Alpha Travel	793-8424	770-988-9982	21
Brendan Air	491-9633	800-491-9633	136
Centrav, Inc.	874-2033	612-948-8400	139
Guardian Travel Service Inc.	741-3050	813-367-5622	55
HTI Tours	441-4411	215-563-8484	157
New Frontiers	366-6387	212-779-0600	80
Travac Tours & Charters	TRAV-800	212-563-3303	106
Up & Away Travel	275-8001	212-889-2345	114

Marseille

AESU	638-7640	410-323-4416	15
Air Travel Discounts, Inc.	888-2621	212-922-1326	18
Alpha Travel	793-8424	770-988-9982	21
Brendan Air	491-9633	800-491-9633	136
Council Charter	800-8222	212-661-0311	144
New Frontiers	366-6387	212-779-0600	80
Picasso Travel	PICASSO	310-645-4400	88
Travac Tours & Charters	TRAV-800	212-563-3303	106
Up & Away Travel	275-8001	212-889-2345	114

Nice

AESU	638-7640	410-323-4416	15
Air Travel Discounts, Inc.	888-2621	212-922-1326	18
Airplan	866-7526	412-257-3199	130
Alpha Travel	793-8424	770-988-9982	21
American Intl. Consolidators	888-5774	914-592-0206	131
Brendan Air	491-9633	800-491-9633	136
Council Charter	800-8222	212-661-0311	144
D-FW Tours	527-2589	214-980-4540	146
Guardian Travel Service Inc.	741-3050	813-367-5622	55
Jetset Tours Inc.	638-3273	312-362-9960	160
Millrun Tours	645-5786	312-641-5914	78
New Frontiers	366-6387	212-779-0600	80
Picasso Travel	PICASSO	310-645-4400	88
Trans Am Travel	822-7600	703-998-7676	184
Travac Tours & Charters	TRAV-800	212-563-3303	106
Up & Away Travel	275-8001	212-889-2345	114

Firm name	1-800-phone	Phone	Page
Europe			
France			
Nice			
World Travel & Tours, Inc.	886-4WTT	703-379-6363	195
Paris			
AESU	638-7640	410-323-4416	15
Agents Advantage	816-2211	908-355-2222	128
Air Travel Discounts, Inc.	888-2621	212-922-1326	18
Airplan	866-7526	412-257-3199	130
Alpha Travel	793-8424	770-988-9982	21
American Intl. Consolidators	888-5774	914-592-0206	131
Brendan Air	491-9633	800-491-9633	136
British Network, LTD	274-8583	201-744-8814	26
Central Tours	783-9882	201-344-2489	31
Centrav, Inc.	874-2033	612-948-8400	139
Council Charter	800-8222	212-661-0311	144
D-FW Tours	527-2589	214-980-4540	146
Fantastiques Tours		310-577-6711	150
Fantasy Holidays	645-2555	516-935-8500	44
Favored Holidays Inc.		718-934-8881	46
Guardian Travel Service Inc.	741-3050	813-367-5622	55
Jetset Tours Inc.	638-3273	312-362-9960	160
Millrun Tours	645-5786	312-641-5914	78
New Frontiers	366-6387	212-779-0600	80
Persvoyage Inc	455-7377	212-719-0900	87
Picasso Travel	PICASSO	310-645-4400	88
Skylink Travel	247-6659	212-573-8980	176
Skytours	246-8687	415-777-3544	96
Solar Tours	388-7652	202-861-6864	177
Supertravel		310-301-4567	102
Trans Am Travel	822-7600	703-998-7676	184
Travac Tours & Charters	TRAV-800	212-563-3303	106
Travel Associates	992-7388	213-933-7388	107
Travel Center	419-0960	212-545-7474	109
Tulips Travel	882-3383	212-490-3388	112
World Travel & Tours, Inc.	886-4WTT	703-379-6363	195
Toulouse			
Alpha Travel	793-8424	770-988-9982	21
Brendan Air	491-9633	800-491-9633	136
Centrav, Inc.	874-2033	612-948-8400	139

Firm name	1-800-phone	Phone	Page

Europe

France

Toulouse

Firm name	1-800-phone	Phone	Page
Travac Tours & Charters	TRAV-800	212-563-3303	106

Germany

Firm name	1-800-phone	Phone	Page
4th Dimension Tours	343-0020	305-279-0014	123
AESU	638-7640	410-323-4416	15
Agents Advantage	816-2211	908-355-2222	128
Air Travel Discounts, Inc.	888-2621	212-922-1326	18
Airplan	866-7526	412-257-3199	130
Alpha Travel	793-8424	770-988-9982	21
Brendan Air	491-9633	800-491-9633	136
Campus Travel Center/Euroflgt	328-3359	612-338-5616	28
Council Charter	800-8222	212-661-0311	144
Fantasy Holidays	645-2555	516-935-8500	44
Favored Holidays Inc.		718-934-8881	46
Gate 1	682-3333	215-572-7676	153
Guardian Travel Service Inc.	741-3050	813-367-5622	55
Kompas Travel	233-6422	305-771-9200	70
Picasso Travel	PICASSO	310-645-4400	88
Pleasure Break Vacations, Inc.	777-1566	708-670-6300	170
Skylink Travel	247-6659	212-573-8980	176
Specialty Tours Int'l USA Inc.	421-3913	310-568-8709	99
Trans Am Travel	822-7600	703-998-7676	184
Travac Tours & Charters	TRAV-800	212-563-3303	106
Travel Expressions, Inc.	724-6274	212-338-9730	110
Value Holidays	558-6850	414-241-6373	115
Worldvision Travel	545-7118	201-736-8210	117

Berlin

Firm name	1-800-phone	Phone	Page
AESU	638-7640	410-323-4416	15
Agents Advantage	816-2211	908-355-2222	128
Air Travel Discounts, Inc.	888-2621	212-922-1326	18
Airplan	866-7526	412-257-3199	130
Alpha Travel	793-8424	770-988-9982	21
Brendan Air	491-9633	800-491-9633	136
Centrav, Inc.	874-2033	612-948-8400	139
D-FW Tours	527-2589	214-980-4540	146
Fantastiques Tours		310-577-6711	150
Guardian Travel Service Inc.	741-3050	813-367-5622	55
Millrun Tours	645-5786	312-641-5914	78

Firm name	1-800-phone	Phone	Page

Firms are listed by region, country, then city, according to the firm's specifications. Firms serving entire region are listed at the beginning of each region section.

Europe

Germany

Berlin

Firm name	1-800-phone	Phone	Page
Picasso Travel	PICASSO	310-645-4400	88
Skylink Travel	247-6659	212-573-8980	176
Skytours	246-8687	415-777-3544	96
Supertravel		310-301-4567	102
Trans Am Travel	822-7600	703-998-7676	184
Travac Tours & Charters	TRAV-800	212-563-3303	106
United Tours Corp	245-0203	212-245-1100	193
Up & Away Travel	275-8001	212-889-2345	114

Cologne

Firm name	1-800-phone	Phone	Page
AESU	638-7640	410-323-4416	15
D-FW Tours	527-2589	214-980-4540	146
Up & Away Travel	275-8001	212-889-2345	114

Dusseldorf

Firm name	1-800-phone	Phone	Page
AESU	638-7640	410-323-4416	15
Air Travel Discounts, Inc.	888-2621	212-922-1326	18
Airplan	866-7526	412-257-3199	130
Alpha Travel	793-8424	770-988-9982	21
Brendan Air	491-9633	800-491-9633	136
Centrav, Inc.	874-2033	612-948-8400	139
Council Charter	800-8222	212-661-0311	144
D-FW Tours	527-2589	214-980-4540	146
Fantasy Holidays	645-2555	516-935-8500	44
Favored Holidays Inc.		718-934-8881	46
Guardian Travel Service Inc.	741-3050	813-367-5622	55
Picasso Travel	PICASSO	310-645-4400	88
Solar Tours	388-7652	202-861-6864	177
Trans Am Travel	822-7600	703-998-7676	184
Travac Tours & Charters	TRAV-800	212-563-3303	106
Up & Away Travel	275-8001	212-889-2345	114

Frankfurt

Firm name	1-800-phone	Phone	Page
AESU	638-7640	410-323-4416	15
Agents Advantage	816-2211	908-355-2222	128
Air Travel Discounts, Inc.	888-2621	212-922-1326	18
Airplan	866-7526	412-257-3199	130
Alpha Travel	793-8424	770-988-9982	21
American Intl. Consolidators	888-5774	914-592-0206	131
Brendan Air	491-9633	800-491-9633	136

Firm name	1-800-phone	Phone	Page

Europe

Germany

Frankfurt

Firm name	1-800-phone	Phone	Page
British Network, LTD	274-8583	201-744-8814	26
Centrav, Inc.	874-2033	612-948-8400	139
Council Charter	800-8222	212-661-0311	144
D-FW Tours	527-2589	214-980-4540	146
DERAIR	717-4247	310-479-4411	37
Fantastiques Tours		310-577-6711	150
Fantasy Holidays	645-2555	516-935-8500	44
Favored Holidays Inc.		718-934-8881	46
Guardian Travel Service Inc.	741-3050	813-367-5622	55
HTI Tours	441-4411	215-563-8484	157
Jetset Tours Inc.	638-3273	312-362-9960	160
New Frontiers	366-6387	212-779-0600	80
Persvoyage Inc	455-7377	212-719-0900	87
Picasso Travel	PICASSO	310-645-4400	88
Skylink Travel	247-6659	212-573-8980	176
Skytours	246-8687	415-777-3544	96
Solar Tours	388-7652	202-861-6864	177
Sunrise Tours	872-3801	212-947-3617	101
Supertravel		310-301-4567	102
Trans Am Travel	822-7600	703-998-7676	184
Travac Tours & Charters	TRAV-800	212-563-3303	106
Travel Associates	992-7388	213-933-7388	107
Travel Center	419-0960	212-545-7474	109
Tulips Travel	882-3383	212-490-3388	112
Up & Away Travel	275-8001	212-889-2345	114
World Travel & Tours, Inc.	886-4WTT	703-379-6363	195

Hamburg

Firm name	1-800-phone	Phone	Page
AESU	638-7640	410-323-4416	15
Air Travel Discounts, Inc.	888-2621	212-922-1326	18
Alpha Travel	793-8424	770-988-9982	21
Brendan Air	491-9633	800-491-9633	136
Centrav, Inc.	874-2033	612-948-8400	139
D-FW Tours	527-2589	214-980-4540	146
Favored Holidays Inc.		718-934-8881	46
Guardian Travel Service Inc.	741-3050	813-367-5622	55
Picasso Travel	PICASSO	310-645-4400	88
Trans Am Travel	822-7600	703-998-7676	184
Travac Tours & Charters	TRAV-800	212-563-3303	106

Part IV - Consolidators and Wholesalers by Destination

Firm name	1-800-phone	Phone	Page

Europe
Germany
Hamburg

| Up & Away Travel | 275-8001 | 212-889-2345 | 114 |

Hanover

AESU	638-7640	410-323-4416	15
Air Travel Discounts, Inc.	888-2621	212-922-1326	18
Alpha Travel	793-8424	770-988-9982	21
Brendan Air	491-9633	800-491-9633	136
Centrav, Inc.	874-2033	612-948-8400	139
Picasso Travel	PICASSO	310-645-4400	88
Up & Away Travel	275-8001	212-889-2345	114

Munich

AESU	638-7640	410-323-4416	15
Air Travel Discounts, Inc.	888-2621	212-922-1326	18
Alpha Travel	793-8424	770-988-9982	21
Brendan Air	491-9633	800-491-9633	136
Centrav, Inc.	874-2033	612-948-8400	139
D-FW Tours	527-2589	214-980-4540	146
Favored Holidays Inc.		718-934-8881	46
HTI Tours	441-4411	215-563-8484	157
Jetset Tours Inc.	638-3273	312-362-9960	160
Leisure Resources	729-9051	203-874-4965	161
Picasso Travel	PICASSO	310-645-4400	88
Solar Tours	388-7652	202-861-6864	177
Trans Am Travel	822-7600	703-998-7676	184
Up & Away Travel	275-8001	212-889-2345	114

Stuttgart

AESU	638-7640	410-323-4416	15
Alpha Travel	793-8424	770-988-9982	21
Brendan Air	491-9633	800-491-9633	136
Centrav, Inc.	874-2033	612-948-8400	139
D-FW Tours	527-2589	214-980-4540	146
Favored Holidays Inc.		718-934-8881	46
Travac Tours & Charters	TRAV-800	212-563-3303	106
Up & Away Travel	275-8001	212-889-2345	114

Greece
Athens

| 4th Dimension Tours | 343-0020 | 305-279-0014 | 123 |

237

Firms are listed by region, country, then city, according to the firm's specifications. Firms serving entire region are listed at the beginning of each region section.			
Firm name	1-800-phone	Phone	Page

Europe

Greece

Athens

Firm name	1-800-phone	Phone	Page
AESU	638-7640	410-323-4416	15
Abratours	227-2887	914-949-3300	126
Agents Advantage	816-2211	908-355-2222	128
Air Brokers Int'l, Inc.	883-3273	415-397-1383	17
Airplan	866-7526	412-257-3199	130
Alpha Travel	793-8424	770-988-9982	21
American Intl. Consolidators	888-5774	914-592-0206	131
Brendan Air	491-9633	800-491-9633	136
Campus Travel Center/Euroflgt	328-3359	612-338-5616	28
Cathay Travel		818-571-6727	29
Central Holidays	935-5000		138
Centrav, Inc.	874-2033	612-948-8400	139
Cosmopolitan TVC Ctr	548-7206	305-523-0973	143
D-FW Tours	527-2589	214-980-4540	146
Fantastiques Tours		310-577-6711	150
Fantasy Holidays	645-2555	516-935-8500	44
Favored Holidays Inc.		718-934-8881	46
Gate 1	682-3333	215-572-7676	153
HTI Tours	441-4411	215-563-8484	157
Homeric Tours, Inc.	223-5570	212-753-1100	60
Interworld Travel	468-3796	305-443-4929	65
Jetset Tours Inc.	638-3273	312-362-9960	160
Kompas Travel	233-6422	305-771-9200	70
Lotus	998-6116	212-213-1625	71
Lucky Tours	932-6654	308-762-3957	72
Picasso Travel	PICASSO	310-645-4400	88
Pleasure Break Vacations, Inc.	777-1566	708-670-6300	170
Skylink Travel	247-6659	212-573-8980	176
Sunny Land Tours	783-7839	201-487-2150	178
Supertravel		310-301-4567	102
Tourlite International Inc.	272-7600	212-599-2727	182
Trans Am Travel	822-7600	703-998-7676	184
Travac Tours & Charters	TRAV-800	212-563-3303	106
Travel Associates	992-7388	213-933-7388	107
United Tours Corp	245-0203	212-245-1100	193
Up & Away Travel	275-8001	212-889-2345	114
World Travel & Tours, Inc.	886-4WTT	703-379-6363	195
Worldvision Travel	545-7118	201-736-8210	117

Firms are listed by region, country, then city, according to the firm's specifications. Firms serving entire region are listed at the beginning of each region section.			
Firm name	1-800-phone	Phone	Page

Europe

Greece

Athens

Wright Travel Holidays	877-3240	212-570-0969	196

Thessaloniki

AESU	638-7640	410-323-4416	15
Homeric Tours, Inc.	223-5570	212-753-1100	60
Tourlite International Inc.	272-7600	212-599-2727	182

Holland

Amsterdam

4th Dimension Tours	343-0020	305-279-0014	123
AESU	638-7640	410-323-4416	15
Agents Advantage	816-2211	908-355-2222	128
Air Travel Discounts, Inc.	888-2621	212-922-1326	18
Airplan	866-7526	412-257-3199	130
Alpha Travel	793-8424	770-988-9982	21
American Intl. Consolidators	888-5774	914-592-0206	131
Brendan Air	491-9633	800-491-9633	136
Centrav, Inc.	874-2033	612-948-8400	139
Council Charter	800-8222	212-661-0311	144
D-FW Tours	527-2589	214-980-4540	146
Fantasy Holidays	645-2555	516-935-8500	44
Favored Holidays Inc.		718-934-8881	46
Guardian Travel Service Inc.	741-3050	813-367-5622	55
HTI Tours	441-4411	215-563-8484	157
Jetset Tours Inc.	638-3273	312-362-9960	160
Kompas Travel	233-6422	305-771-9200	70
Millrun Tours	645-5786	312-641-5914	78
New Frontiers	366-6387	212-779-0600	80
Picasso Travel	PICASSO	310-645-4400	88
Pleasure Break Vacations, Inc.	777-1566	708-670-6300	170
Skylink Travel	247-6659	212-573-8980	176
Sunrise Tours	872-3801	212-947-3617	101
Trans Am Travel	822-7600	703-998-7676	184
Travac Tours & Charters	TRAV-800	212-563-3303	106
Tulips Travel	882-3383	212-490-3388	112
Up & Away Travel	275-8001	212-889-2345	114
Worldvision Travel	545-7118	201-736-8210	117

Firms are listed by region, country, then city, according to the firm's specifications. Firms serving entire region are listed at the beginning of each region section.			
Firm name	*1-800-phone*	*Phone*	*Page*

Europe

Hungary

Budapest

Firm name	1-800-phone	Phone	Page
AESU	638-7640	410-323-4416	15
Adventure Int'l Travel Service	542-2487	216-228-7171	16
Agents Advantage	816-2211	908-355-2222	128
Air Travel Discounts, Inc.	888-2621	212-922-1326	18
Alpha Travel	793-8424	770-988-9982	21
American Intl. Consolidators	888-5774	914-592-0206	131
Brendan Air	491-9633	800-491-9633	136
Cedok Central European Tour	800-8891	212-689-9720	30
Centrav, Inc.	874-2033	612-948-8400	139
Cosmopolitan TVC Ctr	548-7206	305-523-0973	143
D-FW Tours	527-2589	214-980-4540	146
Eastern European Travel Cent		718-339-1100	148
Fantastiques Tours		310-577-6711	150
Favored Holidays Inc.		718-934-8881	46
GTI Travel Consolidators	829-8234	616-396-1234	50
HTI Tours	441-4411	215-563-8484	157
Jetset Tours Inc.	638-3273	312-362-9960	160
Kompas Travel	233-6422	305-771-9200	70
Millrun Tours	645-5786	312-641-5914	78
Orbis Polish Travel, Inc.	87-Orbis	212-867-5011	166
Paul Laifer Tours Inc.	346-6314	201-887-1188	86
Picasso Travel	PICASSO	310-645-4400	88
Pleasure Break Vacations, Inc.	777-1566	708-670-6300	170
Skylink Travel	247-6659	212-573-8980	176
Supertravel		310-301-4567	102
Trans Am Travel	822-7600	703-998-7676	184
Travac Tours & Charters	TRAV-800	212-563-3303	106
United Tours Corp	245-0203	212-245-1100	193
Up & Away Travel	275-8001	212-889-2345	114
Value Holidays	558-6850	414-241-6373	115
Worldvision Travel	545-7118	201-736-8210	117

Ireland

Firm name	1-800-phone	Phone	Page
AESU	638-7640	410-323-4416	15
Agents Advantage	816-2211	908-355-2222	128
Brendan Air	491-9633	800-491-9633	136
HTI Tours	441-4411	215-563-8484	157
Hudson Holidays	323-6855	708-452-0600	62

Part IV - Consolidators and Wholesalers by Destination

Firm name	1-800-phone	Phone	Page
Europe			
Ireland			
Pleasure Break Vacations, Inc.	777-1566	708-670-6300	170
Travac Tours & Charters	TRAV-800	212-563-3303	106
Value Holidays	558-6850	414-241-6373	115
Worldvision Travel	545-7118	201-736-8210	117
Belfast			
AESU	638-7640	410-323-4416	15
Agents Advantage	816-2211	908-355-2222	128
Brendan Air	491-9633	800-491-9633	136
Centrav, Inc.	874-2033	612-948-8400	139
Fantastiques Tours		310-577-6711	150
Jetset Tours Inc.	638-3273	312-362-9960	160
Supertravel		310-301-4567	102
Travac Tours & Charters	TRAV-800	212-563-3303	106
Up & Away Travel	275-8001	212-889-2345	114
Dublin			
AESU	638-7640	410-323-4416	15
Agents Advantage	816-2211	908-355-2222	128
Brendan Air	491-9633	800-491-9633	136
D-FW Tours	527-2589	214-980-4540	146
Fantastiques Tours		310-577-6711	150
Guardian Travel Service Inc.	741-3050	813-367-5622	55
Hudson Holidays	323-6855	708-452-0600	62
Supertravel		310-301-4567	102
Travac Tours & Charters	TRAV-800	212-563-3303	106
Shannon			
AESU	638-7640	410-323-4416	15
Brendan Air	491-9633	800-491-9633	136
GTI Travel Consolidators	829-8234	616-396-1234	50
Hudson Holidays	323-6855	708-452-0600	62
Travac Tours & Charters	TRAV-800	212-563-3303	106
Italy			
4th Dimension Tours	343-0020	305-279-0014	123
AESU	638-7640	410-323-4416	15
Agents Advantage	816-2211	908-355-2222	128
Air Travel Discounts, Inc.	888-2621	212-922-1326	18
Airplan	866-7526	412-257-3199	130

Firms are listed by region, country, then city, according to the firm's specifications. Firms serving entire region are listed at the beginning of each region section.			
Firm name	*1-800-phone*	*Phone*	*Page*

Europe
Italy

Firm name	1-800-phone	Phone	Page
Alpha Travel	793-8424	770-988-9982	21
American Intl. Consolidators	888-5774	914-592-0206	131
Brendan Air	491-9633	800-491-9633	136
Campus Travel Center/Euroflgt	328-3359	612-338-5616	28
Central Holidays	935-5000		138
Council Charter	800-8222	212-661-0311	144
Fantasy Holidays	645-2555	516-935-8500	44
Favored Holidays Inc.		718-934-8881	46
Gate 1	682-3333	215-572-7676	153
Guardian Travel Service Inc.	741-3050	813-367-5622	55
HTI Tours	441-4411	215-563-8484	157
Hudson Holidays	323-6855	708-452-0600	62
Millrun Tours	645-5786	312-641-5914	78
Persvoyage Inc	455-7377	212-719-0900	87
Picasso Travel	PICASSO	310-645-4400	88
Pleasure Break Vacations, Inc.	777-1566	708-670-6300	170
Skylink Travel	247-6659	212-573-8980	176
Trans Am Travel	822-7600	703-998-7676	184
Travac Tours & Charters	TRAV-800	212-563-3303	106
Travel Expressions, Inc.	724-6274	212-338-9730	110
Value Holidays	558-6850	414-241-6373	115
Worldvision Travel	545-7118	201-736-8210	117

Bari

Firm name	1-800-phone	Phone	Page
Central Holidays	935-5000		138

Bologna

Firm name	1-800-phone	Phone	Page
AESU	638-7640	410-323-4416	15
Central Holidays	935-5000		138
Fantasy Holidays	645-2555	516-935-8500	44
Jetset Tours Inc.	638-3273	312-362-9960	160
Travac Tours & Charters	TRAV-800	212-563-3303	106
Up & Away Travel	275-8001	212-889-2345	114

Catania

Firm name	1-800-phone	Phone	Page
Central Holidays	935-5000		138

Florence

Firm name	1-800-phone	Phone	Page
Air Travel Discounts, Inc.	888-2621	212-922-1326	18
Central Holidays	935-5000		138
Leisure Resources	729-9051	203-874-4965	161

Firms are listed by region, country, then city, according to the firm's specifications. Firms serving entire region are listed at the beginning of each region section.			
Firm name	1-800-phone	Phone	Page

Europe
Italy
Genoa

Firm name	1-800-phone	Phone	Page
AESU	638-7640	410-323-4416	15
Central Holidays	935-5000		138
Up & Away Travel	275-8001	212-889-2345	114

Milan

Firm name	1-800-phone	Phone	Page
AESU	638-7640	410-323-4416	15
Air Travel Discounts, Inc.	888-2621	212-922-1326	18
Airplan	866-7526	412-257-3199	130
Alpha Travel	793-8424	770-988-9982	21
American Intl. Consolidators	888-5774	914-592-0206	131
Brendan Air	491-9633	800-491-9633	136
Central Holidays	935-5000		138
Centrav, Inc.	874-2033	612-948-8400	139
Council Charter	800-8222	212-661-0311	144
D-FW Tours	527-2589	214-980-4540	146
Fantastiques Tours		310-577-6711	150
Fantasy Holidays	645-2555	516-935-8500	44
Favored Holidays Inc.		718-934-8881	46
HTI Tours	441-4411	215-563-8484	157
Jetset Tours Inc.	638-3273	312-362-9960	160
Kompas Travel	233-6422	305-771-9200	70
New Frontiers	366-6387	212-779-0600	80
Persvoyage Inc	455-7377	212-719-0900	87
Picasso Travel	PICASSO	310-645-4400	88
Skylink Travel	247-6659	212-573-8980	176
Solar Tours	388-7652	202-861-6864	177
Supertravel		310-301-4567	102
Trans Am Travel	822-7600	703-998-7676	184
Travac Tours & Charters	TRAV-800	212-563-3303	106
Travel Associates	992-7388	213-933-7388	107
Up & Away Travel	275-8001	212-889-2345	114
World Travel & Tours, Inc.	886-4WTT	703-379-6363	195

Naples

Firm name	1-800-phone	Phone	Page
AESU	638-7640	410-323-4416	15
Airplan	866-7526	412-257-3199	130
Central Holidays	935-5000		138
D-FW Tours	527-2589	214-980-4540	146
Travac Tours & Charters	TRAV-800	212-563-3303	106

Firms are listed by region, country, then city, according to the firm's specifications. Firms serving entire region are listed at the beginning of each region section.

Firm name	1-800-phone	Phone	Page
Europe			
Italy			
Naples			
Up & Away Travel	275-8001	212-889-2345	114
Palermo			
Central Holidays	935-5000		138
Pisa			
AESU	638-7640	410-323-4416	15
Central Holidays	935-5000		138
Travac Tours & Charters	TRAV-800	212-563-3303	106
Up & Away Travel	275-8001	212-889-2345	114
Rome			
AESU	638-7640	410-323-4416	15
Agents Advantage	816-2211	908-355-2222	128
Air Travel Discounts, Inc.	888-2621	212-922-1326	18
Airplan	866-7526	412-257-3199	130
Alpha Travel	793-8424	770-988-9982	21
Brendan Air	491-9633	800-491-9633	136
Central Tours	783-9882	201-344-2489	31
Centrav, Inc.	874-2033	612-948-8400	139
Council Charter	800-8222	212-661-0311	144
D-FW Tours	527-2589	214-980-4540	146
Favored Holidays Inc.		718-934-8881	46
Kompas Travel	233-6422	305-771-9200	70
Millrun Tours	645-5786	312-641-5914	78
New Frontiers	366-6387	212-779-0600	80
Palm Coast Tours & Travel	444-1560	407-433-1558	85
Persvoyage Inc	455-7377	212-719-0900	87
Picasso Travel	PICASSO	310-645-4400	88
Skylink Travel	247-6659	212-573-8980	176
Travac Tours & Charters	TRAV-800	212-563-3303	106
Travel Associates	992-7388	213-933-7388	107
Travel Center	419-0960	212-545-7474	109
Tulips Travel	882-3383	212-490-3388	112
Up & Away Travel	275-8001	212-889-2345	114
World Travel & Tours, Inc.	886-4WTT	703-379-6363	195
Turin			
AESU	638-7640	410-323-4416	15
Alpha Travel	793-8424	770-988-9982	21

Firms are listed by region, country, then city, according to the firm's specifications. Firms serving entire region are listed at the beginning of each region section.			
Firm name	1-800-phone	Phone	Page

Europe

Italy

Turin

Brendan Air	491-9633	800-491-9633	136
Up & Away Travel	275-8001	212-889-2345	114

Venice

AESU	638-7640	410-323-4416	15
Agents Advantage	816-2211	908-355-2222	128
Air Travel Discounts, Inc.	888-2621	212-922-1326	18
Alpha Travel	793-8424	770-988-9982	21
Brendan Air	491-9633	800-491-9633	136
Centrav, Inc.	874-2033	612-948-8400	139
Millrun Tours	645-5786	312-641-5914	78
Picasso Travel	PICASSO	310-645-4400	88
Travac Tours & Charters	TRAV-800	212-563-3303	106
Up & Away Travel	275-8001	212-889-2345	114

Verona

AESU	638-7640	410-323-4416	15

Latvia

Riga

Adventure Int'l Travel Service	542-2487	216-228-7171	16
Air Travel Discounts, Inc.	888-2621	212-922-1326	18
Eastern European Travel Cent		718-339-1100	148
Favored Holidays Inc.		718-934-8881	46
Palm Coast Tours & Travel	444-1560	407-433-1558	85
Rahim Tours	556-5305	407-585-5305	173
United Tours Corp	245-0203	212-245-1100	193

Lithuania

Vilnius

Air Travel Discounts, Inc.	888-2621	212-922-1326	18
American Travel Abroad Inc	228-0877	212-586-5230	132
Eastern European Travel Cent		718-339-1100	148
Favored Holidays Inc.		718-934-8881	46
Millrun Tours	645-5786	312-641-5914	78
Palm Coast Tours & Travel	444-1560	407-433-1558	85
Rahim Tours	556-5305	407-585-5305	173
United Tours Corp	245-0203	212-245-1100	193

Firm name	1-800-phone	Phone	Page

Firms are listed by region, country, then city, according to the firm's specifications. Firms serving entire region are listed at the beginning of each region section.

Europe
Luxembourg
Luxembourg

Firm name	1-800-phone	Phone	Page
AESU	638-7640	410-323-4416	15
Alpha Travel	793-8424	770-988-9982	21
Brendan Air	491-9633	800-491-9633	136
Centrav, Inc.	874-2033	612-948-8400	139
D-FW Tours	527-2589	214-980-4540	146
HTI Tours	441-4411	215-563-8484	157
Millrun Tours	645-5786	312-641-5914	78
Picasso Travel	PICASSO	310-645-4400	88

Macedonian Republic
Skopje

Firm name	1-800-phone	Phone	Page
Balkan Holidays	852-0944	212-573-5530	134

Malta

Firm name	1-800-phone	Phone	Page
Cosmopolitan TVC Ctr	548-7206	305-523-0973	143
Lotus	998-6116	212-213-1625	71
Pinto Basto USA	526-8539	212-226-9056	90

Norway
Oslo

Firm name	1-800-phone	Phone	Page
AESU	638-7640	410-323-4416	15
Agents Advantage	816-2211	908-355-2222	128
Air Travel Discounts, Inc.	888-2621	212-922-1326	18
Alpha Travel	793-8424	770-988-9982	21
Brendan Air	491-9633	800-491-9633	136
Centrav, Inc.	874-2033	612-948-8400	139
D-FW Tours	527-2589	214-980-4540	146
Favored Holidays Inc.		718-934-8881	46
Guardian Travel Service Inc.	741-3050	813-367-5622	55
HTI Tours	441-4411	215-563-8484	157
Jetset Tours Inc.	638-3273	312-362-9960	160
Millrun Tours	645-5786	312-641-5914	78
Picasso Travel	PICASSO	310-645-4400	88
Pleasure Break Vacations, Inc.	777-1566	708-670-6300	170
Rahim Tours	556-5305	407-585-5305	173
Skylink Travel	247-6659	212-573-8980	176
Skytours	246-8687	415-777-3544	96
Trans Am Travel	822-7600	703-998-7676	184
Travac Tours & Charters	TRAV-800	212-563-3303	106

Firms are listed by region, country, then city, according to the firm's specifications. Firms serving entire region are listed at the beginning of each region section.			
Firm name	1-800-phone	Phone	Page

Europe

Norway

Oslo

Up & Away Travel	275-8001	212-889-2345	114
Worldvision Travel	545-7118	201-736-8210	117

Poland

Warsaw

Agents Advantage	816-2211	908-355-2222	128
Air Travel Discounts, Inc.	888-2621	212-922-1326	18
Alpha Travel	793-8424	770-988-9982	21
American Intl. Consolidators	888-5774	914-592-0206	131
American Travel Abroad Inc	228-0877	212-586-5230	132
Brendan Air	491-9633	800-491-9633	136
Centrav, Inc.	874-2033	612-948-8400	139
Consolidated Tours, Inc.	228-0877	212-586-5230	142
D-FW Tours	527-2589	214-980-4540	146
Favored Holidays Inc.		718-934-8881	46
GTI Travel Consolidators	829-8234	616-396-1234	50
HTI Tours	441-4411	215-563-8484	157
Jetset Tours Inc.	638-3273	312-362-9960	160
Kompas Travel	233-6422	305-771-9200	70
Millrun Tours	645-5786	312-641-5914	78
Orbis Polish Travel, Inc.	87-Orbis	212-867-5011	166
Palm Coast Tours & Travel	444-1560	407-433-1558	85
Paul Laifer Tours Inc.	346-6314	201-887-1188	86
Picasso Travel	PICASSO	310-645-4400	88
Pleasure Break Vacations, Inc.	777-1566	708-670-6300	170
Plus Ultra Tours	FOR-SPAIN	212-242-0393	171
Rahim Tours	556-5305	407-585-5305	173
Skylink Travel	247-6659	212-573-8980	176
Travac Tours & Charters	TRAV-800	212-563-3303	106
United Tours Corp	245-0203	212-245-1100	193
Up & Away Travel	275-8001	212-889-2345	114
Worldvision Travel	545-7118	201-736-8210	117

Portugal

Lisbon

4th Dimension Tours	343-0020	305-279-0014	123
AESU	638-7640	410-323-4416	15
Agents Advantage	816-2211	908-355-2222	128
Airplan	866-7526	412-257-3199	130

Part IV - Consolidators and Wholesalers by Destination

Firm name	1-800-phone	Phone	Page
Europe			
Portugal			
Lisbon			
Alpha Travel	793-8424	770-988-9982	21
Alta Tours	338-4191	415-777-1307	22
American Intl. Consolidators	888-5774	914-592-0206	131
Brendan Air	491-9633	800-491-9633	136
Central Holidays	935-5000		138
Central Tours	783-9882	201-344-2489	31
Centrav, Inc.	874-2033	612-948-8400	139
D-FW Tours	527-2589	214-980-4540	146
Fantasy Holidays	645-2555	516-935-8500	44
HTI Tours	441-4411	215-563-8484	157
Homeric Tours, Inc.	223-5570	212-753-1100	60
Jetset Tours Inc.	638-3273	312-362-9960	160
Millrun Tours	645-5786	312-641-5914	78
Picasso Travel	PICASSO	310-645-4400	88
Pinto Basto USA	526-8539	212-226-9056	90
Pleasure Break Vacations, Inc.	777-1566	708-670-6300	170
Trans Am Travel	822-7600	703-998-7676	184
Travac Tours & Charters	TRAV-800	212-563-3303	106
Travel Associates	992-7388	213-933-7388	107
Up & Away Travel	275-8001	212-889-2345	114
Worldvision Travel	545-7118	201-736-8210	117
Romania			
Bucharest			
GTI Travel Consolidators	829-8234	616-396-1234	50
HTI Tours	441-4411	215-563-8484	157
Pleasure Break Vacations, Inc.	777-1566	708-670-6300	170
Up & Away Travel	275-8001	212-889-2345	114
Worldvision Travel	545-7118	201-736-8210	117
Russia			
AESU	638-7640	410-323-4416	15
AIT Anderson International	365-1929	517-337-1300	124
Air Travel Discounts, Inc.	888-2621	212-922-1326	18
Alpha Travel	793-8424	770-988-9982	21
AmeriCorp Travel Professional	299-LATI	214-956-9112	23
Eastern European Travel Cent		718-339-1100	148
Favored Holidays Inc.		718-934-8881	46
Gate 1	682-3333	215-572-7676	153

Firms are listed by region, country, then city, according to the firm's specifications. Firms serving entire region are listed at the beginning of each region section.

Firm name	1-800-phone	Phone	Page
Europe			
Russia			
General Tours	221-2216	603-357-5033	52
Hari World Travels, Inc.		212-957-3000	57
Hostway Tours	327-3207	305-966-8500	61
ITS Tours & Travel	533-8688	409-964-9400	63
Lotus	998-6116	212-213-1625	71
Orbis Polish Travel, Inc.	87-Orbis	212-867-5011	166
Palm Coast Tours & Travel	444-1560	407-433-1558	85
Picasso Travel	PICASSO	310-645-4400	88
Pleasure Break Vacations, Inc.	777-1566	708-670-6300	170
Rahim Tours	556-5305	407-585-5305	173
Skylink Travel	247-6659	212-573-8980	176
Sunrise Tours	872-3801	212-947-3617	101
Travac Tours & Charters	TRAV-800	212-563-3303	106
Travel Wholesalers	487-8944	703-359-8855	189
Value Holidays	558-6850	414-241-6373	115
Worldvision Travel	545-7118	201-736-8210	117
Zig Zag Travel	726-0249	516-887-0776	120
Khabarovsk			
Eastern European Travel Cent		718-339-1100	148
Moscow			
AESU	638-7640	410-323-4416	15
Agents Advantage	816-2211	908-355-2222	128
Air Travel Discounts, Inc.	888-2621	212-922-1326	18
Alpha Travel	793-8424	770-988-9982	21
American Travel Abroad Inc	228-0877	212-586-5230	132
Brendan Air	491-9633	800-491-9633	136
Centrav, Inc.	874-2033	612-948-8400	139
Cosmopolitan TVC Ctr	548-7206	305-523-0973	143
D-FW Tours	527-2589	214-980-4540	146
Eastern European Travel Cent		718-339-1100	148
Favored Holidays Inc.		718-934-8881	46
GTI Travel Consolidators	829-8234	616-396-1234	50
HTI Tours	441-4411	215-563-8484	157
Jetset Tours Inc.	638-3273	312-362-9960	160
Palm Coast Tours & Travel	444-1560	407-433-1558	85
Panorama Tours	527-4888	801-328-5390	168
Picasso Travel	PICASSO	310-645-4400	88
Skylink Travel	247-6659	212-573-8980	176

Firms are listed by region, country, then city, according to the firm's specifications. Firms serving entire region are listed at the beginning of each region section.

Firm name	1-800-phone	Phone	Page
Europe			
Russia			
Moscow			
Sunny Land Tours	783-7839	201-487-2150	178
Sunrise Tours	872-3801	212-947-3617	101
Trans Am Travel	822-7600	703-998-7676	184
Travac Tours & Charters	TRAV-800	212-563-3303	106
United Tours Corp	245-0203	212-245-1100	193
Up & Away Travel	275-8001	212-889-2345	114
Zig Zag Travel	726-0249	516-887-0776	120
St. Petersburg			
AESU	638-7640	410-323-4416	15
Adventure Int'l Travel Service	542-2487	216-228-7171	16
Air Travel Discounts, Inc.	888-2621	212-922-1326	18
Alpha Travel	793-8424	770-988-9982	21
American Travel Abroad Inc	228-0877	212-586-5230	132
Centrav, Inc.	874-2033	612-948-8400	139
D-FW Tours	527-2589	214-980-4540	146
Eastern European Travel Cent		718-339-1100	148
Favored Holidays Inc.		718-934-8881	46
GTI Travel Consolidators	829-8234	616-396-1234	50
Millrun Tours	645-5786	312-641-5914	78
Palm Coast Tours & Travel	444-1560	407-433-1558	85
Picasso Travel	PICASSO	310-645-4400	88
Skylink Travel	247-6659	212-573-8980	176
Sunrise Tours	872-3801	212-947-3617	101
Travac Tours & Charters	TRAV-800	212-563-3303	106
Up & Away Travel	275-8001	212-889-2345	114
Zig Zag Travel	726-0249	516-887-0776	120
Slovakia			
Bratislava			
Adventure Int'l Travel Service	542-2487	216-228-7171	16
Cedok Central European Tour	800-8891	212-689-9720	30
HTI Tours	441-4411	215-563-8484	157
Orbis Polish Travel, Inc.	87-Orbis	212-867-5011	166
Sunrise Tours	872-3801	212-947-3617	101
Spain			
4th Dimension Tours	343-0020	305-279-0014	123
AESU	638-7640	410-323-4416	15

Firms are listed by region, country, then city, according to the firm's specifications. Firms serving entire region are listed at the beginning of each region section.

Firm name	1-800-phone	Phone	Page
Europe			
Spain			
Air Travel Discounts, Inc.	888-2621	212-922-1326	18
Alpha Travel	793-8424	770-988-9982	21
Alta Tours	338-4191	415-777-1307	22
Brendan Air	491-9633	800-491-9633	136
Campus Travel Center/Euroflgt	328-3359	612-338-5616	28
Central Holidays	935-5000		138
Central Tours	783-9882	201-344-2489	31
Council Charter	800-8222	212-661-0311	144
Fantasy Holidays	645-2555	516-935-8500	44
Gate 1	682-3333	215-572-7676	153
Mena Tours & Travel	937-6362	312-275-2125	76
Picasso Travel	PICASSO	310-645-4400	88
Pleasure Break Vacations, Inc.	777-1566	708-670-6300	170
Plus Ultra Tours	FOR-SPAIN	212-242-0393	171
Worldvision Travel	545-7118	201-736-8210	117
Barcelona			
AESU	638-7640	410-323-4416	15
Air Travel Discounts, Inc.	888-2621	212-922-1326	18
Airplan	866-7526	412-257-3199	130
Alpha Travel	793-8424	770-988-9982	21
Brendan Air	491-9633	800-491-9633	136
Central Tours	783-9882	201-344-2489	31
Centrav, Inc.	874-2033	612-948-8400	139
City Tours	238-2489	201-939-6572	141
Cosmopolitan TVC Ctr	548-7206	305-523-0973	143
Council Charter	800-8222	212-661-0311	144
D-FW Tours	527-2589	214-980-4540	146
Fantastiques Tours		310-577-6711	150
Fantasy Holidays	645-2555	516-935-8500	44
Jetset Tours Inc.	638-3273	312-362-9960	160
Leisure Resources	729-9051	203-874-4965	161
New Frontiers	366-6387	212-779-0600	80
Picasso Travel	PICASSO	310-645-4400	88
Plus Ultra Tours	FOR-SPAIN	212-242-0393	171
Skytours	246-8687	415-777-3544	96
Supertravel		310-301-4567	102
Trans Am Travel	822-7600	703-998-7676	184
Travac Tours & Charters	TRAV-800	212-563-3303	106

251

Firm name	1-800-phone	Phone	Page

Europe
Spain
Barcelona

| Travel Associates | 992-7388 | 213-933-7388 | 107 |
| Up & Away Travel | 275-8001 | 212-889-2345 | 114 |

Costa Del Sol

| Plus Ultra Tours | FOR-SPAIN | 212-242-0393 | 171 |

Madrid

AESU	638-7640	410-323-4416	15
Agents Advantage	816-2211	908-355-2222	128
Air Travel Discounts, Inc.	888-2621	212-922-1326	18
Airplan	866-7526	412-257-3199	130
Alpha Travel	793-8424	770-988-9982	21
American Intl. Consolidators	888-5774	914-592-0206	131
Brendan Air	491-9633	800-491-9633	136
British Network, LTD	274-8583	201-744-8814	26
Central Tours	783-9882	201-344-2489	31
Centrav, Inc.	874-2033	612-948-8400	139
City Tours	238-2489	201-939-6572	141
Council Charter	800-8222	212-661-0311	144
D-FW Tours	527-2589	214-980-4540	146
Fantastiques Tours		310-577-6711	150
Fantasy Holidays	645-2555	516-935-8500	44
HTI Tours	441-4411	215-563-8484	157
Jetset Tours Inc.	638-3273	312-362-9960	160
Millrun Tours	645-5786	312-641-5914	78
New Frontiers	366-6387	212-779-0600	80
Picasso Travel	PICASSO	310-645-4400	88
Plus Ultra Tours	FOR-SPAIN	212-242-0393	171
Skylink Travel	247-6659	212-573-8980	176
Skytours	246-8687	415-777-3544	96
Solar Tours	388-7652	202-861-6864	177
Supertravel		310-301-4567	102
Trans Am Travel	822-7600	703-998-7676	184
Travac Tours & Charters	TRAV-800	212-563-3303	106
Travel Associates	992-7388	213-933-7388	107
Up & Away Travel	275-8001	212-889-2345	114
World Travel & Tours, Inc.	886-4WTT	703-379-6363	195

Malaga

| AESU | 638-7640 | 410-323-4416 | 15 |

Firms are listed by region, country, then city, according to the firm's specifications. Firms serving entire region are listed at the beginning of each region section.			
Firm name	**1-800-phone**	**Phone**	**Page**

Europe

Spain

Malaga

Brendan Air	491-9633	800-491-9633	136
Up & Away Travel	275-8001	212-889-2345	114

Palma

Brendan Air	491-9633	800-491-9633	136

Santiago De Compostela

Plus Ultra Tours	FOR-SPAIN	212-242-0393	171

Tenerife, Canary Islands

Brendan Air	491-9633	800-491-9633	136
Plus Ultra Tours	FOR-SPAIN	212-242-0393	171
Sunny Land Tours	783-7839	201-487-2150	178

Sweden

Stockholm

AESU	638-7640	410-323-4416	15
Agents Advantage	816-2211	908-355-2222	128
Air Travel Discounts, Inc.	888-2621	212-922-1326	18
Airplan	866-7526	412-257-3199	130
Alpha Travel	793-8424	770-988-9982	21
Brendan Air	491-9633	800-491-9633	136
Centrav, Inc.	874-2033	612-948-8400	139
D-FW Tours	527-2589	214-980-4540	146
Fantastiques Tours		310-577-6711	150
Fantasy Holidays	645-2555	516-935-8500	44
Favored Holidays Inc.		718-934-8881	46
Guardian Travel Service Inc.	741-3050	813-367-5622	55
HTI Tours	441-4411	215-563-8484	157
J & O Air	877-8111	619-282-4124	159
Jetset Tours Inc.	638-3273	312-362-9960	160
Millrun Tours	645-5786	312-641-5914	78
New Frontiers	366-6387	212-779-0600	80
Palm Coast Tours & Travel	444-1560	407-433-1558	85
Picasso Travel	PICASSO	310-645-4400	88
Pleasure Break Vacations, Inc.	777-1566	708-670-6300	170
Rahim Tours	556-5305	407-585-5305	173
Skylink Travel	247-6659	212-573-8980	176
Skytours	246-8687	415-777-3544	96
Solar Tours	388-7652	202-861-6864	177

Firm name	1-800-phone	Phone	Page

Firms are listed by region, country, then city, according to the firm's specifications. Firms serving entire region are listed at the beginning of each region section.

Europe

Sweden

Stockholm

Firm name	1-800-phone	Phone	Page
Supertravel		310-301-4567	102
Trans Am Travel	822-7600	703-998-7676	184
Travac Tours & Charters	TRAV-800	212-563-3303	106
Tulips Travel	882-3383	212-490-3388	112
Worldvision Travel	545-7118	201-736-8210	117

Sveg

Firm name	1-800-phone	Phone	Page
GTI Travel Consolidators	829-8234	616-396-1234	50

Switzerland

Firm name	1-800-phone	Phone	Page
4th Dimension Tours	343-0020	305-279-0014	123
AESU	638-7640	410-323-4416	15
Agents Advantage	816-2211	908-355-2222	128
Air Travel Discounts, Inc.	888-2621	212-922-1326	18
Alpha Travel	793-8424	770-988-9982	21
Brendan Air	491-9633	800-491-9633	136
Campus Travel Center/Euroflgt	328-3359	612-338-5616	28
Favored Holidays Inc.		718-934-8881	46
Gate 1	682-3333	215-572-7676	153
HTI Tours	441-4411	215-563-8484	157
Picasso Travel	PICASSO	310-645-4400	88
Pleasure Break Vacations, Inc.	777-1566	708-670-6300	170
Trans Am Travel	822-7600	703-998-7676	184
Travac Tours & Charters	TRAV-800	212-563-3303	106
Value Holidays	558-6850	414-241-6373	115
Worldvision Travel	545-7118	201-736-8210	117

Basel

Firm name	1-800-phone	Phone	Page
Brendan Air	491-9633	800-491-9633	136
Centrav, Inc.	874-2033	612-948-8400	139
Picasso Travel	PICASSO	310-645-4400	88
Travac Tours & Charters	TRAV-800	212-563-3303	106

Geneva

Firm name	1-800-phone	Phone	Page
AESU	638-7640	410-323-4416	15
Agents Advantage	816-2211	908-355-2222	128
Air Travel Discounts, Inc.	888-2621	212-922-1326	18
Airplan	866-7526	412-257-3199	130
Alpha Travel	793-8424	770-988-9982	21
American Intl. Consolidators	888-5774	914-592-0206	131

Firm name	1-800-phone	Phone	Page

Europe
Switzerland
Geneva

Firm name	1-800-phone	Phone	Page
Brendan Air	491-9633	800-491-9633	136
Centrav, Inc.	874-2033	612-948-8400	139
D-FW Tours	527-2589	214-980-4540	146
Fantastiques Tours		310-577-6711	150
Favored Holidays Inc.		718-934-8881	46
Jetset Tours Inc.	638-3273	312-362-9960	160
Kompas Travel	233-6422	305-771-9200	70
Millrun Tours	645-5786	312-641-5914	78
New Frontiers	366-6387	212-779-0600	80
Picasso Travel	PICASSO	310-645-4400	88
Skytours	246-8687	415-777-3544	96
Supertravel		310-301-4567	102
Trans Am Travel	822-7600	703-998-7676	184
Travac Tours & Charters	TRAV-800	212-563-3303	106
Tulips Travel	882-3383	212-490-3388	112
Up & Away Travel	275-8001	212-889-2345	114
World Travel & Tours, Inc.	886-4WTT	703-379-6363	195

Zurich

Firm name	1-800-phone	Phone	Page
AESU	638-7640	410-323-4416	15
Agents Advantage	816-2211	908-355-2222	128
Air Travel Discounts, Inc.	888-2621	212-922-1326	18
Airplan	866-7526	412-257-3199	130
Alpha Travel	793-8424	770-988-9982	21
Brendan Air	491-9633	800-491-9633	136
Centrav, Inc.	874-2033	612-948-8400	139
Council Charter	800-8222	212-661-0311	144
D-FW Tours	527-2589	214-980-4540	146
Fantasy Holidays	645-2555	516-935-8500	44
Favored Holidays Inc.		718-934-8881	46
Guardian Travel Service Inc.	741-3050	813-367-5622	55
Jetset Tours Inc.	638-3273	312-362-9960	160
Kompas Travel	233-6422	305-771-9200	70
New Frontiers	366-6387	212-779-0600	80
Picasso Travel	PICASSO	310-645-4400	88
Skylink Travel	247-6659	212-573-8980	176
Skytours	246-8687	415-777-3544	96
Solar Tours	388-7652	202-861-6864	177
Trans Am Travel	822-7600	703-998-7676	184

Firms are listed by region, country, then city, according to the firm's specifications. Firms serving entire region are listed at the beginning of each region section.			
Firm name	*1-800-phone*	*Phone*	*Page*

Europe

Switzerland

Zurich

Firm name	1-800-phone	Phone	Page
Travac Tours & Charters	TRAV-800	212-563-3303	106
Up & Away Travel	275-8001	212-889-2345	114
World Travel & Tours, Inc.	886-4WTT	703-379-6363	195

Turkey

Istanbul

Firm name	1-800-phone	Phone	Page
4th Dimension Tours	343-0020	305-279-0014	123
AESU	638-7640	410-323-4416	15
Abratours	227-2887	914-949-3300	126
Air Brokers Int'l, Inc.	883-3273	415-397-1383	17
Air Travel Discounts, Inc.	888-2621	212-922-1326	18
Alpha Travel	793-8424	770-988-9982	21
Brendan Air	491-9633	800-491-9633	136
Centrav, Inc.	874-2033	612-948-8400	139
Cosmopolitan TVC Ctr	548-7206	305-523-0973	143
D-FW Tours	527-2589	214-980-4540	146
Favored Holidays Inc.		718-934-8881	46
Gate 1	682-3333	215-572-7676	153
Homeric Tours, Inc.	223-5570	212-753-1100	60
Jetset Tours Inc.	638-3273	312-362-9960	160
Kompas Travel	233-6422	305-771-9200	70
Lotus	998-6116	212-213-1625	71
Lucky Tours	932-6654	308-762-3957	72
P & F International Inc.	822-3063	718-383-5630	83
Persvoyage Inc	455-7377	212-719-0900	87
Picasso Travel	PICASSO	310-645-4400	88
Skylink Travel	247-6659	212-573-8980	176
Sunny Land Tours	783-7839	201-487-2150	178
Tourlite International Inc.	272-7600	212-599-2727	182
Travac Tours & Charters	TRAV-800	212-563-3303	106
Up & Away Travel	275-8001	212-889-2345	114

Ukraine

Firm name	1-800-phone	Phone	Page
Adventure Int'l Travel Service	542-2487	216-228-7171	16
American Travel Abroad Inc	228-0877	212-586-5230	132
Eastern European Travel Cent		718-339-1100	148
Favored Holidays Inc.		718-934-8881	46
Orbis Polish Travel, Inc.	87-Orbis	212-867-5011	166
P & F International Inc.	822-3063	718-383-5630	83

Part IV - Consolidators and Wholesalers by Destination

Firm name	1-800-phone	Phone	Page
Europe			
Ukraine			
United Tours Corp	245-0203	212-245-1100	193
Kiev			
Adventure Int'l Travel Service	542-2487	216-228-7171	16
Air Travel Discounts, Inc.	888-2621	212-922-1326	18
Alpha Travel	793-8424	770-988-9982	21
American Travel Abroad Inc	228-0877	212-586-5230	132
Balkan Holidays	852-0944	212-573-5530	134
Brendan Air	491-9633	800-491-9633	136
Centrav, Inc.	874-2033	612-948-8400	139
Eastern European Travel Cent		718-339-1100	148
Favored Holidays Inc.		718-934-8881	46
GTI Travel Consolidators	829-8234	616-396-1234	50
HTI Tours	441-4411	215-563-8484	157
Millrun Tours	645-5786	312-641-5914	78
P & F International Inc.	822-3063	718-383-5630	83
Picasso Travel	PICASSO	310-645-4400	88
Skylink Travel	247-6659	212-573-8980	176
Sunrise Tours	872-3801	212-947-3617	101
Lvov			
Adventure Int'l Travel Service	542-2487	216-228-7171	16
American Travel Abroad Inc	228-0877	212-586-5230	132
Eastern European Travel Cent		718-339-1100	148
Favored Holidays Inc.		718-934-8881	46
P & F International Inc.	822-3063	718-383-5630	83
Mid East			
Cyprus Airways	333-2977	212-714-2190	
APC/American Passenger Con	526-2447	212-972-1558	125
The Africa Desk	284-8796	203-354-9344	127
Agents Advantage	816-2211	908-355-2222	128
Air Travel Discounts, Inc.	888-2621	212-922-1326	18
AirFax Airline Marketing Assoc		404-662-0885	129
Alpha Travel	793-8424	770-988-9982	21
Ariel Tours, Inc.	262-1818	718-633-7900	133
Bon Voyage	826-8500	310-854-8585	135
Brendan Air	491-9633	800-491-9633	136
CL Thomson Express Int'l		213-628-9550	137
CWT/Maharaja	223-6862	212-695-8435	27

Firms are listed by region, country, then city, according to the firm's specifications. Firms serving entire region are listed at the beginning of each region section.

Firm name	1-800-phone	Phone	Page
Mid East			
Centrav, Inc.	874-2033	612-948-8400	139
Charterways	869-2344	408-257-2652	140
Chartours	323-4444	415-495-8881	32
Costa Azul Travel	332-7202	213-525-3331	35
Cut Rate Travel	388-0575	708-405-0587	36
DERAIR	717-4247	310-479-4411	37
Democracy Travel	536-8728	202-965-7200	38
Dial Europe Inc.		212-758-5310	40
Diplomat Tours	727-8687	916-972-1500	147
The Egyptian Connection	334-4477	718-762-3838	149
Euram Tours Inc	848-6789	202-789-2255	42
Everest Travel Inc.		404-231-5222	43
Favored Holidays Inc.		718-934-8881	46
GIT Travel	228-1777	404-399-6404	49
Gate 1	682-3333	215-572-7676	153
Gateway Express Ltd.	334-1188	503-242-0088	154
General Tours	221-2216	603-357-5033	52
Getaway Travel Intl. Inc.	683-6336	305-446-7855	53
Global Travel Consolidators	366-3544	310-581-5610	155
HTI Tours	441-4411	215-563-8484	157
Hari World Travels, Inc.		212-957-3000	57
Interworld Travel	468-3796	305-443-4929	65
Jetset Tours Inc.	638-3273	312-362-9960	160
M & H Travel, Inc.		212-661-7171	73
Magical Holidays, Inc.	433-7773	415-781-1345	74
Marakesh Tourist Company	458-1772	201-435-2800	75
Millrun Tours	645-5786	312-641-5914	78
Overseas Travel	783-7196	303-337-7196	82
P & F International Inc.	822-3063	718-383-5630	83
PERS Travel, Inc.	583-0909	214-458-6877	84
Persvoyage Inc	455-7377	212-719-0900	87
Picasso Travel	PICASSO	310-645-4400	88
Pino Welcome Travel	247-6578	212-682-5400	89
Pleasure Break Vacations, Inc.	777-1566	708-670-6300	170
Premier Travel Services Inc	545-1910	215-893-9966	92
Queue Travel	356-4871	619-260-8577	172
STA Travel	825-3001	213-937-9274	174
Saga Tours	683-4200	212-696-5200	93
Skylink Travel	247-6659	212-573-8980	176
Sunrise Tours	872-3801	212-947-3617	101

Part IV - Consolidators and Wholesalers by Destination

Firm name	1-800-phone	Phone	Page
Mid East			
Supervalue Vacations	879-1218	713-876-6400	103
TCI Travel & Tours	ASAP-FLY	214-630-3344	104
TFI Tours Intl. Ltd.	745-8000	212-736-1140	179
Travac Tours & Charters	TRAV-800	212-563-3303	106
Travel Bargains	247-3273	610-834-8150	108
Travel Expressions, Inc.	724-6274	212-338-9730	110
Travel Leaders, Inc.	323-3218	305-443-7755	187
Travel Wholesalers	487-8944	703-359-8855	189
US Inf Tours	262-0456	908-526-0085	192
Up & Away Travel	275-8001	212-889-2345	114
World Travel & Tours, Inc.	886-4WTT	703-379-6363	195
Worldwide Travel	343-0038	202-659-6430	118
Bahrain			
Bahrain			
Air Travel Discounts, Inc.	888-2621	212-922-1326	18
Alpha Travel	793-8424	770-988-9982	21
Brendan Air	491-9633	800-491-9633	136
D-FW Tours	527-2589	214-980-4540	146
Favored Holidays Inc.		718-934-8881	46
P & F International Inc.	822-3063	718-383-5630	83
Skylink Travel	247-6659	212-573-8980	176
Sunrise Tours	872-3801	212-947-3617	101
World Travel & Tours, Inc.	886-4WTT	703-379-6363	195
Egypt			
Abratours	227-2887	914-949-3300	126
Air Brokers Int'l, Inc.	883-3273	415-397-1383	17
Egypt Tours & Travel	523-4978	312-463-4999	41
The Egyptian Connection	334-4477	718-762-3838	149
Gate 1	682-3333	215-572-7676	153
Katy Van Tours	808-8747	713-492-7032	68
Lucky Tours	932-6654	308-762-3957	72
Marakesh Tourist Company	458-1772	201-435-2800	75
P & F International Inc.	822-3063	718-383-5630	83
Skylink Travel	247-6659	212-573-8980	176
Alexandria			
P & F International Inc.	822-3063	718-383-5630	83
Skylink Travel	247-6659	212-573-8980	176

Firms are listed by region, country, then city, according to the firm's specifications. Firms serving entire region are listed at the beginning of each region section.			
Firm name	1-800-phone	Phone	Page

Mid East

Egypt

Cairo

Air Travel Discounts, Inc.	888-2621	212-922-1326	18
Alpha Travel	793-8424	770-988-9982	21
Ariel Tours, Inc.	262-1818	718-633-7900	133
Brendan Air	491-9633	800-491-9633	136
D-FW Tours	527-2589	214-980-4540	146
Favored Holidays Inc.		718-934-8881	46
Homeric Tours, Inc.	223-5570	212-753-1100	60
Jetset Tours Inc.	638-3273	312-362-9960	160
P & F International Inc.	822-3063	718-383-5630	83
Picasso Travel	PICASSO	310-645-4400	88
Skylink Travel	247-6659	212-573-8980	176
Sunny Land Tours	783-7839	201-487-2150	178
Tourlite International Inc.	272-7600	212-599-2727	182
Travel Associates	992-7388	213-933-7388	107
Travel Expressions, Inc.	724-6274	212-338-9730	110
World Travel & Tours, Inc.	886-4WTT	703-379-6363	195

Iran

Tehran

Alpha Travel	793-8424	770-988-9982	21
Brendan Air	491-9633	800-491-9633	136
The Egyptian Connection	334-4477	718-762-3838	149
Favored Holidays Inc.		718-934-8881	46
Persvoyage Inc	455-7377	212-719-0900	87
Picasso Travel	PICASSO	310-645-4400	88
Skylink Travel	247-6659	212-573-8980	176
Sunrise Tours	872-3801	212-947-3617	101

Israel

Eilat

Ariel Tours, Inc.	262-1818	718-633-7900	133

Tel Aviv

4th Dimension Tours	343-0020	305-279-0014	123
AESU	638-7640	410-323-4416	15
Abratours	227-2887	914-949-3300	126
Air Brokers Int'l, Inc.	883-3273	415-397-1383	17
Air Travel Discounts, Inc.	888-2621	212-922-1326	18
Alpha Travel	793-8424	770-988-9982	21
Ariel Tours, Inc.	262-1818	718-633-7900	133

Firm name	1-800-phone	Phone	Page

Mid East

Israel

Tel Aviv

Firm name	1-800-phone	Phone	Page
Brendan Air	491-9633	800-491-9633	136
Central Holidays	935-5000		138
Central Tours	783-9882	201-344-2489	31
D-FW Tours	527-2589	214-980-4540	146
Egypt Tours & Travel	523-4978	312-463-4999	41
The Egyptian Connection	334-4477	718-762-3838	149
Favored Holidays Inc.		718-934-8881	46
Gate 1	682-3333	215-572-7676	153
Guardian Travel Service Inc.	741-3050	813-367-5622	55
HTI Tours	441-4411	215-563-8484	157
J & O Air	877-8111	619-282-4124	159
Jetset Tours Inc.	638-3273	312-362-9960	160
Katy Van Tours	808-8747	713-492-7032	68
Lotus	998-6116	212-213-1625	71
P & F International Inc.	822-3063	718-383-5630	83
Paul Laifer Tours Inc.	346-6314	201-887-1188	86
Picasso Travel	PICASSO	310-645-4400	88
Skylink Travel	247-6659	212-573-8980	176
Sunny Land Tours	783-7839	201-487-2150	178
Tourlite International Inc.	272-7600	212-599-2727	182
Travac Tours & Charters	TRAV-800	212-563-3303	106
Travel Associates	992-7388	213-933-7388	107
Travel Expressions, Inc.	724-6274	212-338-9730	110
World Travel & Tours, Inc.	886-4WTT	703-379-6363	195
Zig Zag Travel	726-0249	516-887-0776	120

Jordan

Amman

Firm name	1-800-phone	Phone	Page
Abratours	227-2887	914-949-3300	126
Air Travel Discounts, Inc.	888-2621	212-922-1326	18
Alpha Travel	793-8424	770-988-9982	21
Egypt Tours & Travel	523-4978	312-463-4999	41
The Egyptian Connection	334-4477	718-762-3838	149
Favored Holidays Inc.		718-934-8881	46
Gate 1	682-3333	215-572-7676	153
Lucky Tours	932-6654	308-762-3957	72
P & F International Inc.	822-3063	718-383-5630	83
Persvoyage Inc	455-7377	212-719-0900	87
Picasso Travel	PICASSO	310-645-4400	88

Firm name	1-800-phone	Phone	Page

Mid East

Jordan
Amman

Skylink Travel	247-6659	212-573-8980	176
Sunny Land Tours	783-7839	201-487-2150	178

Kuwait
Kuwait

Alpha Travel	793-8424	770-988-9982	21
Brendan Air	491-9633	800-491-9633	136
D-FW Tours	527-2589	214-980-4540	146
The Egyptian Connection	334-4477	718-762-3838	149
Favored Holidays Inc.		718-934-8881	46
P & F International Inc.	822-3063	718-383-5630	83
Persvoyage Inc	455-7377	212-719-0900	87
Picasso Travel	PICASSO	310-645-4400	88
Skylink Travel	247-6659	212-573-8980	176
Sunrise Tours	872-3801	212-947-3617	101
Travac Tours & Charters	TRAV-800	212-563-3303	106

Oman
Muscat

Air Travel Discounts, Inc.	888-2621	212-922-1326	18
Alpha Travel	793-8424	770-988-9982	21
Brendan Air	491-9633	800-491-9633	136
Persvoyage Inc	455-7377	212-719-0900	87
Skylink Travel	247-6659	212-573-8980	176
Sunrise Tours	872-3801	212-947-3617	101

Qatar
Doha

Air Travel Discounts, Inc.	888-2621	212-922-1326	18
Alpha Travel	793-8424	770-988-9982	21
Brendan Air	491-9633	800-491-9633	136
Persvoyage Inc	455-7377	212-719-0900	87

Saudi Arabia

Air Travel Discounts, Inc.	888-2621	212-922-1326	18
Alpha Travel	793-8424	770-988-9982	21
Brendan Air	491-9633	800-491-9633	136
The Egyptian Connection	334-4477	718-762-3838	149
Favored Holidays Inc.		718-934-8881	46
P & F International Inc.	822-3063	718-383-5630	83

Firms are listed by region, country, then city, according to the firm's specifications. Firms serving entire region are listed at the beginning of each region section.

Firm name	1-800-phone	Phone	Page
Mid East			
Saudi Arabia			
Skylink Travel	247-6659	212-573-8980	176
Sunrise Tours	872-3801	212-947-3617	101
Travac Tours & Charters	TRAV-800	212-563-3303	106
World Travel & Tours, Inc.	886-4WTT	703-379-6363	195
Dhahran			
Air Travel Discounts, Inc.	888-2621	212-922-1326	18
Alpha Travel	793-8424	770-988-9982	21
Brendan Air	491-9633	800-491-9633	136
D-FW Tours	527-2589	214-980-4540	146
P & F International Inc.	822-3063	718-383-5630	83
Persvoyage Inc	455-7377	212-719-0900	87
Skylink Travel	247-6659	212-573-8980	176
Sunrise Tours	872-3801	212-947-3617	101
Travac Tours & Charters	TRAV-800	212-563-3303	106
Jeddah			
Air Travel Discounts, Inc.	888-2621	212-922-1326	18
Alpha Travel	793-8424	770-988-9982	21
Brendan Air	491-9633	800-491-9633	136
D-FW Tours	527-2589	214-980-4540	146
Favored Holidays Inc.		718-934-8881	46
P & F International Inc.	822-3063	718-383-5630	83
Picasso Travel	PICASSO	310-645-4400	88
Skylink Travel	247-6659	212-573-8980	176
Sunrise Tours	872-3801	212-947-3617	101
Riyadh			
Air Travel Discounts, Inc.	888-2621	212-922-1326	18
Ariel Tours, Inc.	262-1818	718-633-7900	133
D-FW Tours	527-2589	214-980-4540	146
Favored Holidays Inc.		718-934-8881	46
P & F International Inc.	822-3063	718-383-5630	83
Skylink Travel	247-6659	212-573-8980	176
Sunrise Tours	872-3801	212-947-3617	101
Travac Tours & Charters	TRAV-800	212-563-3303	106
Syria			
Damascus			
Air Travel Discounts, Inc.	888-2621	212-922-1326	18
Alpha Travel	793-8424	770-988-9982	21

Firm name	1-800-phone	Phone	Page

Mid East

Syria
Damascus

Balkan Holidays	852-0944	212-573-5530	134
D-FW Tours	527-2589	214-980-4540	146
The Egyptian Connection	334-4477	718-762-3838	149
Favored Holidays Inc.		718-934-8881	46
P & F International Inc.	822-3063	718-383-5630	83
Picasso Travel	PICASSO	310-645-4400	88
Skylink Travel	247-6659	212-573-8980	176
Sunny Land Tours	783-7839	201-487-2150	178
Travel Expressions, Inc.	724-6274	212-338-9730	110

United Arab Emirates

Air Travel Discounts, Inc.	888-2621	212-922-1326	18
Alpha Travel	793-8424	770-988-9982	21
Brendan Air	491-9633	800-491-9633	136
The Egyptian Connection	334-4477	718-762-3838	149
Favored Holidays Inc.		718-934-8881	46
Persvoyage Inc	455-7377	212-719-0900	87
Picasso Travel	PICASSO	310-645-4400	88
Skylink Travel	247-6659	212-573-8980	176
Sunrise Tours	872-3801	212-947-3617	101
World Travel & Tours, Inc.	886-4WTT	703-379-6363	195

Abu Dhabi

Air Travel Discounts, Inc.	888-2621	212-922-1326	18
Alpha Travel	793-8424	770-988-9982	21
Brendan Air	491-9633	800-491-9633	136
D-FW Tours	527-2589	214-980-4540	146
Favored Holidays Inc.		718-934-8881	46
P & F International Inc.	822-3063	718-383-5630	83
Persvoyage Inc	455-7377	212-719-0900	87
Picasso Travel	PICASSO	310-645-4400	88
Skylink Travel	247-6659	212-573-8980	176
Sunrise Tours	872-3801	212-947-3617	101
Travac Tours & Charters	TRAV-800	212-563-3303	106

Dubai

Air Travel Discounts, Inc.	888-2621	212-922-1326	18
Alpha Travel	793-8424	770-988-9982	21
Brendan Air	491-9633	800-491-9633	136

Firm name	1-800-phone	Phone	Page

Mid East

United Arab Emirates
Dubai

D-FW Tours	527-2589	214-980-4540	146
Favored Holidays Inc.		718-934-8881	46
P & F International Inc.	822-3063	718-383-5630	83
Persvoyage Inc	455-7377	212-719-0900	87
Picasso Travel	PICASSO	310-645-4400	88
Skylink Travel	247-6659	212-573-8980	176
Sunrise Tours	872-3801	212-947-3617	101

Yemen
Sanaa

Air Travel Discounts, Inc.	888-2621	212-922-1326	18
Sunrise Tours	872-3801	212-947-3617	101

Orient

AIT Anderson International	365-1929	517-337-1300	124
Agents Advantage	816-2211	908-355-2222	128
Air Brokers Int'l, Inc.	883-3273	415-397-1383	17
Air Travel Discounts, Inc.	888-2621	212-922-1326	18
AirFax Airline Marketing Assoc		404-662-0885	129
Airplan	866-7526	412-257-3199	130
Alpha Travel	793-8424	770-988-9982	21
AmeriCorp Travel Professional	299-LATI	214-956-9112	23
Bon Voyage	826-8500	310-854-8585	135
Brendan Air	491-9633	800-491-9633	136
CL Thomson Express Int'l		213-628-9550	137
CWT/Maharaja	223-6862	212-695-8435	27
Cathay Travel		818-571-6727	29
Centrav, Inc.	874-2033	612-948-8400	139
Charterways	869-2344	408-257-2652	140
Chartours	323-4444	415-495-8881	32
Chisholm Travel, Inc.	631-2824	312-263-7900	33
City Tours	238-2489	201-939-6572	141
Creative Marketing Manageme	458-6663	212-557-1530	145
Cut Rate Travel	388-0575	708-405-0587	36
D-FW Tours	527-2589	214-980-4540	146
Democracy Travel	536-8728	202-965-7200	38
Destinations Unlimited	338-7987	619-299-5161	39
Diplomat Tours	727-8687	916-972-1500	147
The Egyptian Connection	334-4477	718-762-3838	149

Firm name	1-800-phone	Phone	Page

Firms are listed by region, country, then city, according to the firm's specifications. Firms serving entire region are listed at the beginning of each region section.

Orient

Firm name	1-800-phone	Phone	Page
Euram Tours Inc	848-6789	202-789-2255	42
Everest Travel Inc.		404-231-5222	43
Fare Deals Ltd.	347-7006	410-581-8787	45
Festival of Asia	533-9953	415-693-0880	151
Four Seasons Travel		910-292-1887	47
GTI Travel Consolidators	829-8234	616-396-1234	50
Garden State Travel	537-2420	201-333-1232	51
Gateway Express Ltd.	334-1188	503-242-0088	154
General Tours	221-2216	603-357-5033	52
Getaway Travel Intl. Inc.	683-6336	305-446-7855	53
Global Travel Consolidators	366-3544	310-581-5610	155
Golden Pacific #1 Travel	500-8021	813-684-6365	156
Group & Leisure	874-6608	816-224-3717	54
HTI Tours	441-4411	215-563-8484	157
Hana Travel Inc.	962-8044	708-913-1177	56
Hari World Travels, Inc.		212-957-3000	57
J & O Air	877-8111	619-282-4124	159
Jetset Tours Inc.	638-3273	312-362-9960	160
Kambi Travel Intl.	220-2192	301-925-9012	67
Katy Van Tours	808-8747	713-492-7032	68
Lotus	998-6116	212-213-1625	71
M & H Travel, Inc.		212-661-7171	73
MT&T		612-784-3226	163
Midtown Travel Consultants	548-8904	404-872-8308	77
Millrun Tours	645-5786	312-641-5914	78
National Travel Centre	228-6886	312-939-2190	79
Northwest World Vacations	727-1111	612-474-2540	165
Overseas Express	343-4873		81
Overseas Travel	783-7196	303-337-7196	82
PCS	367-8833	213-239-2424	167
Palm Coast Tours & Travel	444-1560	407-433-1558	85
Passport Travel Mgmt Group	950-5864	813-931-3166	169
Pino Welcome Travel	247-6578	212-682-5400	89
Premier Travel Services Inc	545-1910	215-893-9966	92
Queue Travel	356-4871	619-260-8577	172
STA Travel	825-3001	213-937-9274	174
STT Worldwide Travel, Inc.	348-0886	503-671-0494	175
Saga Tours	683-4200	212-696-5200	93
Sharp Travel Washington	969-7427	703-941-2323	95
Skylink Travel	247-6659	212-573-8980	176

Firm name	1-800-phone	Phone	Page

Orient

Specialty Tours Int'l USA Inc.	421-3913	310-568-8709	99
Sunrise Tours	872-3801	212-947-3617	101
Supervalue Vacations	879-1218	713-876-6400	103
TCI Travel & Tours	ASAP-FLY	214-630-3344	104
TFI Tours Intl. Ltd.	745-8000	212-736-1140	179
Thrifty Air	423-4488	310-337-9982	180
Ticketworld/SAF Travel World	394-8587	215-440-7200	105
Time Travel	847-7026	708-595-8463	181
Trans Am Travel	822-7600	703-998-7676	184
Travac Tours & Charters	TRAV-800	212-563-3303	106
Travel Bargains	247-3273	610-834-8150	108
Travel Expressions, Inc.	724-6274	212-338-9730	110
The Travel Group	836-6269	210-698-0100	186
Travel Leaders, Inc.	323-3218	305-443-7755	187
Travel N Tours	854-5400	914-838-2600	188
Travel Wholesalers	487-8944	703-359-8855	189
Travelogue, Inc.	542-9446	910-855-1735	190
Travnet Inc.	359-6388	312-759-9200	191
Unitravel	325-2222	314-569-0900	194
Up & Away Travel	275-8001	212-889-2345	114
Winggate Travel		913-451-9200	116
Zig Zag International Travel	226-9383	309-637-9647	119

Bangladesh
Dacca

Festival of Asia	533-9953	415-693-0880	151

Burma
Rangoon

Festival of Asia	533-9953	415-693-0880	151
Sunrise Tours	872-3801	212-947-3617	101

Yangon

Festival of Asia	533-9953	415-693-0880	151

Cambodia
Phnom Penh

Air Brokers Int'l, Inc.	883-3273	415-397-1383	17
Festival of Asia	533-9953	415-693-0880	151
Passport Travel Mgmt Group	950-5864	813-931-3166	169
Skylink Travel	247-6659	212-573-8980	176
Sunrise Tours	872-3801	212-947-3617	101

Firms are listed by region, country, then city, according to the firm's specifications. Firms serving entire region are listed at the beginning of each region section.

Firm name	1-800-phone	Phone	Page
Orient			
Cambodia			
Phnom Penh			
Thrifty Air	423-4488	310-337-9982	180
Ticketworld/SAF Travel World	394-8587	215-440-7200	105
China			
Airplan	866-7526	412-257-3199	130
Brendan Air	491-9633	800-491-9633	136
Cathay Travel		818-571-6727	29
Creative Marketing Manageme	458-6663	212-557-1530	145
Festival of Asia	533-9953	415-693-0880	151
Hana Travel Inc.	962-8044	708-913-1177	56
Lucky Tours	932-6654	308-762-3957	72
Rahim Tours	556-5305	407-585-5305	173
Thrifty Air	423-4488	310-337-9982	180
Trans Am Travel	822-7600	703-998-7676	184
Travel Expressions, Inc.	724-6274	212-338-9730	110
Value Holidays	558-6850	414-241-6373	115
Beijing			
Brendan Air	491-9633	800-491-9633	136
Creative Marketing Manageme	458-6663	212-557-1530	145
D-FW Tours	527-2589	214-980-4540	146
Favored Holidays Inc.		718-934-8881	46
Festival of Asia	533-9953	415-693-0880	151
Golden Pacific #1 Travel	500-8021	813-684-6365	156
Hana Travel Inc.	962-8044	708-913-1177	56
P & F International Inc.	822-3063	718-383-5630	83
Sharp Travel Washington	969-7427	703-941-2323	95
Skylink Travel	247-6659	212-573-8980	176
Sunrise Tours	872-3801	212-947-3617	101
Trans Am Travel	822-7600	703-998-7676	184
Worldvision Travel	545-7118	201-736-8210	117
Shanghai			
Air Travel Discounts, Inc.	888-2621	212-922-1326	18
Brendan Air	491-9633	800-491-9633	136
City Tours	238-2489	201-939-6572	141
Creative Marketing Manageme	458-6663	212-557-1530	145
D-FW Tours	527-2589	214-980-4540	146
Festival of Asia	533-9953	415-693-0880	151

Firms are listed by region, country, then city, according to the firm's specifications. Firms serving entire region are listed at the beginning of each region section.

Firm name	1-800-phone	Phone	Page
Orient			
China			
Shanghai			
Hana Travel Inc.	962-8044	708-913-1177	56
Sharp Travel Washington	969-7427	703-941-2323	95
Sunrise Tours	872-3801	212-947-3617	101
Trans Am Travel	822-7600	703-998-7676	184
Travnet Inc.	359-6388	312-759-9200	191
Worldvision Travel	545-7118	201-736-8210	117
Hong Kong			
Air Travel Discounts, Inc.	888-2621	212-922-1326	18
Airplan	866-7526	412-257-3199	130
Brendan Air	491-9633	800-491-9633	136
Cathay Travel		818-571-6727	29
Centrav, Inc.	874-2033	612-948-8400	139
City Tours	238-2489	201-939-6572	141
Creative Marketing Manageme	458-6663	212-557-1530	145
D-FW Tours	527-2589	214-980-4540	146
Festival of Asia	533-9953	415-693-0880	151
GTI Travel Consolidators	829-8234	616-396-1234	50
Gateway Express Ltd.	334-1188	503-242-0088	154
Golden Pacific #1 Travel	500-8021	813-684-6365	156
HTI Tours	441-4411	215-563-8484	157
Hana Travel Inc.	962-8044	708-913-1177	56
Jetset Tours Inc.	638-3273	312-362-9960	160
Palm Coast Tours & Travel	444-1560	407-433-1558	85
Sharp Travel Washington	969-7427	703-941-2323	95
Skylink Travel	247-6659	212-573-8980	176
Thrifty Air	423-4488	310-337-9982	180
Trans Am Travel	822-7600	703-998-7676	184
Travel Center	419-0960	212-545-7474	109
Travel Expressions, Inc.	724-6274	212-338-9730	110
Travelogue, Inc.	542-9446	910-855-1735	190
Travnet Inc.	359-6388	312-759-9200	191
Tulips Travel	882-3383	212-490-3388	112
Value Holidays	558-6850	414-241-6373	115
India			
Air Brokers Int'l, Inc.	883-3273	415-397-1383	17
City Tours	238-2489	201-939-6572	141
Creative Marketing Manageme	458-6663	212-557-1530	145

Firms are listed by region, country, then city, according to the firm's specifications. Firms serving entire region are listed at the beginning of each region section.			
Firm name	1-800-phone	Phone	Page

Orient
India

Firm name	1-800-phone	Phone	Page
Festival of Asia	533-9953	415-693-0880	151
Four Seasons Travel		910-292-1887	47
Gateway Express Ltd.	334-1188	503-242-0088	154
General Tours	221-2216	603-357-5033	52
Golden Pacific #1 Travel	500-8021	813-684-6365	156
HTI Tours	441-4411	215-563-8484	157
Lucky Tours	932-6654	308-762-3957	72
MT&T		612-784-3226	163
Magical Holidays, Inc.	433-7773	415-781-1345	74
Marakesh Tourist Company	458-1772	201-435-2800	75
Midtown Travel Consultants	548-8904	404-872-8308	77
Millrun Tours	645-5786	312-641-5914	78
PERS Travel, Inc.	583-0909	214-458-6877	84
Picasso Travel	PICASSO	310-645-4400	88
Queue Travel	356-4871	619-260-8577	172
Thrifty Air	423-4488	310-337-9982	180
Travel Center	419-0960	212-545-7474	109
Travelogue, Inc.	542-9446	910-855-1735	190
World Travel & Tours, Inc.	886-4WTT	703-379-6363	195
Worldwide Travel	343-0038	202-659-6430	118

Ahmedabad

Firm name	1-800-phone	Phone	Page
Four Seasons Travel		910-292-1887	47

Bombay

Firm name	1-800-phone	Phone	Page
Air Travel Discounts, Inc.	888-2621	212-922-1326	18
City Tours	238-2489	201-939-6572	141
Creative Marketing Manageme	458-6663	212-557-1530	145
Festival of Asia	533-9953	415-693-0880	151
Four Seasons Travel		910-292-1887	47
Gateway Express Ltd.	334-1188	503-242-0088	154
MT&T		612-784-3226	163
Millrun Tours	645-5786	312-641-5914	78
Picasso Travel	PICASSO	310-645-4400	88
Travel Center	419-0960	212-545-7474	109
Up & Away Travel	275-8001	212-889-2345	114
World Travel & Tours, Inc.	886-4WTT	703-379-6363	195

Calcutta

Firm name	1-800-phone	Phone	Page
Balkan Holidays	852-0944	212-573-5530	134

270

Firms are listed by region, country, then city, according to the firm's specifications. Firms serving entire region are listed at the beginning of each region section.			
Firm name	1-800-phone	Phone	Page

Orient

India

Calcutta

D-FW Tours	527-2589	214-980-4540	146
Festival of Asia	533-9953	415-693-0880	151
Gateway Express Ltd.	334-1188	503-242-0088	154
MT&T		612-784-3226	163
Millrun Tours	645-5786	312-641-5914	78
Picasso Travel	PICASSO	310-645-4400	88
Up & Away Travel	275-8001	212-889-2345	114
World Travel & Tours, Inc.	886-4WTT	703-379-6363	195

Delhi

Air Travel Discounts, Inc.	888-2621	212-922-1326	18
City Tours	238-2489	201-939-6572	141
Creative Marketing Manageme	458-6663	212-557-1530	145
D-FW Tours	527-2589	214-980-4540	146
Festival of Asia	533-9953	415-693-0880	151
Gateway Express Ltd.	334-1188	503-242-0088	154
MT&T		612-784-3226	163
Millrun Tours	645-5786	312-641-5914	78
Picasso Travel	PICASSO	310-645-4400	88
Sunrise Tours	872-3801	212-947-3617	101
Travel Center	419-0960	212-545-7474	109
Up & Away Travel	275-8001	212-889-2345	114
World Travel & Tours, Inc.	886-4WTT	703-379-6363	195

Hyderabad

Four Seasons Travel		910-292-1887	47

Madras

City Tours	238-2489	201-939-6572	141
Festival of Asia	533-9953	415-693-0880	151
MT&T		612-784-3226	163

Japan

Air Travel Discounts, Inc.	888-2621	212-922-1326	18
Airplan	866-7526	412-257-3199	130
Alpha Travel	793-8424	770-988-9982	21
Brendan Air	491-9633	800-491-9633	136
Creative Marketing Manageme	458-6663	212-557-1530	145
Hana Travel Inc.	962-8044	708-913-1177	56
Hari World Travels, Inc.		212-957-3000	57

Firms are listed by region, country, then city, according to the firm's specifications. Firms serving entire region are listed at the beginning of each region section.

Firm name	1-800-phone	Phone	Page
Orient			
Japan			
Jetset Tours Inc.	638-3273	312-362-9960	160
Lucky Tours	932-6654	308-762-3957	72
Sharp Travel Washington	969-7427	703-941-2323	95
Skylink Travel	247-6659	212-573-8980	176
Specialty Tours Int'l USA Inc.	421-3913	310-568-8709	99
Thrifty Air	423-4488	310-337-9982	180
Trans Am Travel	822-7600	703-998-7676	184
Travel Expressions, Inc.	724-6274	212-338-9730	110
Travnet Inc.	359-6388	312-759-9200	191
Fukuoka			
Air Travel Discounts, Inc.	888-2621	212-922-1326	18
Brendan Air	491-9633	800-491-9633	136
Centrav, Inc.	874-2033	612-948-8400	139
Creative Marketing Manageme	458-6663	212-557-1530	145
Sharp Travel Washington	969-7427	703-941-2323	95
Skylink Travel	247-6659	212-573-8980	176
Trans Am Travel	822-7600	703-998-7676	184
Travnet Inc.	359-6388	312-759-9200	191
Nagoya			
Air Travel Discounts, Inc.	888-2621	212-922-1326	18
Brendan Air	491-9633	800-491-9633	136
Centrav, Inc.	874-2033	612-948-8400	139
Creative Marketing Manageme	458-6663	212-557-1530	145
Hana Travel Inc.	962-8044	708-913-1177	56
Sharp Travel Washington	969-7427	703-941-2323	95
Skylink Travel	247-6659	212-573-8980	176
Trans Am Travel	822-7600	703-998-7676	184
Okinawa			
Air Travel Discounts, Inc.	888-2621	212-922-1326	18
Brendan Air	491-9633	800-491-9633	136
Creative Marketing Manageme	458-6663	212-557-1530	145
Sharp Travel Washington	969-7427	703-941-2323	95
Skylink Travel	247-6659	212-573-8980	176
Trans Am Travel	822-7600	703-998-7676	184
Osaka			
Air Travel Discounts, Inc.	888-2621	212-922-1326	18
Airplan	866-7526	412-257-3199	130

Firm name	1-800-phone	Phone	Page
Orient			
Japan			
Osaka			
Alpha Travel	793-8424	770-988-9982	21
Brendan Air	491-9633	800-491-9633	136
Creative Marketing Manageme	458-6663	212-557-1530	145
HTI Tours	441-4411	215-563-8484	157
Hana Travel Inc.	962-8044	708-913-1177	56
Sharp Travel Washington	969-7427	703-941-2323	95
Skylink Travel	247-6659	212-573-8980	176
Trans Am Travel	822-7600	703-998-7676	184
Travel Expressions, Inc.	724-6274	212-338-9730	110
Travnet Inc.	359-6388	312-759-9200	191
Tulips Travel	882-3383	212-490-3388	112
Tokyo			
Air Travel Discounts, Inc.	888-2621	212-922-1326	18
Airplan	866-7526	412-257-3199	130
Alpha Travel	793-8424	770-988-9982	21
Brendan Air	491-9633	800-491-9633	136
Centrav, Inc.	874-2033	612-948-8400	139
City Tours	238-2489	201-939-6572	141
Creative Marketing Manageme	458-6663	212-557-1530	145
D-FW Tours	527-2589	214-980-4540	146
Fantastiques Tours		310-577-6711	150
Favored Holidays Inc.		718-934-8881	46
Festival of Asia	533-9953	415-693-0880	151
Four Seasons Travel		910-292-1887	47
Gateway Express Ltd.	334-1188	503-242-0088	154
Golden Pacific #1 Travel	500-8021	813-684-6365	156
Hana Travel Inc.	962-8044	708-913-1177	56
J & O Air	877-8111	619-282-4124	159
MT&T		612-784-3226	163
Sharp Travel Washington	969-7427	703-941-2323	95
Skylink Travel	247-6659	212-573-8980	176
Sunrise Tours	872-3801	212-947-3617	101
Supertravel		310-301-4567	102
Trans Am Travel	822-7600	703-998-7676	184
Travel Expressions, Inc.	724-6274	212-338-9730	110
Travnet Inc.	359-6388	312-759-9200	191
Tulips Travel	882-3383	212-490-3388	112

Firms are listed by region, country, then city, according to the firm's specifications. Firms serving entire region are listed at the beginning of each region section.			
Firm name	1-800-phone	Phone	Page

Orient

Korea

Seoul

Air Travel Discounts, Inc.	888-2621	212-922-1326	18
Airplan	866-7526	412-257-3199	130
Alpha Travel	793-8424	770-988-9982	21
Brendan Air	491-9633	800-491-9633	136
Creative Marketing Manageme	458-6663	212-557-1530	145
D-FW Tours	527-2589	214-980-4540	146
Fantastiques Tours		310-577-6711	150
Four Seasons Travel		910-292-1887	47
Gateway Express Ltd.	334-1188	503-242-0088	154
Golden Pacific #1 Travel	500-8021	813-684-6365	156
Hana Travel Inc.	962-8044	708-913-1177	56
Hari World Travels, Inc.		212-957-3000	57
J & O Air	877-8111	619-282-4124	159
Palm Coast Tours & Travel	444-1560	407-433-1558	85
Sharp Travel Washington	969-7427	703-941-2323	95
Skylink Travel	247-6659	212-573-8980	176
South Pacific Express Travels	321-7739	415-982-6833	98
Specialty Tours Int'l USA Inc.	421-3913	310-568-8709	99
Supertravel		310-301-4567	102
Thrifty Air	423-4488	310-337-9982	180
Trans Am Travel	822-7600	703-998-7676	184
Travel Expressions, Inc.	724-6274	212-338-9730	110
Travnet Inc.	359-6388	312-759-9200	191

Laos

Vientiane

Festival of Asia	533-9953	415-693-0880	151
Ticketworld/SAF Travel World	394-8587	215-440-7200	105

Pakistan

Karachi

D-FW Tours	527-2589	214-980-4540	146
Favored Holidays Inc.		718-934-8881	46
Festival of Asia	533-9953	415-693-0880	151
MT&T		612-784-3226	163
Picasso Travel	PICASSO	310-645-4400	88
Travelogue, Inc.	542-9446	910-855-1735	190

Firms are listed by region, country, then city, according to the firm's specifications. Firms serving entire region are listed at the beginning of each region section.			
Firm name	1-800-phone	Phone	Page

Orient

Singapore
Singapore

Firm name	1-800-phone	Phone	Page
Air Travel Discounts, Inc.	888-2621	212-922-1326	18
Alpha Travel	793-8424	770-988-9982	21
Brendan Air	491-9633	800-491-9633	136
Centrav, Inc.	874-2033	612-948-8400	139
City Tours	238-2489	201-939-6572	141
Creative Marketing Manageme	458-6663	212-557-1530	145
Favored Holidays Inc.		718-934-8881	46
Festival of Asia	533-9953	415-693-0880	151
GTI Travel Consolidators	829-8234	616-396-1234	50
Gateway Express Ltd.	334-1188	503-242-0088	154
Golden Pacific #1 Travel	500-8021	813-684-6365	156
Hana Travel Inc.	962-8044	708-913-1177	56
Jetset Tours Inc.	638-3273	312-362-9960	160
Sharp Travel Washington	969-7427	703-941-2323	95
Skylink Travel	247-6659	212-573-8980	176
Thrifty Air	423-4488	310-337-9982	180
Trans Am Travel	822-7600	703-998-7676	184
Travel Expressions, Inc.	724-6274	212-338-9730	110
Travelogue, Inc.	542-9446	910-855-1735	190
Travnet Inc.	359-6388	312-759-9200	191
Tulips Travel	882-3383	212-490-3388	112

Sri Lanka
Colombo

Firm name	1-800-phone	Phone	Page
Air Travel Discounts, Inc.	888-2621	212-922-1326	18
Alpha Travel	793-8424	770-988-9982	21
D-FW Tours	527-2589	214-980-4540	146
Festival of Asia	533-9953	415-693-0880	151
Persvoyage Inc	455-7377	212-719-0900	87
Sunrise Tours	872-3801	212-947-3617	101
Up & Away Travel	275-8001	212-889-2345	114

Taiwan
Taipei

Firm name	1-800-phone	Phone	Page
Brendan Air	491-9633	800-491-9633	136
Cathay Travel		818-571-6727	29
City Tours	238-2489	201-939-6572	141
Creative Marketing Manageme	458-6663	212-557-1530	145
D-FW Tours	527-2589	214-980-4540	146

Firm name	1-800-phone	Phone	Page

Firms are listed by region, country, then city, according to the firm's specifications. Firms serving entire region are listed at the beginning of each region section.

Orient

Taiwan

Taipei

Firm name	1-800-phone	Phone	Page
Festival of Asia	533-9953	415-693-0880	151
GTI Travel Consolidators	829-8234	616-396-1234	50
HTI Tours	441-4411	215-563-8484	157
Hana Travel Inc.	962-8044	708-913-1177	56
MT&T		612-784-3226	163
Sharp Travel Washington	969-7427	703-941-2323	95
Skylink Travel	247-6659	212-573-8980	176
Thrifty Air	423-4488	310-337-9982	180
Trans Am Travel	822-7600	703-998-7676	184
Travnet Inc.	359-6388	312-759-9200	191

Thailand

Bangkok

Firm name	1-800-phone	Phone	Page
Air Travel Discounts, Inc.	888-2621	212-922-1326	18
Airplan	866-7526	412-257-3199	130
Alpha Travel	793-8424	770-988-9982	21
Brendan Air	491-9633	800-491-9633	136
Centrav, Inc.	874-2033	612-948-8400	139
City Tours	238-2489	201-939-6572	141
Creative Marketing Manageme	458-6663	212-557-1530	145
D-FW Tours	527-2589	214-980-4540	146
Favored Holidays Inc.		718-934-8881	46
Festival of Asia	533-9953	415-693-0880	151
Four Seasons Travel		910-292-1887	47
GTI Travel Consolidators	829-8234	616-396-1234	50
Gateway Express Ltd.	334-1188	503-242-0088	154
Golden Pacific #1 Travel	500-8021	813-684-6365	156
Hana Travel Inc.	962-8044	708-913-1177	56
Jetset Tours Inc.	638-3273	312-362-9960	160
Palm Coast Tours & Travel	444-1560	407-433-1558	85
Sharp Travel Washington	969-7427	703-941-2323	95
Skylink Travel	247-6659	212-573-8980	176
Thrifty Air	423-4488	310-337-9982	180
Trans Am Travel	822-7600	703-998-7676	184
Travel Expressions, Inc.	724-6274	212-338-9730	110
Travnet Inc.	359-6388	312-759-9200	191
Tulips Travel	882-3383	212-490-3388	112

Firms are listed by region, country, then city, according to the firm's specifications. Firms serving entire region are listed at the beginning of each region section.			
Firm name	1-800-phone	Phone	Page

Orient
Vietnam

Firm name	1-800-phone	Phone	Page
Air Brokers Int'l, Inc.	883-3273	415-397-1383	17
Brendan Air	491-9633	800-491-9633	136
Festival of Asia	533-9953	415-693-0880	151
Golden Pacific #1 Travel	500-8021	813-684-6365	156
Thrifty Air	423-4488	310-337-9982	180

Hanoi

Firm name	1-800-phone	Phone	Page
Brendan Air	491-9633	800-491-9633	136
Festival of Asia	533-9953	415-693-0880	151
Thrifty Air	423-4488	310-337-9982	180

Ho-Chi-Minh City

Firm name	1-800-phone	Phone	Page
Alpha Travel	793-8424	770-988-9982	21
Brendan Air	491-9633	800-491-9633	136
Festival of Asia	533-9953	415-693-0880	151
GTI Travel Consolidators	829-8234	616-396-1234	50
MT&T		612-784-3226	163
Picasso Travel	PICASSO	310-645-4400	88
Sharp Travel Washington	969-7427	703-941-2323	95
Skylink Travel	247-6659	212-573-8980	176
Ticketworld/SAF Travel World	394-8587	215-440-7200	105
Trans Am Travel	822-7600	703-998-7676	184
Travelogue, Inc.	542-9446	910-855-1735	190

Africa

Firm name	1-800-phone	Phone	Page
AIT Anderson International	365-1929	517-337-1300	124
The Africa Desk	284-8796	203-354-9344	127
AirFax Airline Marketing Assoc		404-662-0885	129
Alpha Travel	793-8424	770-988-9982	21
AmeriCorp Travel Professional	299-LATI	214-956-9112	23
American Intl. Consolidators	888-5774	914-592-0206	131
Bon Voyage	826-8500	310-854-8585	135
Brendan Air	491-9633	800-491-9633	136
CL Thomson Express Int'l		213-628-9550	137
CWT/Maharaja	223-6862	212-695-8435	27
Centrav, Inc.	874-2033	612-948-8400	139
Charterways	869-2344	408-257-2652	140
Chartours	323-4444	415-495-8881	32
Costa Azul Travel	332-7202	213-525-3331	35
DERAIR	717-4247	310-479-4411	37

Firms are listed by region, country, then city, according to the firm's specifications. Firms serving entire region are listed at the beginning of each region section.

Firm name	1-800-phone	Phone	Page
Africa			
Democracy Travel	536-8728	202-965-7200	38
Diplomat Tours	727-8687	916-972-1500	147
The Egyptian Connection	334-4477	718-762-3838	149
Euram Tours Inc	848-6789	202-789-2255	42
Everest Travel Inc.		404-231-5222	43
Fare Deals Ltd.	347-7006	410-581-8787	45
GIT Travel	228-1777	404-399-6404	49
Gateway Express Ltd.	334-1188	503-242-0088	154
General Tours	221-2216	603-357-5033	52
Getaway Travel Intl. Inc.	683-6336	305-446-7855	53
Global Travel Consolidators	366-3544	310-581-5610	155
HTI Tours	441-4411	215-563-8484	157
Hari World Travels, Inc.		212-957-3000	57
Holbrook Travel Inc.	451-7111	904-377-7111	58
Interworld Travel	468-3796	305-443-4929	65
J & O Air	877-8111	619-282-4124	159
Jetset Tours Inc.	638-3273	312-362-9960	160
Kambi Travel Intl.	220-2192	301-925-9012	67
Leisure Resources	729-9051	203-874-4965	161
M & H Travel, Inc.		212-661-7171	73
Magical Holidays, Inc.	433-7773	415-781-1345	74
Marakesh Tourist Company	458-1772	201-435-2800	75
Midtown Travel Consultants	548-8904	404-872-8308	77
Millrun Tours	645-5786	312-641-5914	78
Overseas Express	343-4873		81
Overseas Travel	783-7196	303-337-7196	82
PERS Travel, Inc.	583-0909	214-458-6877	84
Picasso Travel	PICASSO	310-645-4400	88
Pino Welcome Travel	247-6578	212-682-5400	89
Premier Travel Services Inc	545-1910	215-893-9966	92
Queue Travel	356-4871	619-260-8577	172
STA Travel	825-3001	213-937-9274	174
STT Worldwide Travel, Inc.	348-0886	503-671-0494	175
Saga Tours	683-4200	212-696-5200	93
Spector Travel of Boston	879-2374	617-338-0111	100
Sunrise Tours	872-3801	212-947-3617	101
Supervalue Vacations	879-1218	713-876-6400	103
TFI Tours Intl. Ltd.	745-8000	212-736-1140	179
Time Travel	847-7026	708-595-8463	181
Travac Tours & Charters	TRAV-800	212-563-3303	106

Firms are listed by region, country, then city, according to the firm's specifications. Firms serving entire region are listed at the beginning of each region section.			
Firm name	1-800-phone	Phone	Page

Africa

Travel Beyond	876-3131	612-475-2565	185
Travel Expressions, Inc.	724-6274	212-338-9730	110
The Travel Group	836-6269	210-698-0100	186
Travel Leaders, Inc.	323-3218	305-443-7755	187
Travel N Tours	854-5400	914-838-2600	188
Travelogue, Inc.	542-9446	910-855-1735	190
US Inf Tours	262-0456	908-526-0085	192
Unitravel	325-2222	314-569-0900	194
Up & Away Travel	275-8001	212-889-2345	114
World Travel & Tours, Inc.	886-4WTT	703-379-6363	195
Worldvision Travel	545-7118	201-736-8210	117
Worldwide Travel	343-0038	202-659-6430	118
Zig Zag International Travel	226-9383	309-637-9647	119

Algeria

Millrun Tours	645-5786	312-641-5914	78
Spector Travel of Boston	879-2374	617-338-0111	100

Angola
Luanda

Millrun Tours	645-5786	312-641-5914	78
Premier Travel Services Inc	545-1910	215-893-9966	92
Spector Travel of Boston	879-2374	617-338-0111	100
Worldvision Travel	545-7118	201-736-8210	117

Benin
Cotonou

Overseas Express	343-4873		81
Premier Travel Services Inc	545-1910	215-893-9966	92

Botswana
Gaborone

Airplan	866-7526	412-257-3199	130
Magical Holidays, Inc.	433-7773	415-781-1345	74
Overseas Express	343-4873		81
Premier Travel Services Inc	545-1910	215-893-9966	92
Spector Travel of Boston	879-2374	617-338-0111	100
Travel Expressions, Inc.	724-6274	212-338-9730	110

Burkina Faso
Ougadougou

Magical Holidays, Inc.	433-7773	415-781-1345	74

Firms are listed by region, country, then city, according to the firm's specifications. Firms serving entire region are listed at the beginning of each region section.

Firm name	1-800-phone	Phone	Page
Africa			
Burkina Faso			
Ougadougou			
Overseas Express	343-4873		81
Burundi			
Bujumbura			
Millrun Tours	645-5786	312-641-5914	78
Spector Travel of Boston	879-2374	617-338-0111	100
World Travel & Tours, Inc.	886-4WTT	703-379-6363	195
Cameroon			
Douala			
Magical Holidays, Inc.	433-7773	415-781-1345	74
Millrun Tours	645-5786	312-641-5914	78
Overseas Express	343-4873		81
Spector Travel of Boston	879-2374	617-338-0111	100
Worldvision Travel	545-7118	201-736-8210	117
Congo			
Brazzaville			
Millrun Tours	645-5786	312-641-5914	78
Overseas Express	343-4873		81
Spector Travel of Boston	879-2374	617-338-0111	100
World Travel & Tours, Inc.	886-4WTT	703-379-6363	195
Cote D'Ivoire			
Abidjan			
The Africa Desk	284-8796	203-354-9344	127
Kambi Travel Intl.	220-2192	301-925-9012	67
Magical Holidays, Inc.	433-7773	415-781-1345	74
Millrun Tours	645-5786	312-641-5914	78
Overseas Express	343-4873		81
Premier Travel Services Inc	545-1910	215-893-9966	92
Spector Travel of Boston	879-2374	617-338-0111	100
World Travel & Tours, Inc.	886-4WTT	703-379-6363	195
Worldvision Travel	545-7118	201-736-8210	117
Ethiopia			
Addis Ababa			
Millrun Tours	645-5786	312-641-5914	78
Overseas Express	343-4873		81
Premier Travel Services Inc	545-1910	215-893-9966	92

Firms are listed by region, country, then city, according to the firm's specifications. Firms serving entire region are listed at the beginning of each region section.

Firm name	1-800-phone	Phone	Page
Africa			
Ethiopia			
Addis Ababa			
Skylink Travel	247-6659	212-573-8980	176
Spector Travel of Boston	879-2374	617-338-0111	100
World Travel & Tours, Inc.	886-4WTT	703-379-6363	195
Gabon			
Liberville			
Overseas Express	343-4873		81
Gambia			
Banjul			
The Africa Desk	284-8796	203-354-9344	127
Millrun Tours	645-5786	312-641-5914	78
Overseas Express	343-4873		81
Spector Travel of Boston	879-2374	617-338-0111	100
Ghana			
Accra			
The Africa Desk	284-8796	203-354-9344	127
Alpha Travel	793-8424	770-988-9982	21
American Intl. Consolidators	888-5774	914-592-0206	131
D-FW Tours	527-2589	214-980-4540	146
Magical Holidays, Inc.	433-7773	415-781-1345	74
Overseas Express	343-4873		81
Premier Travel Services Inc	545-1910	215-893-9966	92
Skylink Travel	247-6659	212-573-8980	176
Up & Away Travel	275-8001	212-889-2345	114
World Travel & Tours, Inc.	886-4WTT	703-379-6363	195
Worldvision Travel	545-7118	201-736-8210	117
Guinea			
Conakry			
Alpha Travel	793-8424	770-988-9982	21
Millrun Tours	645-5786	312-641-5914	78
Overseas Express	343-4873		81
Premier Travel Services Inc	545-1910	215-893-9966	92
Spector Travel of Boston	879-2374	617-338-0111	100
World Travel & Tours, Inc.	886-4WTT	703-379-6363	195

Firms are listed by region, country, then city, according to the firm's specifications. Firms serving entire region are listed at the beginning of each region section.

Firm name	1-800-phone	Phone	Page
Africa			
Kenya			
Nairobi			
The Africa Desk	284-8796	203-354-9344	127
Air Brokers Int'l, Inc.	883-3273	415-397-1383	17
Air Travel Discounts, Inc.	888-2621	212-922-1326	18
Airplan	866-7526	412-257-3199	130
Alpha Travel	793-8424	770-988-9982	21
American Intl. Consolidators	888-5774	914-592-0206	131
Brendan Air	491-9633	800-491-9633	136
D-FW Tours	527-2589	214-980-4540	146
J & O Air	877-8111	619-282-4124	159
Magical Holidays, Inc.	433-7773	415-781-1345	74
Millrun Tours	645-5786	312-641-5914	78
Overseas Express	343-4873		81
Picasso Travel	PICASSO	310-645-4400	88
Premier Travel Services Inc	545-1910	215-893-9966	92
Skylink Travel	247-6659	212-573-8980	176
Spector Travel of Boston	879-2374	617-338-0111	100
Sunny Land Tours	783-7839	201-487-2150	178
Travac Tours & Charters	TRAV-800	212-563-3303	106
Travel Expressions, Inc.	724-6274	212-338-9730	110
Travelogue, Inc.	542-9446	910-855-1735	190
Up & Away Travel	275-8001	212-889-2345	114
World Travel & Tours, Inc.	886-4WTT	703-379-6363	195
Worldvision Travel	545-7118	201-736-8210	117
Liberia			
Millrun Tours	645-5786	312-641-5914	78
Spector Travel of Boston	879-2374	617-338-0111	100
Malawi			
Lilongwe			
Airplan	866-7526	412-257-3199	130
Alpha Travel	793-8424	770-988-9982	21
Brendan Air	491-9633	800-491-9633	136
Magical Holidays, Inc.	433-7773	415-781-1345	74
Overseas Express	343-4873		81
Premier Travel Services Inc	545-1910	215-893-9966	92
Travel Expressions, Inc.	724-6274	212-338-9730	110
World Travel & Tours, Inc.	886-4WTT	703-379-6363	195
Worldvision Travel	545-7118	201-736-8210	117

Firms are listed by region, country, then city, according to the firm's specifications. Firms serving entire region are listed at the beginning of each region section.

Firm name	1-800-phone	Phone	Page
Africa			
Mali			
Bamako			
Magical Holidays, Inc.	433-7773	415-781-1345	74
Overseas Express	343-4873		81
Premier Travel Services Inc	545-1910	215-893-9966	92
Mauritius			
Festival of Asia	533-9953	415-693-0880	151
Travel Expressions, Inc.	724-6274	212-338-9730	110
Morocco			
Central Holidays	935-5000		138
Lucky Tours	932-6654	308-762-3957	72
Millrun Tours	645-5786	312-641-5914	78
Spector Travel of Boston	879-2374	617-338-0111	100
Casablanca			
Air Travel Discounts, Inc.	888-2621	212-922-1326	18
Alpha Travel	793-8424	770-988-9982	21
Brendan Air	491-9633	800-491-9633	136
Favored Holidays Inc.		718-934-8881	46
Homeric Tours, Inc.	223-5570	212-753-1100	60
Marakesh Tourist Company	458-1772	201-435-2800	75
Picasso Travel	PICASSO	310-645-4400	88
Sunny Land Tours	783-7839	201-487-2150	178
World Travel & Tours, Inc.	886-4WTT	703-379-6363	195
Tangiers			
Worldvision Travel	545-7118	201-736-8210	117
Mozambique			
Maputo			
Overseas Express	343-4873		81
Premier Travel Services Inc	545-1910	215-893-9966	92
Spector Travel of Boston	879-2374	617-338-0111	100
Namibia			
Windhoek			
Brendan Air	491-9633	800-491-9633	136
Millrun Tours	645-5786	312-641-5914	78
Overseas Express	343-4873		81
Spector Travel of Boston	879-2374	617-338-0111	100

Firm name	1-800-phone	Phone	Page

Africa

Namibia

Windhoek

| Travel Expressions, Inc. | 724-6274 | 212-338-9730 | 110 |

Niger

Niamey

| Overseas Express | 343-4873 | | 81 |

Nigeria

Alpha Travel	793-8424	770-988-9982	21
Millrun Tours	645-5786	312-641-5914	78
Premier Travel Services Inc	545-1910	215-893-9966	92
Spector Travel of Boston	879-2374	617-338-0111	100

Kano

| Alpha Travel | 793-8424 | 770-988-9982 | 21 |
| Picasso Travel | PICASSO | 310-645-4400 | 88 |

Lagos

Air Travel Discounts, Inc.	888-2621	212-922-1326	18
Alpha Travel	793-8424	770-988-9982	21
American Intl. Consolidators	888-5774	914-592-0206	131
Balkan Holidays	852-0944	212-573-5530	134
Brendan Air	491-9633	800-491-9633	136
D-FW Tours	527-2589	214-980-4540	146
Magical Holidays, Inc.	433-7773	415-781-1345	74
Overseas Express	343-4873		81
Up & Away Travel	275-8001	212-889-2345	114
World Travel & Tours, Inc.	886-4WTT	703-379-6363	195
Worldvision Travel	545-7118	201-736-8210	117

Rwanda

| Millrun Tours | 645-5786 | 312-641-5914 | 78 |
| Spector Travel of Boston | 879-2374 | 617-338-0111 | 100 |

Senegal

Dakar

The Africa Desk	284-8796	203-354-9344	127
Brendan Air	491-9633	800-491-9633	136
Favored Holidays Inc.		718-934-8881	46
HTI Tours	441-4411	215-563-8484	157
Kambi Travel Intl.	220-2192	301-925-9012	67

Firm name	1-800-phone	Phone	Page

Africa

Senegal

Dakar

Firm name	1-800-phone	Phone	Page
Magical Holidays, Inc.	433-7773	415-781-1345	74
Millrun Tours	645-5786	312-641-5914	78
Overseas Express	343-4873		81
Premier Travel Services Inc	545-1910	215-893-9966	92
Spector Travel of Boston	879-2374	617-338-0111	100
World Travel & Tours, Inc.	886-4WTT	703-379-6363	195
Worldvision Travel	545-7118	201-736-8210	117

Sierra Leone

Freetown

Firm name	1-800-phone	Phone	Page
Alpha Travel	793-8424	770-988-9982	21
HTI Tours	441-4411	215-563-8484	157
Kambi Travel Intl.	220-2192	301-925-9012	67
Millrun Tours	645-5786	312-641-5914	78
Overseas Express	343-4873		81
Picasso Travel	PICASSO	310-645-4400	88
Spector Travel of Boston	879-2374	617-338-0111	100
World Travel & Tours, Inc.	886-4WTT	703-379-6363	195

South Africa

Firm name	1-800-phone	Phone	Page
The Africa Desk	284-8796	203-354-9344	127
Air Brokers Int'l, Inc.	883-3273	415-397-1383	17
Airplan	866-7526	412-257-3199	130
Alpha Travel	793-8424	770-988-9982	21
Brendan Air	491-9633	800-491-9633	136
Millrun Tours	645-5786	312-641-5914	78
Picasso Travel	PICASSO	310-645-4400	88
Spector Travel of Boston	879-2374	617-338-0111	100
Travel Expressions, Inc.	724-6274	212-338-9730	110
Worldvision Travel	545-7118	201-736-8210	117

Capetown

Firm name	1-800-phone	Phone	Page
The Africa Desk	284-8796	203-354-9344	127
Alpha Travel	793-8424	770-988-9982	21
Brendan Air	491-9633	800-491-9633	136
D-FW Tours	527-2589	214-980-4540	146
Picasso Travel	PICASSO	310-645-4400	88
Premier Travel Services Inc	545-1910	215-893-9966	92
Trans Am Travel	822-7600	703-998-7676	184

Firms are listed by region, country, then city, according to the firm's specifications. Firms serving entire region are listed at the beginning of each region section.			
Firm name	1-800-phone	Phone	Page

Africa

South Africa

Capetown

Firm name	1-800-phone	Phone	Page
Travel Expressions, Inc.	724-6274	212-338-9730	110
World Travel & Tours, Inc.	886-4WTT	703-379-6363	195
Worldvision Travel	545-7118	201-736-8210	117

Durban

Firm name	1-800-phone	Phone	Page
Travel Expressions, Inc.	724-6274	212-338-9730	110

Johannesburg

Firm name	1-800-phone	Phone	Page
The Africa Desk	284-8796	203-354-9344	127
Alpha Travel	793-8424	770-988-9982	21
American Intl. Consolidators	888-5774	914-592-0206	131
Balkan Holidays	852-0944	212-573-5530	134
Brendan Air	491-9633	800-491-9633	136
Cosmopolitan TVC Ctr	548-7206	305-523-0973	143
D-FW Tours	527-2589	214-980-4540	146
Magical Holidays, Inc.	433-7773	415-781-1345	74
Overseas Express	343-4873		81
Picasso Travel	PICASSO	310-645-4400	88
Premier Travel Services Inc	545-1910	215-893-9966	92
Skylink Travel	247-6659	212-573-8980	176
Trans Am Travel	822-7600	703-998-7676	184
Travel Expressions, Inc.	724-6274	212-338-9730	110
World Travel & Tours, Inc.	886-4WTT	703-379-6363	195
Worldvision Travel	545-7118	201-736-8210	117

Swaziland

Manzini

Firm name	1-800-phone	Phone	Page
Overseas Express	343-4873		81
Travel Expressions, Inc.	724-6274	212-338-9730	110

Tanzania

Firm name	1-800-phone	Phone	Page
Airplan	866-7526	412-257-3199	130
Alpha Travel	793-8424	770-988-9982	21
Brendan Air	491-9633	800-491-9633	136
Millrun Tours	645-5786	312-641-5914	78
Spector Travel of Boston	879-2374	617-338-0111	100

Arusha, Kilimanjaro

Firm name	1-800-phone	Phone	Page
Alpha Travel	793-8424	770-988-9982	21
Brendan Air	491-9633	800-491-9633	136

Firms are listed by region, country, then city, according to the firm's specifications. Firms serving entire region are listed at the beginning of each region section.			
Firm name	1-800-phone	Phone	Page

Africa

Tanzania

Arusha, Kilimanjaro

Overseas Express	343-4873		81
Picasso Travel	PICASSO	310-645-4400	88
Travelogue, Inc.	542-9446	910-855-1735	190

Dar Es Salaam

Air Travel Discounts, Inc.	888-2621	212-922-1326	18
Alpha Travel	793-8424	770-988-9982	21
American Intl. Consolidators	888-5774	914-592-0206	131
Brendan Air	491-9633	800-491-9633	136
D-FW Tours	527-2589	214-980-4540	146
Overseas Express	343-4873		81
Premier Travel Services Inc	545-1910	215-893-9966	92
Travac Tours & Charters	TRAV-800	212-563-3303	106
Travel Expressions, Inc.	724-6274	212-338-9730	110
Travelogue, Inc.	542-9446	910-855-1735	190
Up & Away Travel	275-8001	212-889-2345	114
World Travel & Tours, Inc.	886-4WTT	703-379-6363	195

Togo

Lome

Alpha Travel	793-8424	770-988-9982	21
Brendan Air	491-9633	800-491-9633	136
Magical Holidays, Inc.	433-7773	415-781-1345	74
Overseas Express	343-4873		81

Tunisia

Tunis

Air Travel Discounts, Inc.	888-2621	212-922-1326	18
Alpha Travel	793-8424	770-988-9982	21
Brendan Air	491-9633	800-491-9633	136
Favored Holidays Inc.		718-934-8881	46
Lotus	998-6116	212-213-1625	71
Picasso Travel	PICASSO	310-645-4400	88
World Travel & Tours, Inc.	886-4WTT	703-379-6363	195

Uganda

Entebbe

Airplan	866-7526	412-257-3199	130
Millrun Tours	645-5786	312-641-5914	78
Overseas Express	343-4873		81

Firms are listed by region, country, then city, according to the firm's specifications. Firms serving entire region are listed at the beginning of each region section.

Firm name	1-800-phone	Phone	Page
Africa			
Uganda			
Entebbe			
Premier Travel Services Inc	545-1910	215-893-9966	92
Spector Travel of Boston	879-2374	617-338-0111	100
Travac Tours & Charters	TRAV-800	212-563-3303	106
Travel Expressions, Inc.	724-6274	212-338-9730	110
Travelogue, Inc.	542-9446	910-855-1735	190
Up & Away Travel	275-8001	212-889-2345	114
Worldvision Travel	545-7118	201-736-8210	117
Zaire			
Kinshasa			
Magical Holidays, Inc.	433-7773	415-781-1345	74
Millrun Tours	645-5786	312-641-5914	78
Spector Travel of Boston	879-2374	617-338-0111	100
Zambia			
Lusaka			
Airplan	866-7526	412-257-3199	130
American Intl. Consolidators	888-5774	914-592-0206	131
Brendan Air	491-9633	800-491-9633	136
Magical Holidays, Inc.	433-7773	415-781-1345	74
Millrun Tours	645-5786	312-641-5914	78
Overseas Express	343-4873		81
Premier Travel Services Inc	545-1910	215-893-9966	92
Spector Travel of Boston	879-2374	617-338-0111	100
Travac Tours & Charters	TRAV-800	212-563-3303	106
Travel Expressions, Inc.	724-6274	212-338-9730	110
Up & Away Travel	275-8001	212-889-2345	114
World Travel & Tours, Inc.	886-4WTT	703-379-6363	195
Zimbabwe			
Harare			
Air Travel Discounts, Inc.	888-2621	212-922-1326	18
Airplan	866-7526	412-257-3199	130
Alpha Travel	793-8424	770-988-9982	21
American Intl. Consolidators	888-5774	914-592-0206	131
Brendan Air	491-9633	800-491-9633	136
Magical Holidays, Inc.	433-7773	415-781-1345	74
Millrun Tours	645-5786	312-641-5914	78
Overseas Express	343-4873		81
Premier Travel Services Inc	545-1910	215-893-9966	92

Firms are listed by region, country, then city, according to the firm's specifications. Firms serving entire region are listed at the beginning of each region section.			
Firm name	1-800-phone	Phone	Page

Africa
Zimbabwe
Harare

Skylink Travel	247-6659	212-573-8980	176
Spector Travel of Boston	879-2374	617-338-0111	100
Travac Tours & Charters	TRAV-800	212-563-3303	106
Travel Expressions, Inc.	724-6274	212-338-9730	110
Up & Away Travel	275-8001	212-889-2345	114
World Travel & Tours, Inc.	886-4WTT	703-379-6363	195
Worldvision Travel	545-7118	201-736-8210	117

Victoria Falls

Brendan Air	491-9633	800-491-9633	136
Worldvision Travel	545-7118	201-736-8210	117

Latin America

4th Dimension Tours	343-0020	305-279-0014	123
AIT Anderson International	365-1929	517-337-1300	124
Agents Advantage	816-2211	908-355-2222	128
AirFax Airline Marketing Assoc		404-662-0885	129
Airplan	866-7526	412-257-3199	130
Alta Tours	338-4191	415-777-1307	22
AmeriCorp Travel Professional	299-LATI	214-956-9112	23
Asensio Tours & Travel Corp	221-7679	212-213-4310	24
Bon Voyage	826-8500	310-854-8585	135
Brendan Air	491-9633	800-491-9633	136
CL Thomson Express Int'l		213-628-9550	137
CWT/Maharaja	223-6862	212-695-8435	27
Central Tours	783-9882	201-344-2489	31
Centrav, Inc.	874-2033	612-948-8400	139
Charterways	869-2344	408-257-2652	140
Chartours	323-4444	415-495-8881	32
City Tours	238-2489	201-939-6572	141
Cosmopolitan TVC Ctr	548-7206	305-523-0973	143
Costa Azul Travel	332-7202	213-525-3331	35
Cut Rate Travel	388-0575	708-405-0587	36
D-FW Tours	527-2589	214-980-4540	146
Democracy Travel	536-8728	202-965-7200	38
Diplomat Tours	727-8687	916-972-1500	147
Euram Tours Inc	848-6789	202-789-2255	42
Everest Travel Inc.		404-231-5222	43
Fantastiques Tours		310-577-6711	150

Firm name	1-800-phone	Phone	Page

Latin America

Firm name	1-800-phone	Phone	Page
Fare Deals Ltd.	347-7006	410-581-8787	45
Four Seasons Travel		910-292-1887	47
GIT Travel	228-1777	404-399-6404	49
Gateway Express Ltd.	334-1188	503-242-0088	154
Getaway Travel Intl. Inc.	683-6336	305-446-7855	53
Global Travel Consolidators	366-3544	310-581-5610	155
Group & Leisure	874-6608	816-224-3717	54
HTI Tours	441-4411	215-563-8484	157
Hari World Travels, Inc.		212-957-3000	57
Holbrook Travel Inc.	451-7111	904-377-7111	58
Hostway Tours	327-3207	305-966-8500	61
Interworld Travel	468-3796	305-443-4929	65
J & O Air	877-8111	619-282-4124	159
Jetset Tours Inc.	638-3273	312-362-9960	160
MLT Vacations	328-0025	612-474-2540	162
Magical Holidays, Inc.	433-7773	415-781-1345	74
Marnella Tours Inc.	937-6999	516-271-6969	164
Mena Tours & Travel	937-6362	312-275-2125	76
Midtown Travel Consultants	548-8904	404-872-8308	77
Overseas Express	343-4873		81
PCS	367-8833	213-239-2424	167
Palm Coast Tours & Travel	444-1560	407-433-1558	85
Panorama Tours	527-4888	801-328-5390	168
Pino Welcome Travel	247-6578	212-682-5400	89
Pinto Basto USA	526-8539	212-226-9056	90
Pioneer Tours	228-2107	408-648-8800	91
Pleasure Break Vacations, Inc.	777-1566	708-670-6300	170
Premier Travel Services Inc	545-1910	215-893-9966	92
Queue Travel	356-4871	619-260-8577	172
STA Travel	825-3001	213-937-9274	174
STT Worldwide Travel, Inc.	348-0886	503-671-0494	175
Saga Tours	683-4200	212-696-5200	93
Solar Tours	388-7652	202-861-6864	177
South American Fiesta	334-3782	804-825-9000	97
Sunny Land Tours	783-7839	201-487-2150	178
Sunrise Tours	872-3801	212-947-3617	101
Supertravel		310-301-4567	102
Supervalue Vacations	879-1218	713-876-6400	103
TFI Tours Intl. Ltd.	745-8000	212-736-1140	179
Tours International Inc.	247-7965	713-293-0809	183

Firm name	1-800-phone	Phone	Page
Latin America			
Trans Am Travel	822-7600	703-998-7676	184
Travel Bargains	247-3273	610-834-8150	108
Travel Expressions, Inc.	724-6274	212-338-9730	110
Travel Leaders, Inc.	323-3218	305-443-7755	187
Travel N Tours	854-5400	914-838-2600	188
Travel Wholesalers	487-8944	703-359-8855	189
Tread Lightly LTD.	643-0060	203-868-1710	111
Unitravel	325-2222	314-569-0900	194
Up & Away Travel	275-8001	212-889-2345	114
Wright Travel Holidays	877-3240	212-570-0969	196
Zig Zag International Travel	226-9383	309-637-9647	119
Argentina			
Buenos Aires			
4th Dimension Tours	343-0020	305-279-0014	123
Air Travel Discounts, Inc.	888-2621	212-922-1326	18
Airplan	866-7526	412-257-3199	130
Brendan Air	491-9633	800-491-9633	136
City Tours	238-2489	201-939-6572	141
Cosmopolitan TVC Ctr	548-7206	305-523-0973	143
D-FW Tours	527-2589	214-980-4540	146
Fantastiques Tours		310-577-6711	150
Getaway Travel Intl. Inc.	683-6336	305-446-7855	53
HTI Tours	441-4411	215-563-8484	157
Hostway Tours	327-3207	305-966-8500	61
J & O Air	877-8111	619-282-4124	159
Katy Van Tours	808-8747	713-492-7032	68
Marnella Tours Inc.	937-6999	516-271-6969	164
Mena Tours & Travel	937-6362	312-275-2125	76
Millrun Tours	645-5786	312-641-5914	78
Panorama Tours	527-4888	801-328-5390	168
Pinto Basto USA	526-8539	212-226-9056	90
Solar Tours	388-7652	202-861-6864	177
Sunny Land Tours	783-7839	201-487-2150	178
Supertravel		310-301-4567	102
Thrifty Air	423-4488	310-337-9982	180
Tourlite International Inc.	272-7600	212-599-2727	182
Tours International Inc.	247-7965	713-293-0809	183
Trans Am Travel	822-7600	703-998-7676	184

Firms are listed by region, country, then city, according to the firm's specifications. Firms serving entire region are listed at the beginning of each region section.

Firm name	1-800-phone	Phone	Page
Latin America			
Belize			
Belize City			
4th Dimension Tours	343-0020	305-279-0014	123
D-FW Tours	527-2589	214-980-4540	146
Marnella Tours Inc.	937-6999	516-271-6969	164
Mena Tours & Travel	937-6362	312-275-2125	76
Panorama Tours	527-4888	801-328-5390	168
Pinto Basto USA	526-8539	212-226-9056	90
Pioneer Tours	228-2107	408-648-8800	91
Pleasure Break Vacations, Inc.	777-1566	708-670-6300	170
Solar Tours	388-7652	202-861-6864	177
Bolivia			
4th Dimension Tours	343-0020	305-279-0014	123
Getaway Travel Intl. Inc.	683-6336	305-446-7855	53
Marnella Tours Inc.	937-6999	516-271-6969	164
Mena Tours & Travel	937-6362	312-275-2125	76
Panorama Tours	527-4888	801-328-5390	168
Solar Tours	388-7652	202-861-6864	177
Sunny Land Tours	783-7839	201-487-2150	178
Tours International Inc.	247-7965	713-293-0809	183
La Paz			
Fantastiques Tours		310-577-6711	150
Marnella Tours Inc.	937-6999	516-271-6969	164
Supertravel		310-301-4567	102
Santa Cruz			
Marnella Tours Inc.	937-6999	516-271-6969	164
Brazil			
4th Dimension Tours	343-0020	305-279-0014	123
Air Brokers Int'l, Inc.	883-3273	415-397-1383	17
Airplan	866-7526	412-257-3199	130
Brendan Air	491-9633	800-491-9633	136
City Tours	238-2489	201-939-6572	141
Getaway Travel Intl. Inc.	683-6336	305-446-7855	53
J & O Air	877-8111	619-282-4124	159
Marnella Tours Inc.	937-6999	516-271-6969	164
Mena Tours & Travel	937-6362	312-275-2125	76
Millrun Tours	645-5786	312-641-5914	78

Firms are listed by region, country, then city, according to the firm's specifications. Firms serving entire region are listed at the beginning of each region section.

Firm name	1-800-phone	Phone	Page
Latin America			
Brazil			
Panorama Tours	527-4888	801-328-5390	168
Solar Tours	388-7652	202-861-6864	177
Sunny Land Tours	783-7839	201-487-2150	178
Thrifty Air	423-4488	310-337-9982	180
Tourlite International Inc.	272-7600	212-599-2727	182
Tours International Inc.	247-7965	713-293-0809	183
Trans Am Travel	822-7600	703-998-7676	184
Travel Center	419-0960	212-545-7474	109
Fortaleza			
Brendan Air	491-9633	800-491-9633	136
Marnella Tours Inc.	937-6999	516-271-6969	164
Manaus			
Brendan Air	491-9633	800-491-9633	136
City Tours	238-2489	201-939-6572	141
Marnella Tours Inc.	937-6999	516-271-6969	164
Solar Tours	388-7652	202-861-6864	177
Recife			
Brendan Air	491-9633	800-491-9633	136
Marnella Tours Inc.	937-6999	516-271-6969	164
Rio De Janeiro			
Air Travel Discounts, Inc.	888-2621	212-922-1326	18
Brendan Air	491-9633	800-491-9633	136
City Tours	238-2489	201-939-6572	141
D-FW Tours	527-2589	214-980-4540	146
Hostway Tours	327-3207	305-966-8500	61
J & O Air	877-8111	619-282-4124	159
Marnella Tours Inc.	937-6999	516-271-6969	164
Millrun Tours	645-5786	312-641-5914	78
Pinto Basto USA	526-8539	212-226-9056	90
Solar Tours	388-7652	202-861-6864	177
Sunny Land Tours	783-7839	201-487-2150	178
Tourlite International Inc.	272-7600	212-599-2727	182
Trans Am Travel	822-7600	703-998-7676	184
Travel Center	419-0960	212-545-7474	109
Sao Paulo			
Brendan Air	491-9633	800-491-9633	136

Firms are listed by region, country, then city, according to the firm's specifications. Firms serving entire region are listed at the beginning of each region section.		

Firm name	1-800-phone	Phone	Page

Latin America

Brazil

Sao Paulo

D-FW Tours	527-2589	214-980-4540	146
Destinations Unlimited	338-7987	619-299-5161	39
J & O Air	877-8111	619-282-4124	159
Marnella Tours Inc.	937-6999	516-271-6969	164
Millrun Tours	645-5786	312-641-5914	78
Solar Tours	388-7652	202-861-6864	177
Sunny Land Tours	783-7839	201-487-2150	178
Tourlite International Inc.	272-7600	212-599-2727	182
Trans Am Travel	822-7600	703-998-7676	184
Travel Center	419-0960	212-545-7474	109

Chile

Santiago

4th Dimension Tours	343-0020	305-279-0014	123
Airplan	866-7526	412-257-3199	130
Brendan Air	491-9633	800-491-9633	136
City Tours	238-2489	201-939-6572	141
D-FW Tours	527-2589	214-980-4540	146
Fantastiques Tours		310-577-6711	150
Getaway Travel Intl. Inc.	683-6336	305-446-7855	53
HTI Tours	441-4411	215-563-8484	157
Katy Van Tours	808-8747	713-492-7032	68
Marnella Tours Inc.	937-6999	516-271-6969	164
Mena Tours & Travel	937-6362	312-275-2125	76
Millrun Tours	645-5786	312-641-5914	78
Panorama Tours	527-4888	801-328-5390	168
Pinto Basto USA	526-8539	212-226-9056	90
Solar Tours	388-7652	202-861-6864	177
Sunny Land Tours	783-7839	201-487-2150	178
Supertravel		310-301-4567	102
Tours International Inc.	247-7965	713-293-0809	183
Trans Am Travel	822-7600	703-998-7676	184

Colombia

Getaway Travel Intl. Inc.	683-6336	305-446-7855	53
Marnella Tours Inc.	937-6999	516-271-6969	164
Mena Tours & Travel	937-6362	312-275-2125	76
PERS Travel, Inc.	583-0909	214-458-6877	84
Panorama Tours	527-4888	801-328-5390	168

Firms are listed by region, country, then city, according to the firm's specifications. Firms serving entire region are listed at the beginning of each region section.

Firm name	1-800-phone	Phone	Page
Latin America			
Colombia			
Solar Tours	388-7652	202-861-6864	177
Bogota			
Brendan Air	491-9633	800-491-9633	136
D-FW Tours	527-2589	214-980-4540	146
Marnella Tours Inc.	937-6999	516-271-6969	164
Millrun Tours	645-5786	312-641-5914	78
Sunny Land Tours	783-7839	201-487-2150	178
Medellin			
Marnella Tours Inc.	937-6999	516-271-6969	164
Costa Rica			
San Jose			
4th Dimension Tours	343-0020	305-279-0014	123
Adventure Int'l Travel Service	542-2487	216-228-7171	16
Air Brokers Int'l, Inc.	883-3273	415-397-1383	17
American Intl. Consolidators	888-5774	914-592-0206	131
Brendan Air	491-9633	800-491-9633	136
City Tours	238-2489	201-939-6572	141
Cut Rate Travel	388-0575	708-405-0587	36
D-FW Tours	527-2589	214-980-4540	146
HTI Tours	441-4411	215-563-8484	157
Marnella Tours Inc.	937-6999	516-271-6969	164
Mena Tours & Travel	937-6362	312-275-2125	76
Panorama Tours	527-4888	801-328-5390	168
Pinto Basto USA	526-8539	212-226-9056	90
Pioneer Tours	228-2107	408-648-8800	91
Pleasure Break Vacations, Inc.	777-1566	708-670-6300	170
Solar Tours	388-7652	202-861-6864	177
Sunny Land Tours	783-7839	201-487-2150	178
Sunrise Tours	872-3801	212-947-3617	101
Tourlite International Inc.	272-7600	212-599-2727	182
Trans Am Travel	822-7600	703-998-7676	184
Ecuador			
4th Dimension Tours	343-0020	305-279-0014	123
Getaway Travel Intl. Inc.	683-6336	305-446-7855	53
Marnella Tours Inc.	937-6999	516-271-6969	164
Mena Tours & Travel	937-6362	312-275-2125	76

Firm name	1-800-phone	Phone	Page
Latin America			
Ecuador			
Panorama Tours	527-4888	801-328-5390	168
Tours International Inc.	247-7965	713-293-0809	183
Galapagos Islands			
4th Dimension Tours	343-0020	305-279-0014	123
Marnella Tours Inc.	937-6999	516-271-6969	164
Quito			
Brendan Air	491-9633	800-491-9633	136
D-FW Tours	527-2589	214-980-4540	146
Fantastiques Tours		310-577-6711	150
Marnella Tours Inc.	937-6999	516-271-6969	164
Millrun Tours	645-5786	312-641-5914	78
Solar Tours	388-7652	202-861-6864	177
Sunny Land Tours	783-7839	201-487-2150	178
Supertravel		310-301-4567	102
El Salvador			
San Salvador			
D-FW Tours	527-2589	214-980-4540	146
Fantastiques Tours		310-577-6711	150
Marnella Tours Inc.	937-6999	516-271-6969	164
Mena Tours & Travel	937-6362	312-275-2125	76
Millrun Tours	645-5786	312-641-5914	78
Panorama Tours	527-4888	801-328-5390	168
Pinto Basto USA	526-8539	212-226-9056	90
Solar Tours	388-7652	202-861-6864	177
Sunrise Tours	872-3801	212-947-3617	101
Supertravel		310-301-4567	102
Trans Am Travel	822-7600	703-998-7676	184
Guatemala			
Guatemala City			
4th Dimension Tours	343-0020	305-279-0014	123
Brendan Air	491-9633	800-491-9633	136
Cut Rate Travel	388-0575	708-405-0587	36
D-FW Tours	527-2589	214-980-4540	146
Katy Van Tours	808-8747	713-492-7032	68
Marnella Tours Inc.	937-6999	516-271-6969	164
Mena Tours & Travel	937-6362	312-275-2125	76
Millrun Tours	645-5786	312-641-5914	78

Firms are listed by region, country, then city, according to the firm's specifications. Firms serving entire region are listed at the beginning of each region section.			
Firm name	**1-800-phone**	**Phone**	**Page**

Latin America

Guatemala

Guatemala City

Panorama Tours	527-4888	801-328-5390	168
Pinto Basto USA	526-8539	212-226-9056	90
Pioneer Tours	228-2107	408-648-8800	91
Solar Tours	388-7652	202-861-6864	177
Sunny Land Tours	783-7839	201-487-2150	178
Sunrise Tours	872-3801	212-947-3617	101
Trans Am Travel	822-7600	703-998-7676	184

Honduras

Marnella Tours Inc.	937-6999	516-271-6969	164
Mena Tours & Travel	937-6362	312-275-2125	76
Panorama Tours	527-4888	801-328-5390	168
Pioneer Tours	228-2107	408-648-8800	91
Sunny Land Tours	783-7839	201-487-2150	178

Roatan

Marnella Tours Inc.	937-6999	516-271-6969	164

San Pedro Sula

D-FW Tours	527-2589	214-980-4540	146
Pinto Basto USA	526-8539	212-226-9056	90
Solar Tours	388-7652	202-861-6864	177

Teguigalpa

D-FW Tours	527-2589	214-980-4540	146
Marnella Tours Inc.	937-6999	516-271-6969	164

Nicaragua

Managua

D-FW Tours	527-2589	214-980-4540	146
Marnella Tours Inc.	937-6999	516-271-6969	164
Mena Tours & Travel	937-6362	312-275-2125	76
Millrun Tours	645-5786	312-641-5914	78
Panorama Tours	527-4888	801-328-5390	168
Pinto Basto USA	526-8539	212-226-9056	90
Solar Tours	388-7652	202-861-6864	177
Sunny Land Tours	783-7839	201-487-2150	178

Panama

Panama City

4th Dimension Tours	343-0020	305-279-0014	123

Firms are listed by region, country, then city, according to the firm's specifications. Firms serving entire region are listed at the beginning of each region section.

Firm name	1-800-phone	Phone	Page

Latin America

Panama

Panama City

American Intl. Consolidators	888-5774	914-592-0206	131
D-FW Tours	527-2589	214-980-4540	146
Marnella Tours Inc.	937-6999	516-271-6969	164
Mena Tours & Travel	937-6362	312-275-2125	76
Millrun Tours	645-5786	312-641-5914	78
Panorama Tours	527-4888	801-328-5390	168
Pinto Basto USA	526-8539	212-226-9056	90
Solar Tours	388-7652	202-861-6864	177
Sunny Land Tours	783-7839	201-487-2150	178
Trans Am Travel	822-7600	703-998-7676	184

Paraguay

Asuncion

4th Dimension Tours	343-0020	305-279-0014	123
Brendan Air	491-9633	800-491-9633	136
Getaway Travel Intl. Inc.	683-6336	305-446-7855	53
Marnella Tours Inc.	937-6999	516-271-6969	164
Mena Tours & Travel	937-6362	312-275-2125	76
Panorama Tours	527-4888	801-328-5390	168
Solar Tours	388-7652	202-861-6864	177
Sunny Land Tours	783-7839	201-487-2150	178
Tours International Inc.	247-7965	713-293-0809	183

Peru

Air Brokers Int'l, Inc.	883-3273	415-397-1383	17
Getaway Travel Intl. Inc.	683-6336	305-446-7855	53
Mena Tours & Travel	937-6362	312-275-2125	76
Panorama Tours	527-4888	801-328-5390	168
Tours International Inc.	247-7965	713-293-0809	183

Amazon

Marnella Tours Inc.	937-6999	516-271-6969	164
Sunny Land Tours	783-7839	201-487-2150	178

Lima

Brendan Air	491-9633	800-491-9633	136
Fantastiques Tours		310-577-6711	150
Solar Tours	388-7652	202-861-6864	177
Supertravel		310-301-4567	102

Firms are listed by region, country, then city, according to the firm's specifications. Firms serving entire region are listed at the beginning of each region section.

Firm name	1-800-phone	Phone	Page
Latin America			
Uruguay			
Montevideo			
4th Dimension Tours	343-0020	305-279-0014	123
Brendan Air	491-9633	800-491-9633	136
CL Thomson Express Int'l		213-628-9550	137
Cosmopolitan TVC Ctr	548-7206	305-523-0973	143
D-FW Tours	527-2589	214-980-4540	146
Getaway Travel Intl. Inc.	683-6336	305-446-7855	53
J & O Air	877-8111	619-282-4124	159
Marnella Tours Inc.	937-6999	516-271-6969	164
Mena Tours & Travel	937-6362	312-275-2125	76
Panorama Tours	527-4888	801-328-5390	168
Pinto Basto USA	526-8539	212-226-9056	90
Solar Tours	388-7652	202-861-6864	177
Sunny Land Tours	783-7839	201-487-2150	178
Tours International Inc.	247-7965	713-293-0809	183
Trans Am Travel	822-7600	703-998-7676	184
Venezuela			
4th Dimension Tours	343-0020	305-279-0014	123
Getaway Travel Intl. Inc.	683-6336	305-446-7855	53
Inter Island Tours	245-3434	212-686-4868	64
Marnella Tours Inc.	937-6999	516-271-6969	164
PERS Travel, Inc.	583-0909	214-458-6877	84
Panorama Tours	527-4888	801-328-5390	168
Sunrise Tours	872-3801	212-947-3617	101
Tours International Inc.	247-7965	713-293-0809	183
Barcelona			
Inter Island Tours	245-3434	212-686-4868	64
Betania			
Marnella Tours Inc.	937-6999	516-271-6969	164
Caracus			
Cut Rate Travel	388-0575	708-405-0587	36
D-FW Tours	527-2589	214-980-4540	146
Inter Island Tours	245-3434	212-686-4868	64
Marnella Tours Inc.	937-6999	516-271-6969	164
Millrun Tours	645-5786	312-641-5914	78
Pinto Basto USA	526-8539	212-226-9056	90
Solar Tours	388-7652	202-861-6864	177

Firms are listed by region, country, then city, according to the firm's specifications. Firms serving entire region are listed at the beginning of each region section.

Firm name	1-800-phone	Phone	Page

Latin America
Venezuela
Caracus

Firm name	1-800-phone	Phone	Page
Sunny Land Tours	783-7839	201-487-2150	178
Sunrise Tours	872-3801	212-947-3617	101
Trans Am Travel	822-7600	703-998-7676	184
Wright Travel Holidays	877-3240	212-570-0969	196

Macuto

Firm name	1-800-phone	Phone	Page
Marnella Tours Inc.	937-6999	516-271-6969	164

Margarita Island

Firm name	1-800-phone	Phone	Page
Sunrise Tours	872-3801	212-947-3617	101
Wright Travel Holidays	877-3240	212-570-0969	196

Porlamar

Firm name	1-800-phone	Phone	Page
Inter Island Tours	245-3434	212-686-4868	64

South Pacific

Firm name	1-800-phone	Phone	Page
Air Brokers Int'l, Inc.	883-3273	415-397-1383	17
Air Travel Discounts, Inc.	888-2621	212-922-1326	18
AirFax Airline Marketing Assoc		404-662-0885	129
Bon Voyage	826-8500	310-854-8585	135
Brendan Air	491-9633	800-491-9633	136
CL Thomson Express Int'l		213-628-9550	137
CWT/Maharaja	223-6862	212-695-8435	27
Campus Travel Center/Euroflgt	328-3359	612-338-5616	28
Centrav, Inc.	874-2033	612-948-8400	139
Charterways	869-2344	408-257-2652	140
Chartours	323-4444	415-495-8881	32
Chisholm Travel, Inc.	631-2824	312-263-7900	33
Creative Marketing Manageme	458-6663	212-557-1530	145
Cut Rate Travel	388-0575	708-405-0587	36
Democracy Travel	536-8728	202-965-7200	38
Diplomat Tours	727-8687	916-972-1500	147
Euram Tours Inc	848-6789	202-789-2255	42
Everest Travel Inc.		404-231-5222	43
Fare Deals Ltd.	347-7006	410-581-8787	45
Festival of Asia	533-9953	415-693-0880	151
Gateway Express Ltd.	334-1188	503-242-0088	154
Global Travel Consolidators	366-3544	310-581-5610	155
HTI Tours	441-4411	215-563-8484	157

Firms are listed by region, country, then city, according to the firm's specifications. Firms serving entire region are listed at the beginning of each region section.

Firm name	1-800-phone	Phone	Page
South Pacific			
Hana Travel Inc.	962-8044	708-913-1177	56
Hari World Travels, Inc.		212-957-3000	57
J & O Air	877-8111	619-282-4124	159
Jetset Tours Inc.	638-3273	312-362-9960	160
MT&T		612-784-3226	163
Overseas Travel	783-7196	303-337-7196	82
Passport Travel Mgmt Group	950-5864	813-931-3166	169
Pino Welcome Travel	247-6578	212-682-5400	89
Premier Travel Services Inc	545-1910	215-893-9966	92
Queue Travel	356-4871	619-260-8577	172
STA Travel	825-3001	213-937-9274	174
STT Worldwide Travel, Inc.	348-0886	503-671-0494	175
Saga Tours	683-4200	212-696-5200	93
Specialty Tours Int'l USA Inc.	421-3913	310-568-8709	99
Supervalue Vacations	879-1218	713-876-6400	103
TFI Tours Intl. Ltd.	745-8000	212-736-1140	179
Thrifty Air	423-4488	310-337-9982	180
Time Travel	847-7026	708-595-8463	181
Trans Am Travel	822-7600	703-998-7676	184
The Travel Group	836-6269	210-698-0100	186
Travnet Inc.	359-6388	312-759-9200	191
Up & Away Travel	275-8001	212-889-2345	114
Zig Zag International Travel	226-9383	309-637-9647	119
Australia			
Air Brokers Int'l, Inc.	883-3273	415-397-1383	17
Air Travel Discounts, Inc.	888-2621	212-922-1326	18
Brendan Air	491-9633	800-491-9633	136
Festival of Asia	533-9953	415-693-0880	151
J & O Air	877-8111	619-282-4124	159
Lotus	998-6116	212-213-1625	71
Lucky Tours	932-6654	308-762-3957	72
Specialty Tours Int'l USA Inc.	421-3913	310-568-8709	99
Trans Am Travel	822-7600	703-998-7676	184
Travel Expressions, Inc.	724-6274	212-338-9730	110
Value Holidays	558-6850	414-241-6373	115
Brisbane			
Brendan Air	491-9633	800-491-9633	136
South Pacific Express Travels	321-7739	415-982-6833	98

Firms are listed by region, country, then city, according to the firm's specifications. Firms serving entire region are listed at the beginning of each region section.

Firm name	1-800-phone	Phone	Page
South Pacific			
Australia			
Brisbane			
Trans Am Travel	822-7600	703-998-7676	184
Cairns			
Brendan Air	491-9633	800-491-9633	136
South Pacific Express Travels	321-7739	415-982-6833	98
Trans Am Travel	822-7600	703-998-7676	184
Melbourne			
Air Travel Discounts, Inc.	888-2621	212-922-1326	18
Brendan Air	491-9633	800-491-9633	136
South Pacific Express Travels	321-7739	415-982-6833	98
Trans Am Travel	822-7600	703-998-7676	184
Perth			
Brendan Air	491-9633	800-491-9633	136
Festival of Asia	533-9953	415-693-0880	151
J & O Air	877-8111	619-282-4124	159
Sunrise Tours	872-3801	212-947-3617	101
Sydney			
Air Travel Discounts, Inc.	888-2621	212-922-1326	18
American Intl. Consolidators	888-5774	914-592-0206	131
Brendan Air	491-9633	800-491-9633	136
Festival of Asia	533-9953	415-693-0880	151
HTI Tours	441-4411	215-563-8484	157
J & O Air	877-8111	619-282-4124	159
South Pacific Express Travels	321-7739	415-982-6833	98
Sunrise Tours	872-3801	212-947-3617	101
Trans Am Travel	822-7600	703-998-7676	184
Travel Center	419-0960	212-545-7474	109
Travnet Inc.	359-6388	312-759-9200	191
Fiji			
Nadi			
Global Travel Consolidators	366-3544	310-581-5610	155
J & O Air	877-8111	619-282-4124	159
South Pacific Express Travels	321-7739	415-982-6833	98
Guam			
Hana Travel Inc.	962-8044	708-913-1177	56
South Pacific Express Travels	321-7739	415-982-6833	98

Firm name	1-800-phone	Phone	Page

South Pacific

Guam

| Trans Am Travel | 822-7600 | 703-998-7676 | 184 |

Indonesia

Air Brokers Int'l, Inc.	883-3273	415-397-1383	17
Alpha Travel	793-8424	770-988-9982	21
Cathay Travel		818-571-6727	29
Festival of Asia	533-9953	415-693-0880	151
Golden Pacific #1 Travel	500-8021	813-684-6365	156
Jetset Tours Inc.	638-3273	312-362-9960	160
Thrifty Air	423-4488	310-337-9982	180
Trans Am Travel	822-7600	703-998-7676	184

Bali, Denpasar

Air Travel Discounts, Inc.	888-2621	212-922-1326	18
Alpha Travel	793-8424	770-988-9982	21
Brendan Air	491-9633	800-491-9633	136
D-FW Tours	527-2589	214-980-4540	146
Festival of Asia	533-9953	415-693-0880	151
Ticketworld/SAF Travel World	394-8587	215-440-7200	105
Trans Am Travel	822-7600	703-998-7676	184

Jakarta

Air Travel Discounts, Inc.	888-2621	212-922-1326	18
Alpha Travel	793-8424	770-988-9982	21
City Tours	238-2489	201-939-6572	141
Creative Marketing Manageme	458-6663	212-557-1530	145
D-FW Tours	527-2589	214-980-4540	146
Festival of Asia	533-9953	415-693-0880	151
GTI Travel Consolidators	829-8234	616-396-1234	50
Gateway Express Ltd.	334-1188	503-242-0088	154
Hana Travel Inc.	962-8044	708-913-1177	56
Millrun Tours	645-5786	312-641-5914	78
Sharp Travel Washington	969-7427	703-941-2323	95
Skylink Travel	247-6659	212-573-8980	176
Trans Am Travel	822-7600	703-998-7676	184

Malaysia

Brendan Air	491-9633	800-491-9633	136
Jetset Tours Inc.	638-3273	312-362-9960	160
Thrifty Air	423-4488	310-337-9982	180

Firm name	1-800-phone	Phone	Page

Firms are listed by region, country, then city, according to the firm's specifications. Firms serving entire region are listed at the beginning of each region section.

South Pacific

Malaysia

Trans Am Travel	822-7600	703-998-7676	184

Kuala Lumpur

Air Brokers Int'l, Inc.	883-3273	415-397-1383	17
Air Travel Discounts, Inc.	888-2621	212-922-1326	18
Alpha Travel	793-8424	770-988-9982	21
Borgsmiller Travels	228-0585	618-529-5511	25
Brendan Air	491-9633	800-491-9633	136
City Tours	238-2489	201-939-6572	141
Creative Marketing Manageme	458-6663	212-557-1530	145
D-FW Tours	527-2589	214-980-4540	146
Festival of Asia	533-9953	415-693-0880	151
GTI Travel Consolidators	829-8234	616-396-1234	50
Gateway Express Ltd.	334-1188	503-242-0088	154
HTI Tours	441-4411	215-563-8484	157
Hana Travel Inc.	962-8044	708-913-1177	56
Millrun Tours	645-5786	312-641-5914	78
Sharp Travel Washington	969-7427	703-941-2323	95
Skylink Travel	247-6659	212-573-8980	176
Trans Am Travel	822-7600	703-998-7676	184

Penang

Brendan Air	491-9633	800-491-9633	136
Trans Am Travel	822-7600	703-998-7676	184

Nepal

Kathmandu

Air Brokers Int'l, Inc.	883-3273	415-397-1383	17
Air Travel Discounts, Inc.	888-2621	212-922-1326	18
D-FW Tours	527-2589	214-980-4540	146
Festival of Asia	533-9953	415-693-0880	151
Kambi Travel Intl.	220-2192	301-925-9012	67

New Zealand

Brendan Air	491-9633	800-491-9633	136
Festival of Asia	533-9953	415-693-0880	151
HTI Tours	441-4411	215-563-8484	157
Lotus	998-6116	212-213-1625	71
Specialty Tours Int'l USA Inc.	421-3913	310-568-8709	99
Trans Am Travel	822-7600	703-998-7676	184

Firm name	1-800-phone	Phone	Page
South Pacific			
New Zealand			
Travnet Inc.	359-6388	312-759-9200	191
Value Holidays	558-6850	414-241-6373	115
Auckland			
Brendan Air	491-9633	800-491-9633	136
J & O Air	877-8111	619-282-4124	159
MT&T		612-784-3226	163
South Pacific Express Travels	321-7739	415-982-6833	98
Trans Am Travel	822-7600	703-998-7676	184
Christchurch			
Brendan Air	491-9633	800-491-9633	136
Trans Am Travel	822-7600	703-998-7676	184
Wellington			
Brendan Air	491-9633	800-491-9633	136
Trans Am Travel	822-7600	703-998-7676	184
Papua New Guinea			
Port Moresby			
Festival of Asia	533-9953	415-693-0880	151
Overseas Express	343-4873		81
Philippines			
Cebu City			
GTI Travel Consolidators	829-8234	616-396-1234	50
Manila			
Air Travel Discounts, Inc.	888-2621	212-922-1326	18
Alpha Travel	793-8424	770-988-9982	21
Brendan Air	491-9633	800-491-9633	136
Creative Marketing Manageme	458-6663	212-557-1530	145
D-FW Tours	527-2589	214-980-4540	146
GTI Travel Consolidators	829-8234	616-396-1234	50
Golden Pacific #1 Travel	500-8021	813-684-6365	156
Hana Travel Inc.	962-8044	708-913-1177	56
Hari World Travels, Inc.		212-957-3000	57
Jetset Tours Inc.	638-3273	312-362-9960	160
Sharp Travel Washington	969-7427	703-941-2323	95
Skylink Travel	247-6659	212-573-8980	176
South Pacific Express Travels	321-7739	415-982-6833	98
Thrifty Air	423-4488	310-337-9982	180

Firms are listed by region, country, then city, according to the firm's specifications. Firms serving entire region are listed at the beginning of each region section.

Firm name	1-800-phone	Phone	Page
South Pacific			
Philippines			
Manila			
Trans Am Travel	822-7600	703-998-7676	184
Travelogue, Inc.	542-9446	910-855-1735	190
Tahiti			
South Pacific Express Travels	321-7739	415-982-6833	98
Circle Pacific & Round-the-World			
Air Brokers Int'l, Inc.	883-3273	415-397-1383	17
City Tours	238-2489	201-939-6572	141
Festival of Asia	533-9953	415-693-0880	151
HTI Tours	441-4411	215-563-8484	157
Zig Zag International Travel	226-9383	309-637-9647	119
North America			
APC/American Passenger Con	526-2447	212-972-1558	125
Air Travel Discounts, Inc.	888-2621	212-922-1326	18
Bon Voyage	826-8500	310-854-8585	135
CL Thomson Express Int'l		213-628-9550	137
CWT/Maharaja	223-6862	212-695-8435	27
Chartours	323-4444	415-495-8881	32
Destinations Unlimited	338-7987	619-299-5161	39
Everest Travel Inc.		404-231-5222	43
Fantastiques Tours		310-577-6711	150
Group & Leisure	874-6608	816-224-3717	54
Hari World Travels, Inc.		212-957-3000	57
Hostway Tours	327-3207	305-966-8500	61
MLT Vacations	328-0025	612-474-2540	162
Northwest World Vacations	727-1111	612-474-2540	165
Pino Welcome Travel	247-6578	212-682-5400	89
Queue Travel	356-4871	619-260-8577	172
STA Travel	825-3001	213-937-9274	174
Saga Tours	683-4200	212-696-5200	93
Supertravel		310-301-4567	102
Supervalue Vacations	879-1218	713-876-6400	103
TFI Tours Intl. Ltd.	745-8000	212-736-1140	179
Unitravel	325-2222	314-569-0900	194
Up & Away Travel	275-8001	212-889-2345	114

Firms are listed by region, country, then city, according to the firm's specifications. Firms serving entire region are listed at the beginning of each region section.

Firm name	1-800-phone	Phone	Page
North America			
Canada			
Toronto			
Cathay Travel		818-571-6727	29
Vancouver			
Cathay Travel		818-571-6727	29
Mexico			
AirFax Airline Marketing Assoc		404-662-0885	129
AmeriCorp Travel Professional	299-LATI	214-956-9112	23
Costa Azul Travel	332-7202	213-525-3331	35
Fare Deals Ltd.	347-7006	410-581-8787	45
Group & Leisure	874-6608	816-224-3717	54
MLT Vacations	328-0025	612-474-2540	162
Marnella Tours Inc.	937-6999	516-271-6969	164
Mena Tours & Travel	937-6362	312-275-2125	76
Northwest World Vacations	727-1111	612-474-2540	165
STT Worldwide Travel, Inc.	348-0886	503-671-0494	175
Solar Tours	388-7652	202-861-6864	177
Travel Bargains	247-3273	610-834-8150	108
Cancun			
Solar Tours	388-7652	202-861-6864	177
Mexico City			
Solar Tours	388-7652	202-861-6864	177
Puerto Vallarta			
Solar Tours	388-7652	202-861-6864	177
United States			
Agents Advantage	816-2211	908-355-2222	128
Air Travel Discounts, Inc.	888-2621	212-922-1326	18
American Intl. Consolidators	888-5774	914-592-0206	131
Fare Deals Ltd.	347-7006	410-581-8787	45
Group & Leisure	874-6608	816-224-3717	54
Happy Tours	877-5262	408-461-0150	158
Holiday Travel International	775-7111	412-863-7500	59
Hostway Tours	327-3207	305-966-8500	61
MLT Vacations	328-0025	612-474-2540	162
Northwest World Vacations	727-1111	612-474-2540	165
Queue Travel	356-4871	619-260-8577	172

| Firm name | 1-800-phone | Phone | Page |

North America
United States

South Pacific Express Travels	321-7739	415-982-6833	98
Thrifty Air	423-4488	310-337-9982	180
Travel Associates	992-7388	213-933-7388	107
Travel Center	419-0960	212-545-7474	109
Travel Wholesalers	487-8944	703-359-8855	189
Tulips Travel	882-3383	212-490-3388	112
Worldvision Travel	545-7118	201-736-8210	117

Chicago

| Air Travel Discounts, Inc. | 888-2621 | 212-922-1326 | 18 |
| American Intl. Consolidators | 888-5774 | 914-592-0206 | 131 |

Dallas

| Agents Advantage | 816-2211 | 908-355-2222 | 128 |
| Air Travel Discounts, Inc. | 888-2621 | 212-922-1326 | 18 |

Ft. Lauderdale

Air Travel Discounts, Inc.	888-2621	212-922-1326	18
American Intl. Consolidators	888-5774	914-592-0206	131
Thrifty Air	423-4488	310-337-9982	180

Honolulu

Agents Advantage	816-2211	908-355-2222	128
Air Travel Discounts, Inc.	888-2621	212-922-1326	18
Fare Deals Ltd.	347-7006	410-581-8787	45
Holiday Travel International	775-7111	412-863-7500	59
South Pacific Express Travels	321-7739	415-982-6833	98
Travel Center	419-0960	212-545-7474	109
Worldvision Travel	545-7118	201-736-8210	117

Houston

Air Travel Discounts, Inc.	888-2621	212-922-1326	18
American Intl. Consolidators	888-5774	914-592-0206	131
Hostway Tours	327-3207	305-966-8500	61
Travel Center	419-0960	212-545-7474	109

Las Vegas

Agents Advantage	816-2211	908-355-2222	128
Fare Deals Ltd.	347-7006	410-581-8787	45
Holiday Travel International	775-7111	412-863-7500	59

Firms are listed by region, country, then city, according to the firm's specifications. Firms serving entire region are listed at the beginning of each region section.

Firm name	1-800-phone	Phone	Page
North America			
United States			
Los Angeles			
Agents Advantage	816-2211	908-355-2222	128
Air Travel Discounts, Inc.	888-2621	212-922-1326	18
American Intl. Consolidators	888-5774	914-592-0206	131
Hostway Tours	327-3207	305-966-8500	61
Thrifty Air	423-4488	310-337-9982	180
Travel Center	419-0960	212-545-7474	109
Tulips Travel	882-3383	212-490-3388	112
Maui			
American Intl. Consolidators	888-5774	914-592-0206	131
Hostway Tours	327-3207	305-966-8500	61
Miami			
American Intl. Consolidators	888-5774	914-592-0206	131
New York			
Thrifty Air	423-4488	310-337-9982	180
Orlando			
All Destinations	228-1510	203-744-3100	20
Phoenix			
Agents Advantage	816-2211	908-355-2222	128
San Diego			
Agents Advantage	816-2211	908-355-2222	128
Holiday Travel International	775-7111	412-863-7500	59
San Francisco			
Agents Advantage	816-2211	908-355-2222	128
Holiday Travel International	775-7111	412-863-7500	59
Travel Center	419-0960	212-545-7474	109
Tulips Travel	882-3383	212-490-3388	112
Seattle			
Agents Advantage	816-2211	908-355-2222	128
Caribbean			
AirFax Airline Marketing Assoc		404-662-0885	129
All Destinations	228-1510	203-744-3100	20
Diplomat Tours	727-8687	916-972-1500	147
G. G. Tours		416-487-1146	152

Firms are listed by region, country, then city, according to the firm's specifications. Firms serving entire region are listed at the beginning of each region section.

Firm name	1-800-phone	Phone	Page
Caribbean			
Group & Leisure	874-6608	816-224-3717	54
Inter Island Tours	245-3434	212-686-4868	64
MLT Vacations	328-0025	612-474-2540	162
Marakesh Tourist Company	458-1772	201-435-2800	75
Marnella Tours Inc.	937-6999	516-271-6969	164
Aruba			
Panorama Tours	527-4888	801-328-5390	168
Travel Wholesalers	487-8944	703-359-8855	189
Bonaire			
Panorama Tours	527-4888	801-328-5390	168
Curacao			
Panorama Tours	527-4888	801-328-5390	168
Dominican Republic			
Inter Island Tours	245-3434	212-686-4868	64
Sunrise Tours	872-3801	212-947-3617	101
Grenada			
American Intl. Consolidators	888-5774	914-592-0206	131
Mena Tours & Travel	937-6362	312-275-2125	76
Puerto Rico			
San Juan			
Inter Island Tours	245-3434	212-686-4868	64
Mena Tours & Travel	937-6362	312-275-2125	76
Millrun Tours	645-5786	312-641-5914	78
Queue Travel	356-4871	619-260-8577	172
Sunrise Tours	872-3801	212-947-3617	101
St. Croix			
All Destinations	228-1510	203-744-3100	20
St. Kitts			
All Destinations	228-1510	203-744-3100	20
St. Maarten			
All Destinations	228-1510	203-744-3100	20
Inter Island Tours	245-3434	212-686-4868	64

Firms are listed by region, country, then city, according to the firm's specifications. Firms serving entire region are listed at the beginning of each region section.			
Firm name	*1-800-phone*	*Phone*	*Page*

Caribbean

St. Thomas

Inter Island Tours	245-3434	212-686-4868	64

Virgin Islands

All Destinations	228-1510	203-744-3100	20